3   361.61 ADA

Other titles by Robert Adams:

A *Measure of Diversion? Case Studies in IT* (with S. Allard,
J. Baldwin and J. Thomas)
Prison Riots in Britain and the USA
Problem-solving with Self-help Groups (with G. Lindenfield)
Protests by Pupils: Empowerment, Schooling and the State
*Quality Social Work**
*Social Work: Themes, Issues and Critical Debates** (edited with
L. Dominelli and M. Payne)
Self-help, Social Work and Empowerment
Skilled Work with People
*Social Work and Empowerment**
The Abuses of Punishment
The Personal Social Services: Clients, Consumers or Citizens?
*Critical Practice in Social Work** (edited with L. Dominelli and
. Payne)

lso published by Palgrave

Social Policy for Social Work

ROBERT ADAMS

Consultant Editor: Jo Campling

palgrave

First published 2002 by
PALGRAVE
Houndmills, Basingstoke, Hampshire RG21 6XS and
175 Fifth Avenue, New York, N. Y. 10010
Companies and representatives throughout the world

PALGRAVE is the new global academic imprint of
St. Martin's Press LLC Scholarly and Reference Division and
Palgrave Publishers Ltd (formerly Macmillan Press Ltd).

ISBN 0–333–77473–6 paperback

This book is printed on paper suitable for recycling and
made from fully managed and sustained forest sources.

A catalogue record for this book is available
from the British Library.

10   9   8   7   6   5   4   3   2
11   10   09   08   07   06   05   04   03

Printed and bound in Great Britain by J. W. Arrowsmith Ltd., Bristol

For Yasmeen

Contents

Introduction   x

PART I: CONTEXTS

1 **Changing Perspectives on Social Policy and
   Social Work**   **3**
   Social work consists of more than merely   4
   implementing the law
   How do social workers use social policy in their practice?   5
   What changing contexts affect social policy and   6
   social work?
   What are social policy, social administration, social security,   26
   social services, social care and social work?
   How does social policy relate to social work?   29

PART II: POLICIES

2 **Social Security**   **37**
   Policy context   38
   Key policy changes and related issues   45
   Implications for social workers   53

3 **Employment**   **55**
   Policy context   55
   Key policy changes and related issues   61
   Implications for social workers   69

4 **Housing**   **72**
   Policy context   72
   Key policy changes and related issues   74
   Implications for social workers   89

5   Health and Community Care   **92**
Policy context   93
Key policy changes and related issues   94
Implications for social workers   107

6   Family and Childcare   **110**
Policy context   110
Key policy changes and related issues   112
Implications for social workers   124

7   Youth Justice and Criminal Justice   **127**
Policy context   129
Key policy changes and related issues   137
Implications for social workers   146

PART III: ISSUES

8   Tackling Divisions and Inequalities   **151**
Contexts   152
Key aspects   152
Implications for social workers   171

9   Organising and Delivering Social Services   **173**
Policy context   173
Key changes and related issues   177
Implications for social workers   184

10 Financing Social Services   **186**
Contexts   186
Key aspects   188
Implications for social workers   197

11 Who Controls Social Services?   **200**
Contexts and key aspects   200
Implications for social workers   211

12 Future Trends   **213**
How have social conditions changed since 1981?   213
Can government policies deliver improvements   217
  to the people?
What are the implications for social workers?   224

APPENDICES

1	Abbreviations	229
2	Key Dates: Legislation	234
3	Internet Addresses of Main Sources of Information on Policy and Research	237

Bibliography   239

Index   263

Introduction

Several approaches are possible with a book of this kind, which sets out to provide a particular professional group – social workers – with relevant aspects of social policy. The chapters on each policy area could take a historical approach and the first chapter could attempt a general historical introduction to social policy. Alternatively, the book could undertake a systematic examination of theories and interpretations of social policies. Or the book could go through each area, detailing the legal enactments and procedures and specifying what the practitioner could, or should, be doing.

But in practical terms none of these approaches would be possible in a book of this length. There would not be space to give the required attention to detail in each area. As far as the history was concerned, in the introduction it would be impossible to attempt a complete history of welfare policy since the welfare state began in the 1940s, or to present a history of a more recent period. More important, neither approach would engage necessarily with social work concerns. Examination of general welfare theories and theories and perspectives on each area would be fraught with problems of inadequate space. The problem of relevance, or lack of obvious relevance, to practice would be just as acute. Finally, lists of laws and procedures would consume far more space than the book allows. Any attempt to offer commentary would collapse in the face of the vast body of material in each policy area. Added to this, of course, is the reality that merely listing and describing legislation does not stimulate the reader to reflect and develop a more critical practice. A better basis for this would be to evaluate practice against key European and UN Declarations of Children's Rights, Women's Rights and Human Rights.

Returning to social policy in Britain, there are limits on what can be achieved in the relatively small space, but there is an even more pressing problem, expressed in the question: in what way is this relevant to social work?

I decided to keep asking myself this question while I was writing. I finished up providing a little of each of the above approaches in every chapter, drawing on historical, theoretical and legal aspects where appropriate. So, the book is not a history, but it is historical. It is not a review of theory, but it refers to theories, perspectives and approaches.

And it is not a descriptive survey of all the different policies, but nevertheless I do try to bring most of them into the discussion of the various areas.

The book provides a core of discussion of the nature of the traditionally accepted main areas of welfare policy – employment, social security, health, housing and social services – with the addition of criminal justice. This discussion is informed by reference to material of direct relevance to social work: authoritative commentaries, selected research and other reflective writing. It is hoped that this strategy will encourage the development of questioning and critical approaches to practice.

The book falls into three parts. Part I contains Chapter 1 and gives an overview of social policy and social work, providing a context for the rest of the book. Part II comprises Chapters 2 to 7 and deals with particular aspects of social policy which bear on social work. Part III, Chapters 8 to 12, examines key issues of relevance in social policy and social work. The layout of the chapters is intended to further debate about the contexts and nature of policy, focus on issues in particular policy areas and raise pointers for critical practice in social work. Each chapter concludes with a summary and suggestions for further reading.

Part I

Contexts

1

Changing Perspectives on Social Policy and Social Work

The idea that policy is an organised, coherent, worked out strategy which leads to a readily applied, straightforward plan for practice is attractive but mistaken. As an experienced social policy researcher says:

> it is a view born of a rational, logical approach to the process of planning and policy formulation. Appealing as this view may be, the reality, especially in the field of social policy, is that it tends to be complex, messy and created within a dynamic environment of competing forces and tensions. (Spurgeon, 2000, p. 191)

It is in this context of arguments, differences of perspective, compromises, decisions made at the last minute, plans needing implementing yesterday, that policymakers and politicians construct the laws which empower social services and probation departments, for implementing by overworked managers and practitioners.

The resulting legislation gives practitioners their statutory duties, powers, responsibilities and functions. The Local Authority Social Services Act 1970 establishes the framework for social workers by requiring the local authority to set up and operate a social services department. Within this, particular legislation generates specific duties. The Probation Services Act 1993 requires probation committees in the area covered by each magistrates' court to appoint probation officers who are responsible for carrying out specified functions in the criminal justice system (see Chapter 7). Not surprisingly, given the context of conflict and negotiation in which the laws are framed, the resulting brief for practitioners is often full of dilemmas, uncertainties and contradictions.

Social work consists of more than merely implementing the law

Louis Blom-Cooper wrote in the introduction to the report of the inquiry he chaired into the death of Jasmine Beckford:

> We are strongly of the view that social work can, in fact, be defined *only* (his italics) in terms of the functions required of its practitioners by their employing agency operating within a statutory framework. (Blom-Cooper, 1985, p. 12)

This is tantamount to asserting that practitioners implement the law. That is all they need to know, where to find the law. Why bother with social policy? This *legalistic* model of social work (revisited near the end of this chapter)

> emphasises the need to work within the statutory framework, in contrast to a view that what really matters is social workers using their expertise to help clients. (Brayne and Martin, 1999, p. 15)

But, as we discuss at the end of this chapter, the relationship between social work and the law is more complex and problematic than this. Social policy, like psychology and sociology, offers even wider contexts on people's circumstances, sometimes contributing research which raises vital questions, at other times offering theoretical debates. All these elements make possible critical reflection on our part as practitioners, contribute to our expertise and engage our personal and professional values, activating a moral dimension on our work, a judgement about what sort of society we want and what contribution we believe social policy and social workers should make to it.

As if this is not complicated enough, outside the statutory duties of social workers lies the range of therapeutic, community-based and community work tasks in which some social workers get involved, which are not underpinned directly by legislation. These activities include some of the aspirations of critical practitioners – to encourage advocacy and empower clients, for instance.

So, the law is necessary to social workers; they have to abide by it and carry it out where necessary. But there is more to social work than implementing the law. Social workers are not simply lawyers, working on people's problems. Social workers draw on a range of social science perspectives and research in their practice. As part of this process, social policy contributes to the critical practitioner's grasp of the context of practice. Many years ago, Paul Halmos wrote about the need for the professional to encompass the tensions, conflicts, paradoxes and contradictions embodied in the 'personal' and the 'political' dimensions of people's circumstances (Halmos, 1978). Social policy and social work share these tensions and dilemmas.

Using this book

This chapter forms Part I of this book. It contains general maps of ideas about the links between social policy and social work. You, as a student or practising social worker, may prefer not to start here, but may go to one of the chapters in Part II. You can think of these as larger scale maps of particular aspects of policy. Or, you may consult Part III, pursuing an issue which slices through the other chapters. It will be helpful, though, at some stage to return to the questions dealt with in this chapter under the three main headings below: what changing contexts affect social policy and social work?; what are social policy, social work, social security and the other disciplines with 'social' in them?; how does social policy relate to social work? Before tackling these, we justify the need for all practitioners to have an up-to-date knowledge and critical understanding of social policy by posing a prior question: how do social workers use social policy in their practice?

How do social workers use social policy in their practice?

EXAMPLE

Mrs K is a divorced Asian lone parent who has restricted movement through an arthritic condition made worse by the cold. She lives in rented accommodation with her 16-year-old son who has a learning disability. Mrs K is entitled to housing benefit. She rings social services to complain that her application has been put into the pending tray because she is still living with her former husband.

The social worker who picks up the case visits Mrs K and soon realises that there is no food and no heating in the house and Mrs K's son is too scared to go out. It emerges that he has been cautioned by the police for allegedly throwing a stone through a shop window, an offence he denies, saying a gang of boys keep harassing him, shouting 'Paki' at him, so he prefers to stay indoors. The social worker asks whether Mrs K's former husband pays maintenance. Mrs K does not answer but her son interjects that his father, who is white, owns three shops, drives a Mercedes, calls his son an idle scrounger and gives them nothing.

The social worker realises that this case touches on the policies of the housing department, social security and youth justice. Mrs K may need health and community care services and her lack of everyday means of living adequately needs attending to. There are issues of racism, discrimination, poverty and family and child support. So, it is vital that the social worker feels confident about drawing on up-to-date knowledge and understandings in these areas, including critical research, to inform practice with Mrs K and her son. Social policy does not provide an answer, but may give us a sense of perspective, a context, which helps us to appreciate and interpret what is going on.

Not every case is as complex. But, as Anne Brechin argues in her important chapter which introduces critical practice, it is vital for practitioners to grasp the policy context of the cases they deal with and thereby improve their responses to the constraints and uncertainties which contribute to the complexities of many people's lives (Brechin, 2000, p. 25). This book is devoted to this task.

How can we keep up to date?

- As social workers, we need to keep up to date on the changing contexts of policy and policy changes. These often affect what happens to clients, for example, when they go into offices to seek benefits or services and there has been a change of policy. The social worker needs to be abreast of this and be proactive in work with the client, anticipating rather than responding.
- Books, articles in social policy and social work journals are a good up-to-date source. Another source are organisations offering information, some which are detailed in Appendix Three at the end of this book.
- It helps to take an informed daily newspaper, or a good Sunday paper and maintain files of recent press cuttings. In a period of rapid change, it helps to subscribe to key social work journals and weekly magazines such as *Community Care*.

What changing contexts affect social policy and social work?

Social policy and social work both show signs of the disruption to the welfare state and welfare services which has occurred since the 1970s.

This has eroded, if not actually destroyed, the policies and those health, social work and social care practices derived from them, which were established in the 1940s, and which evolved through the significant social, economic and political changes of the 1950s and 60s.

At the same time, debates about what welfare is, who should have it, whether some services should be free and if so on what basis should this be decided, have broadened, as the language and concepts informing welfare policies and professions have been subject to critical scrutiny. While politicians from the New Right from the late 1970s have questioned the assumptions justifying state provision of health and social services as a right for all, on the basis of need, those receiving services have organised to express collective preferences and challenge established concepts, policies and services. The traditional power relationships between the state and the citizen, people and their welfare, professionals and 'clients' or 'service users', managers and practitioners have been challenged successfully. Children and parents now attend case reviews, service users represent their own views at policy and management levels in the work of the Care Commissioners.

Academics, researchers and practitioners express concern that the centre of gravity of social policy has shifted to the political Right since the 1970s and identify threats to the identity and survival of social work. Undeniably, changes are occurring, but there is little consensus about which are the most significant of these and it is almost impossible to predict how likely they are to persist.

Ideas context: no consensus about values and goals

There is little doubt that welfare services have changed massively during the twentieth century, but it is a more open question as to how far the ideas and values informing the shaping and delivering of these services have been affected by these changes. Debates about this draw on a vast and rapidly growing body of research evidence, as well as the more subjective sources of personal opinion, experience and beliefs. The subject matter of welfare – people's lives – may be subject to independent critical analysis but is prone to value judgements and assumptions based on opinion. To make this more complicated, no simple dichotomy between research and personal experience and prejudice can be drawn. Critical perspectives on social research attest to the inherently problematic nature of traditional, so-called scientific research, often mimicked by social scientists, while qualitative research methodologies are prone to attack by adherents to experimental research for not meeting the basic conditions for the carrying out of respectable research.

A welfare revolution: illusion or a reality?
Another way of posing this question is to ask how revolutionary the massive changes which have occurred in the social services during the twentieth century have been, in terms of their impact on people. Before the First World War, social services were embryonic. In the decade following the outbreak of the Second World War, the welfare state was conceived and set up. The National Assistance Act 1948 replaced the nineteenth-century Poor Laws and instituted the basis on which social services for adults are still provided. The Children Act 1948 represented the first recognition of the duty of local authorities to provide comprehensive services for caring for children who lacked a normal home life. In the 40 years after the Second World War, all aspects of social services were the targets of an unprecedented mass of legislation, much of it creating new powers, duties and responsibilities for social services agencies.

During the last decades of the twentieth century, a second revolution in social policy could be said to have taken place, as many welfare services were reconstituted and privatised and markets were created for the purchase and delivery of services. Local government was subjected to transformation, not just through the creation of unitary local authorities, but also involving the shift from local government to local governance by complex arrangements involving the public, private and voluntary sectors.

Have these changes significantly improved the quality of life of specific groups of people? On the whole, those who already have wealth and are higher earners have fared well. Welfare policies during the twentieth century have left the living conditions of many worse-off people largely unchanged. Chapters 2 to 7 of this book provide evidence that unemployment, inadequate housing, deficient health and community care, low incomes and problems associated with poverty still particularly affect people experiencing physical or learning disabilities, older people, people with mental health problems, lone parents, those with less earning capacity, children in poor families and families living in resource-starved urban and rural districts where access to welfare services is far from adequate. Poor people are still likely to be viewed with a mixture of sympathy and suspicion, depending on the extent to which they are regarded as trying to help themselves. Stereotypes of the beggar, the orphan, the 'morally careless' pregnant young girl, the 'mad' person, the disabled person deemed less capable, or the older person regarded as 'past it' are still dominated by prejudices rather than informed by the realities of their circumstances and the experiences of people themselves. The focus on the undeniable changes in welfare services, and how they are organised, managed and delivered, diverts attention from the unchanging realities of being poor, being a lone parent, experiencing mental health problems, becoming older or living in a society which discriminates against people who are different, whether through class, age, gender, ethnicity, disability or other social divisions.

Up to a third of people in Britain still live in poverty. Many children, especially those living with lone parents, experience poor housing, long-term poverty and inadequate education, health and childcare provision. The gap between rich and poor people at the beginning of 2000 was as great as in 1900.

Demographic context

There are some changes which are less matters of judgement and personal value and more subject to objective measurement. The population of Britain, for instance, has increased overall, but some areas, notably inner cities and some rural regions, have experienced decreases in population, particularly of economically active, better-off people. In 1901, just over 38 million people lived in the UK. By 1961, there were nearly 53 million and by 1997 this figure had increased by a further 12 per cent to 59 million. However, in this latter period, whereas the population of Northern Ireland increased by 17 per cent, that of England increased by 13 per cent, Wales by 11 per cent, whereas the population of Scotland actually fell by 1 per cent (Office for National Statistics, 1999, p. 30).

During the twentieth century, the burden of caring has shifted considerably within families and households. More people are dependent and a smaller proportion are in the workforce. Whereas in 1961, about 12 per cent of the UK population were aged 65 and over and 4 per cent were over 75, in 1997, these figures had risen to 16 and 7 per cent respectively (Office for National Statistics, 1999, p. 31).

Even in the demographic context, there are myths. For instance, it is often said that only since the waves of immigration from the Caribbean and Asian countries from the 1960s onwards, Britain has become a multiracial society. But the reality is that immigrants have figured largely throughout the history of this country. In the mid-nineteenth century, more than a million Irish people were driven by potato famines and poverty to seek a home elsewhere, while almost as many died at home. In the late nineteenth century, Jews and others from Central and Eastern Europe settled in towns such as Manchester, Hull and Leeds. Britain again provided a refuge for Jewish people in the 1930s and 40s. Ugandan Asian people and the so-called 'boat people' from Vietnam settled in smaller numbers from the 1970s. From the 1990s, refugees and people seeking asylum arrived from Central, Southern and Eastern Europe and the Middle East.

International context: globalisation and post-devolution welfare

During the social and political upheavals in Romania and former Yugoslavia in the 1980s and 90s, there were cases of British people travelling to those countries, obtaining orphaned or abandoned children and bringing them back as adopted. Concepts, policies and practices regarding adoption, children's rights and parental responsibility differ widely in different countries. In January 2001, controversy followed the purchase from an Internet adoption agency by Alan and Judith Kilshaw of six-month-old twin girls in Arkansas, USA, taken into care when they arrived at the couple's home in northern England. While it is illegal in the USA to purchase children directly for a fee, adoption procedures often are more abbreviated than in England and a private adoption for a fee paid to the agency can be obtained in Arkansas, provided the relevant authorities and courts are satisfied with the arrangements and the adoptive parents have been resident in that state for a minimum of 30 days.

Devolution
These cases show that social policy and social work in post-devolution England, Northern Ireland, Scotland and Wales cannot be isolated from welfare policies and legislation in other European countries forming the European Union (EU) (Cannan et al., 1992) and the wider social, political, economic and policy contexts provided by the USA as a major world power and other more and less developed countries. Influences on British social policy occupy concentric spaces: macro (global), mezzo (European) and micro (local). At the *macro*, global level, there may be a growing tendency towards international standards being set and sustained. At the other extreme of the *micro* level, the impact of devolution in the UK may mean that local conditions are in the process of fragmentation as the four countries of the United Kingdom – England,

Scotland, Northern Ireland and Wales – gather momentum in expressing their separate identities through policy and practice.

Europe

Between global and national entities, at the *mezzo* level, the EU plays an increasingly influential role in British social policy. European government and legislation superimpose a further layer of duties, powers, responsibilities and roles on central and local governments in Britain. These include a huge mass of laws and regulations relating to the Single European Market and the Social Chapter of the Maastricht Treaty, covering many areas of employment protection and the promotion of equality.

Despite Britain's proximity to the rest of Western Europe, historical, cultural, political and economic factors contribute to the distinctive differences between Britain and its neighbours (Adams et al., 2000). There is evidence, however, of some convergence in welfare policies and levels of welfare spending, 'as lower spending Mediterranean countries with left-wing governments increase provision and Northern governments retrench' (George and Taylor-Gooby, 1996, p. x).

The creation of the European Coal and Steel Community (ECSC) in 1951, the European Atomic Energy Community (Euratom) in 1957 and the European Economic Community (EEC) (1957) began the process of social, economic, financial and political convergence in Europe which led in 1994 to the replacement of the European Community (EC) by the EU. The EU is run by the Executive Commission, the European Parliament, the Council of Ministers and the Court of Justice. The powers of the European Parliament, whose elected members consider issues in a similar way to the parliament in Westminster, are considerably less than those of Westminster. In contrast, the pronouncements of the Court of Justice are binding on member states.

In some senses, the EU operates as a supranational entity, with its own political structures able to make policy and law and impose them on individual member states. In the main, though, member states pool their sovereignty in most areas of policy, retaining the right to make their own decisions about what they do (Kegley and Wittkopf, 1997, p. 163).

Britain and the rest of Western Europe are undergoing a period of major adjustment in the wake of the collapse of the Union of Soviet Socialist Republics (USSR) at the end of the 1980s and the expansion of the EU as former communist states negotiate entry. Such expansion heightens debates about whether greater monetary, economic and policy integration is desirable. Despite the persistence in Britain of a significant cohort of conservative politicians who resist closer political and policy integration on the grounds that it would undermine national sovereignty, there are strong economic and business pressures towards Britain harmonising more closely with Brussels and reformist pressures towards interventionist economics and social policies, stronger protection of people's social rights and needs (through the Social Chapter of the Maastricht Treaty 1991) and minimum wage and maximum working week legislation (through the EC Working Time Directive). There is also the ideological argument that isolationism and nationalism are inconsistent with progressive democratic and social policies aiming to transcend divisions, maximise equality and achieve monetary and financial union.

There are internationalist and nationalist pressures both pulling European countries together and, in some senses, fragmenting their distinct, separate identities. Within some countries, as support for regional government within England shows, there are campaigns for sub-national identities, independence and government.

The USA

Historically, economic and social policy in Britain has been influenced greatly by developments in the USA, in the early years of the Thatcher government. Milton Friedman, a US economist committed to free-market principles, was used in the 1980s by Conservative politicians to justify the monetarist policies of the Thatcher government, one goal being to reduce the role of the public sector in providing health and social services and encourage private and voluntary providers to enlarge their contributions. This political proximity between these two countries was furthered by a convergence of views, the so-called 'special relationship', between the Republican President Ronald Reagan and Prime Minister Margaret Thatcher.

Globalisation

Globalisation is a recognised feature of economic and social systems, as well as social policy and the delivery of welfare services (Mishra, 1999). Björkman and Altenstetter observe that in health policies 'the diffusion of policy ideas is truly global' and there is 'considerable evidence of cross-national borrowing of reforms – or at least (re)labelling of reform proposals – in order to obtain beneficial results' (Björkman and Altenstetter, 1997, p. 1). They agree with Maynard, however, that

> it is remarkable in all health care systems how policy formation reflects fashion and beliefs rather than the knowledge base … The reluctance of physicians to be 'confused' by facts in their everyday practice is paralleled by the reluctance of

'policy makers' to be informed by evidence when 'redisorganising' health care systems in pursuit of perfection ie. equity, efficiency and cost control. (Maynard, 1995, p. 49, quoted in Björkman and Altenstetter, 1997, p. 1)

These observations are applicable to the social care, social services and social work fields, many of whose services are attached to, or form part of, healthcare provision.

As important as the transnational nature of ideas about social policies, the persistence of massive global inequalities of wealth, income, political and economic power makes it ironic that no statutory body has been set up charged specifically with the pursuit of global improvements in associated services. The nearest approach to this is the United Nations (UN), an intergovernmental organisation (IGO) whose members are individual nations. In contrast, there are nongovernmental organisations (NGOs) whose members include groups and private individuals. In 1909, there were 176 NGOs and 37 IGOs, these totals increasing to 4830 and 272 respectively (Kegley and Wittkopf, 1997, p. 146).

United Nations

The UN is the best known IGO, with the broadest range of economic and social responsibilities, only a minority of countries, such as Switzerland, not seeking membership. It grew from the somewhat pathetic initiative of the League of Nations whose major purpose, collective security, was intended to prevent a repetition of the catastrophe of the First World War. The UN was formed in 1946, after the collapse of the League of Nations. The UN's purposes include maintaining international peace and security; developing friendly relations between nations based on principles of equal rights and self-determination of people; solving economic, social, cultural and humanitarian problems; and promoting respect for human rights and fundamental freedoms through international cooperation and harmonising the actions of nations to achieve these goals (Kegley and Wittkopf, 1997, pp. 148–9). Its enactments include the Universal Declaration of Human Rights (1948), European Convention for the Protection of Human Rights and Fundamental Freedoms (1950), Convention Relating to the Status of Refugees (1951), International Convention on the Elimination of All Forms of Racial Discrimination (1965), Convention on the Elimination of All Forms of Discrimination Against Women (1967), Inter-American Convention on Human Rights (1969), Declaration on the Elimination of All Forms of Intolerance and of Discrimination Based on Religion or Belief (1981), Convention Against Torture and Other Cruel, Inhuman, or Degrading Treatment or Punishment (1984), Convention on the

Rights of the Child (1989), Convention on the Elimination of Political, Economic, Social, Cultural, and Civil Discrimination Against Women (1991), Declaration on Principles of International Law on Compensation to Refugees (1992). In addition, the UN has sponsored conferences raising international awareness on many issues affecting social policy, including ageing (1982), crime prevention and treatment of offenders (1985), drug abuse (1987, 1992), child protection (1990), housing (1996) and social development (1995) (Kegley and Wittkopf, 1997, p. 160).

Any international association of states is no stronger than the motivation towards cooperation of its contributing members. The principal weakness of the UN is the lack of legal power in its resolutions and the lack of political and organisational structures to enable it to achieve global governance in any meaningful sense. It is easy for members and non-members to weaken it by turning their backs on it.

Complexity of international context

Whatever uncertainties exist about the political future in Europe and the USA, it is likely that social policies in Britain will continue to be influenced by those in other countries, particularly Europe and the USA, and international associations such as the UN.

The area of children's rights illustrates the extraordinary complexity of legislation and policies at the micro, mezzo and macro levels. At the micro level, the British government passed the Children Act in 1989 and the Human Rights Act in 1998. At the mezzo level, there are decisions in the European Court of Human Rights, for example in the case of *A. v. the United Kingdom*, 1998, which found against the UK, that the law failed to protect a child from inhuman or degrading treatment and therefore violated Article 3 of the European Convention on the Protection of Human Rights and Fundamental Freedoms, 1950. At the macro level, there are the UN declarations of children's rights, referred to above. On occasions, the interpretation of these different enactments may not harmonise, and may actually conflict.

Organisational context: tensions between
state and local government

The responsibilities of central and local government for the personal social services changed considerably during the twentieth century, and these changes accelerated in the second half of the century. Notably, legislation governing services for adults, including those receiving community care, older people, disabled people, people with mental health problems and children and families, has increased the powers, duties and responsibilities of the state and local authorities for ensuring the delivery of a vast and complex range of services.

The last years of the twentieth century saw relations between central and local government changing, as central government laid down increasingly specific standards for the delivery of quality health and welfare services, to be inspected and monitored through the Social Services Inspectorate of the Department of Health.

Local government also experienced a shift from the tradition of the local authority largely monopolising the organisation, management, provision and delivery of services, to a style of governance involving the public, voluntary, private and informal sectors. The local authority became the enabler, as commissioner and *purchaser*, with other agencies as *providers* of an increasing range of services, particularly for adults and in significant areas of family and childcare.

Unitary local authorities were created under the local government reorganisation of 1995–8 (see Chapter 9), amid some concerns about whether the smaller unitaries would be disadvantaging those requiring social services, by not being equipped to provide an equivalent range of choice of services as the larger unitary authorities. Craig and Manthorpe (1999a, 1999b), in their evaluation of the reorganisation, pointed out that the then Conservative government advocates of unitary authorities tended to adopt the argument that 'small is beautiful', stressing the enhancement of opportunities for citizen participation and involvement by elected local councillors in decisions affecting planning, resourcing and service delivery. Robin SeQueira, director of social services for Dorset until local government reorgnisation in April 1997, noted that the smaller unitary authorities could expect more involvement by elected councillors in the day-to-day running of social services. From the viewpoint of professionals and clients, this might be a mixed blessing (SeQueira, 1997, p. 8).

Government control over what local authorities did was exercised not only through the content of their work but also through the way it was resourced from the purse of the state. Central government control over local government was enhanced by tighter monetary regulation. Various funding arrangements, such as those associated with economic regeneration, were subject to central government approval. Local provision was restricted by capping arrangements which restricted choices available at local level. Local government was financially vulnerable in the sense that central government could withhold funding over and above local rates and council taxes and thereby exercise sanctions over the nature and level of appropriate provision.

Historical context

The changing focus of debates about what welfare provision should be made, how much should be provided by the state and how much in the voluntary, private and informal sectors reflects broader shifts in normative values, rooted in political, economic and social trends. Between the 1940s and 2000, there have been three significant watersheds in politics and welfare policy: the significant wave of legislation setting up the welfare state in the 1940s, the partial dismantlement of the welfare state under Thatcherism in the 1980s and the partial synthesis of these ideas in the so-called third way of 'New' Labour from 1997 onwards.

While the first two periods represented turning points for politics and social policy, it would be a mistake to regard them as revolutionary, or as totally new departures, largely disengaged from preceding events. Historians and social policy analysts may emphasise the rapid changes which often separate one era from that which precedes it. However, they often point to continuities which enable rapid change to take place. These seemingly contradictory themes of change and continuity are both necessary to an understanding of changes in politics and social policy.

Beveridge: the birth of the welfare state?
Social work and social services both lie at the heart of the most significant and influential innovation in social policy in the twentieth century, that of the welfare state. This term conveys the impression of a grand plan or holistic set of welfare laws by a munificent state. In some ways, though, the welfare state was never a homogeneous entity, but rather a succession of legal provisions which arose from the complex processes of policymaking, reflecting the range of beliefs of politicians and others involved in bringing in legislation. It was never a prior agreed plan, leading to a generally agreed body of prescriptions becoming law, which met a set of goals with agreed criteria by which its success or otherwise could be evaluated.

The term 'welfare state' was not widely used until the 1940s. The most positive accounts of it present it as:

> a system of social organisation which restricts free market operations in three principal ways; by the designation of certain groups, such as children or factory workers, whose rights are guaranteed and whose welfare is protected by the community; by the delivery of services such as medical care or education, so that no citizen shall be deprived of access to them; and by transfer payments which maintain income in times of exceptional need, such as parenthood, or of interruption of earnings caused by such things as sickness or unemployment. (Fraser, 1984, p. xxi)

It refers to a disparate and at times somewhat confused group of legal enactments, measures, policies, practices and their consequences for individuals and groups of people. According to T H Marshall, for instance, its social security provisions were aimed at providing everybody with the guarantee of a minimum, while its setting up of the National Health Service aimed to provide an optimum level of service (Marshall, 1970, p. 92).

People born during the Second World War have lived through a half century during which the idea of the welfare state has had currency. But beyond that, there is no general agreement about its birth, maturity and dissolution. The welfare state was not conjured from the morass of hardship and disaster of the Second World War. The war certainly contributed, shaping and highlighting certain societal inadequacies and promoting the passing of certain laws. But many historical factors led to its creation, some linked with traditions and forces whose origins cannot be located entirely in the twentieth century.

The Beveridge Report (1942), despite the above comments, is undeniably one of the most influential social policy documents of the twentieth century. Before the war ended, Sir William Beveridge had spelled out his ideals for a full employment society (1944). Beveridge's political affiliations were left of Centre but with liberal rather than Marxist inclinations. In many ways, Beveridge would have had an easy dialogue with Tony Blair over the diagnosis of social ills. Beveridge was no revolutionary. He synthesised many of the existing beliefs and trends of liberals of his day. His ideas came at a period in Britain's wartime history when the mass of people wanted to build a new society.

Some social policies proceed by pragmatism and small, incremental changes. In contrast, both the making of the welfare state in the 1940s, and the unmaking of the welfare state in the 1980s and 90s, have resulted from the coincidence of a huge swathe of social policy changes across the health, social security and welfare services. The spirit of radical reform which gathered impetus through the mass, dehumanising experiences of millions of people during the war was partly the sentiment of 'never again'. There was widespread regret that the First World War had neither been the gateway to a social utopia nor the war to end all wars. Partly also, some people had broader aspirations. Nowhere was this idealism expressed more clearly than in the Hutton Press edition of the magazine *Picture Post* for 4 January 1941, on sale not only in Britain but also distributed to forces overseas. The list of chapter headings is indicative of its scope: A Plan for Britain; This is the Problem; Work for All; Social Security; The New Britain Must be Planned; Plan the

Home; The Land for All; A Plan for Education; Health for All; A Real Medical Service; When Work is Over; this last, incidentally, written by the novelist and playwright J B Priestley. The editorial of this *Picture Post* rooted the rationale for this in the war effort:

> Our plan for a new Britain is not something outside the war, or something *after* the war. It is an essential part of our war aims. It is, indeed, our most positive war aim. The new Britain is the country we are fighting for. And the kind of land we want, the kind of life we think the good life, will exercise an immense attraction over the oppressed peoples of Europe and the friendly peoples of America. What we have done in this number is simply to rough out a plan. We have tried to out-line a fairer, pleasanter, happier, more beautiful Britain than our own – but one based fairly and squarely on the Britain we have now. We have not imagined away South Wales or Tyneside, or our confused system of education. We have tried to show how they can be reconstructed – or at least to *begin* to show it. This new and better Britain could, we believe, be realised – given goodwill – within ten years… We believe that, after this war, certain things will be common ground among all political parties. It will be common ground, for example, that every Briton – man, woman or child – shall be assured of enough food of the right kinds to maintain him in full bodily health and fitness. It will be common ground that we must reform our system of education – so that every child is assured of the fullest edu-cation he can profit by. It will be common ground that our state medical service must be reorganised and developed so as to foster health, not merely battle with disease. (*Picture Post*, 4.1.41, p. 4)

By and large, this optimism was realised in the legislation passed by the Labour government (the Education Act 1944 was the precursor) which swept into power in 1945 (National Health Service Act 1946; Welfare Services Act 1947; Children Act 1948; Criminal Justice Act 1948; National Assistance Act 1948), ousting the wartime leader Winston Churchill.

Thatcherism and the New Right: end of the welfare state?
Derek Fraser's authoritative historical study of the evolution of the welfare state had a short postscript added in the second edition, headed 'The Decline of the Welfare State 1973–83?' (Fraser, 1984, pp. 250–3). It might seem obvious that it took more than a century for the principles and policies embodied in the welfare state in Britain to be expressed in the legislation of the late 1940s, but less than a quarter of that time for it to be dismantled in the closing years of the twentieth century. But the assumption that the welfare state was born in the 1940s and destroyed by the Thatcher government should not be accepted uncritically. Has the cluster of legislation from the 1940s been 'reified' (treated as a fact) with hindsight into 'the welfare state'? Should the Thatcher government

take all the blame for dismantling this apparatus? Surely, the foundations for its undermining were laid during the preceding Labour government (1974–79) and the task was completed by the Blair government (1997 onwards), in its rejection of much of the thinking of the New Left? The 'New Left', incidentally, is a term used by some to refer to Marxists, black power and radical feminist theorists, adherents to anti-psychiatry and critical social policy analysts (Page and Silburn, 1999, pp. 100–1).

Critics of the welfare state   Pressure to reduce the so-called monopoly of services supplied by the welfare state, which apparently denied people freedom of choice, came after the 1960s from 'neo-liberal' economists and the Institute of Economic Affairs, who attacked what they described as the welfare consensus of the 1940s and 50s. There were critics on the Left, too, such as Peter Townsend, who argued that the welfare state had not yet achieved its goal of abolishing want, poverty and the redistribution of wealth (Fraser, 1984, p. 251). Whereas the New Right wanted to develop selective benefits as the way out of the perceived welfare 'crisis', the Left wanted to strengthen universalistic benefits.

The momentum of the Thatcher government from its accession to power in 1979, in implementing monetarist policies and cutting public expenditure, was increased by the policies of the preceding Labour government. Throughout the entire 1970s, there was a notable

> sharp decline in capital expenditure in the major areas of education, housing and health … [a] police pay rise, the extension of police powers in strike-breaking and the formation of para-military squads. Even in the citadel of Thatcherism – monetarism – it is possible to suggest that current practice is simply a more rhetorical version of a trend initiated under previous governments. (Taylor-Gooby, 1981, p. 19)

There is no doubt, though, that Margaret Thatcher's Conservative government gave these New Right policies an unprecedentedly high profile.

Ironically, the emphasis of Thatcherite social policy on an expanded role for the voluntary and informal sectors, as part of a conservative re-emphasis on the mid-Victorian notion of self-help, benefited the advocates of welfare pluralism. They were keen to explore the viability of 'participative alternatives to centralised social services' (Hadley and Hatch, 1981, pp. 170–5) through voluntary and informal activity. Ironically, too, the extensive privatisation of public services and the civil service under the Conservatives, which gathered momentum during the 1980s, and the marketisation of local authority services and key areas of the health and social services, such as community care, were embraced by the Blair government of 1997 onwards. The centre of gravity of the Labour Party had shifted a long way from the days when Labour served the trade union cause first and foremost and regarded itself as the enemy of 'capital' in the form of industrialists, entrepreneurs, business managers and professionals, as well as many middle-class people.

New Labour and the 'third way'

The size of the two landslide victories of New Labour in the 1997 and 2001 general elections took most commentators by surprise. They reflected the success of Labour in detaching itself from its exclusive roots in the interests of the working class, its unique links with certain sectors of trade union movements, especially those in mass production industries, and its expressed commitment to left-wing socialism. Tony Blair and a group of New Labour colleagues reformulated policies with the aim of winning support from a substantial body of what might be described as 'haves' rather than simply the 'have-nots' among traditional Labour supporters. Thus Labour attracted many middle-class voters who had not felt able to support a left-wing Labour agenda, and yet who were disaffected with Tory politics.

New Labour claimed to offer a way between the 'extremes' of conservatism and socialism, beyond the traditional, 'old' Labour politics of confrontation between the trade union sponsored working classes and the ruling capitalists, industrial and business entrepreneurs, portrayed by socialists and Marxists. The Blair government attempted a difficult balancing act, trying not to alienate the traditional working-class supporters of Labour while attempting to recruit support from what was called 'middle England', those who constitute the middle classes, who might otherwise have given their allegiance first to the Conservatives or Liberal Democrats.

The ground had been prepared by John Smith, leader of the Labour Party in opposition, when he set up the Commission on Social Justice in 1992 on the fiftieth anniversary of the publication of the Beveridge Report (Beveridge, 1942). The Commission reported under its chairperson Gordon Borrie in 1994 (Commission on Social Justice, 1994).

Borrie Report

The report of the Commission on Social Justice was published in 1994 shortly after the death of John Smith, leader of the Labour Party, and, significantly, contained the following panegyric on its cover by Tony Blair, who succeeded him and led Labour to victory in the election of May 1997: 'Essential reading for everyone who wants a new way forward for our country'.

Borrie occupied the transitional period between what became known as Old and New Labour. The Commission's membership was a demonstration of the ability of New Labour to bring into the consultation process theorists, pragmatists, radicals, researchers and activists in the voluntary sector. Borrie focused on how to shift from a so-called dependency culture to supporting people in need, while developing the culture of self-reliance and partnership in provision between the state and voluntary, private and informal sectors.

Social welfare reforms under New Labour
Blair's third way contained sufficient former Labour policies to retain the traditional Labour vote and sufficient also to attract people who might otherwise have committed themselves in the ballot box to the Liberal Democratic or Conservative parties. Far-reaching reforms of the social services were in prospect, even though in the immediate wake of the general election, the Queen's Speech which opened the new parliament followed the Labour Party manifesto in not mentioning social services. This contrasted, for instance, with the high profile given to details of intended measures to combat youth crime (Douglas, 1997, p. 11). Yet the Green Paper of March 1998 provided a set of proposals for the comprehensive overhaul of the welfare state (Secretary of State for Social Security and Minister for Welfare Reform, 1998). This was followed by the White Paper in November of the same year (Secretary of State for Health, 1998). A Labour government consultation paper published in 1998 (Ministerial Group on the Family, 1998) aimed to complement these proposals on service provision, in what Jack Straw claimed was the first ever consultation document on the family. This affirmed the government's commitment to the family as the foundation of society (Ministerial Group on the Family, 1998). The consultation document set out a commitment to better financial support for families, better advice on parenting and the prevention of family breakdown, and better services to families with problems. The rationale was partly that a stronger family would promote greater independence from costly state-provided services. At a deeper level, while the Blair government took tight control of the work of civil servants in central government departments, there were continuities with the contract-based market ideology created by the Thatcher government in central government

departments traditionally dominated by civil servants. Thus, the Social Care Group of the Department of Health (DH) had the stated aim:

> to improve the quality, reliability and efficiency of social services in England ... [as] one of the three key business areas within the Department of Health, working alongside the NHS Executive and the Public Health Group. (DH/SSI, 1999, *The Work of the Social Care Group*, DH at http://www.doh.gov.uk, 26.5.00)

The picture is more complex because that part of the DH concerned with the personal social services was distinctive in having close links with agencies and practice, and also in its research and grant-giving functions, with social policy and social work departments in universities. This culture of formal partnership and informal interaction had been built up since the days of the Social Work Service of the DHSS in the early 1970s and interwove personnel who had moved around the triangle linking practice, academic work and the DH in London, the regions, Northern Ireland, Scotland and Wales.

Tackling shortcomings in quality of social services: 'Quality Protects'
Quality assurance procedures in the social services were enforced from the early 1980s by central government, under the umbrella of the Audit Commission and the Social Services Inspectorate (SSI), which grew from the former Social Work Service of the DHSS. These arrangements reflected public and political reactions to a succession of scandals in social services, shown in demands for increased accountability and control of social services staff, including social workers, who by then had a very poor public image (Franklin, 1999). In Wales, the Social Services Inspectorate for Wales developed a performance management framework for social services departments which incorporated performance indicators, Joint Review inspections and regular monitoring (Social Services Inspectorate, 2000a).

Quality Protects (QP), a three-year £375 m programme, was launched in England by the Secretary of State for Health on 21 September 1998 with the aim of transforming social services for children. Local authorities were expected to demonstrate by 2002 their success in meeting specified key performance targets, improving the wellbeing of children in need and looked after children (that is, those for whom the local authority is directly responsible). Management Actions Plans (MAPs) had to be devised indicating how children's services would be modernised and progress reported to the DH. In October 1999, new sub-objectives were published for children's services, under the umbrella of

Quality Protects. One target was to reduce repeated child abuse and neglect by 10 per cent by 2002 (see Chapter 6). The intention to bring in HM Inspectors of Schools to inspect daycare and childminding had been announced in March 1998.

These measures for quality assurance meshed with the contract culture established in the early 1990s with the implementation of the NHS and Community Care Act 1990, under the banner of promoting best practice at the 'best value'. A new Best Value Inspectorate was established to oversee and inspect all local services, with the government intervening promptly to tackle any serious or persistent failures in performance. The regime of compulsory competitive tendering was abolished, and new national performance indicators were set in place, against which the efficiency, cost and quality of services were to be judged.

The White Paper (DH, 1998a) published in November 1998 set out the government's proposals for the reorganisation of the social services in England and consultation documents were published in 1999 on the regulation of private and voluntary healthcare in England and for the regulation and inspection of healthcare and social care services in Wales. A spate of further publications followed. The Local Government Act 1999 introduced the principle of 'best value', increasing the accountability of local authorities by requiring more clearly stated objectives; specific criteria for measuring performance and outcomes; the involvement of citizens in the community, including people receiving services, in assessing the quality of services; and efficiency in using resources.

In April 1999, the Department of Health (1999e) issued a consultation document, *A New Approach to Social Services Performance*. This stated the intention to approach the performance of social services departments more proactively than previously. Forty-six performance indicators (PIs) were put forward as the means to achieve this. Here, as elsewhere, the specification of PIs was regarded by critics as neglecting the tension between purchasing the 'best value' service and maximising the quality of services. Also, the focus on PIs associated directly with practice emphasises the quantitative aspects of services rather than qualitative dimensions, which are crucial, for example, when research, monitoring and perceptions of users and carers need to be taken into account. For example, typical PIs included the stability of placements of looked after children and whether children are reregistered on the Child Protection Register. They also neglect issues associated with educating, training and supervising staff and resourcing services.

Seventeen local authorities were named in November 1999 as 'failing' and, at the launch of new performance assessment tables by John Hutton, Minister of Health, were made subject to special measures and performance indicators.

The Care Standards Bill, introduced to parliament by the Labour government in 1999, heralded a major departure from arrangements dating from the Registered Homes Act 1984 which would be repealed in its entirety. The Bill proposed regulation of community homes, voluntary adoption societies, local authority fostering and adoption services and welfare aspects of all boarding schools and colleges of further education taking children. The resultant Care Standards Act 2000 created new, independent, regulatory bodies in England and Wales for social care and private and voluntary healthcare services. The English body would be known as the National Care Standards Commission. In Wales, this body would be an arm of the National Assembly for Wales. At the same time, new, independent councils were to be set up to register social workers, set social care standards and regulate social workers' education and training in England and Wales, keep an up-to-date list of people judged unsuitable to work with vulnerable adults and reform the regulation of residential, domiciliary and daycare, fostering, adoption and childminder provision.

To some extent, welfare reforms after 1997 were the product of wider concerns of the Labour government, beyond social services, about how to reduce the huge, crisis-level volume of spending on state benefits for people with chronic problems associated with ageing and disability. There was also a crisis in social services. The term 'crisis' may refer to the slow, insidious impact of chronic problems such as lack of resources and financing (see Chapter 10). Or, as happened after the inquiry into the abuse and death of Maria Colwell in the early 1970s and the wave of subsequent scandals and inquiries, there could be said to be a growing crisis of credibility of social work and in the provision of welfare services. There is a crisis from the vantage point of those politicians disenchanted with social workers, impatient with nurses and viewing doctors' complaints about working conditions as unreasonable. There is a crisis from the standpoint of those professionals who feel undervalued, undertrained and underpaid. Patients, clients and service users, who feel they often receive less than adequate services, may also perceive a crisis.

The main achievements claimed by the prime minister by 2000 were not in the personal social services, but in the areas of employment, social security and education:

The New Deal has helped create nearly 100,000 new jobs in metropolitan areas. The Working Families' Tax Credit and Minimum Wage are making work pay for millions of people on low incomes. Schools have sharply improved standards in literacy and numeracy particularly in deprived areas. (Social Exclusion Unit, 2000b, p. 5)

One of the linking themes was the initiative aimed at tackling social exclusion, through the setting up of the Social Exclusion Unit (SEU) (see Chapter 8). In September 1998, the SEU published a report proposing the need for a national strategy for neighbourhood renewal, based on policy development in 18 intersecting areas, with two goals:

to bridge the gap between the most deprived neighbourhoods and the rest of England; and in all the worst neighbourhoods, to achieve lower long-term worklessness; less crime; better health; and better educational qualifications. (Social Exclusion Unit, 2000d, p. 5)

Eighteen Policy Action Teams (PATs) (Table 1.1) were set up, each having a Ministerial Champion but bringing in a range of 'outside experts and people working in deprived areas to ensure the recommendations were evidence-based and reality-tested' (Social Exclusion Unit, 2000d, p. 5). The reports of the PATs were summarised (Social Exclusion Unit, 2000d) and fed into a consultation report (Social Exclusion Unit, 2000b) (see Chapter 12) and summary (Social Exclusion Unit, 2000c) published early in 2000, the responses to which would feed into the government's National Strategy intended to be published later in the year. Some areas which cut across many PATs, notably minority ethnic issues (Social Exclusion Unit, 2000a), were given particular attention during the consultation process in 2000.

As the Blair government began its second term of office in 2001, it did not escape criticism in the light of evidence of the enduring problems of poverty (see Chapter 2). The government claimed that the priority in the

Table 1.1 Policy action teams

1.	Jobs	10.	Arts and Sport
2.	Skills	11.	Schools Plus
3.	Business	12.	Young People
4.	Neighbourhood Management	13.	Shops
5.	Housing Management	14.	Financial Services
6.	Neighbourhood Wardens	15.	Information Technology
7.	Unpopular Housing	16.	Learning Lessons
8.	Antisocial Behaviour	17.	Joining it up Locally
9.	Community Self-help	18.	Better Information

second term would be improving the quality of public services, notably education and health.

What are social policy, social administration, social security, social services, social care and social work?

We have spent much of this chapter using terms with 'social' in them. It is now time to specify what we mean by them. Perhaps the subject of this book could be defined in a sentence: social work is politics and policy made local. This simplification contains some truth but ignores vital distinctions. The terms 'social policy' and 'social work' seem simple yet refer to disciplines, fields of study and practice of great complexity. There is no consensus about what they are, no agreement about the perspective from which they are best viewed and no single preferred way to research, teach or practise them. People from a range of political persuasions are engaged in them and it is not surprising, therefore, that they are often the subject of strenuous debate, controversy and conflict. Since the nineteenth century, there has been a growing vocabulary of terms used to refer to the 'social' perspectives informing research, theorising, politicking, policy, provision and professional practice. There is often confusion about their meanings.

Social policy

This is the term applied to the study of the development, implementation and impact of policies which influence the social situations of people. Social policy may be defined as a discipline in the social sciences, as a field of study, or as 'social action in the real world' (Alcock et al., 1998, p. 7). Social policy is not a static discipline. Its change since the 1970s from the study of social administration to policy studies reflects growing independence from liberal perspectives, a developmental focus and political affiliations with Fabianism and social democracy, rather than the Right or the socialist Left.

Social administration

In the 1960s, Kathleen Slack of the London School of Economics (the first director of the LSE was William Beveridge whose Beveridge Reports

in the 1940s provided the foundations of the welfare state) acknowledged the difficulties of defining the meaning of social administration,
as social policy was then called. She suggested two common uses for
the term 'social administration' – as a subject of study and as a process
'directed to the solution of social problems, the promotion of social
welfare or the implementation of social policy' (Slack, 1966, p. 9). This
process, she acknowledged, 'is furthered by the use of different methods or techniques designed to reach a decision, promote some action or
establish a precedent' (Slack, 1966, pp. 9–10).

Social security

This is the term used to describe those arrangements made for the
support of people in financial need, as examined in detail in Chapter 2.

Social services

Kathleen Slack commented on the confusion over the meaning of the
term 'social services', raising questions about whether they included
all services for the community, or only those for children and families,
mental health services and elderly people (Slack, 1966, p. 11). In the
process, she highlighted the work of Richard Titmuss as portraying the
widest view. Titmuss drew attention in 1955 to the tendency over
the previous 50 years for more and more areas to be drawn into the definition of social services, as 'collective provision for certain "needs"'
(Titmuss, 1976a, p. 40), in contrast with its former limited territory in
poor relief, sanitation and the control of public nuisances. Despite what
he perceived as the elasticity of the boundaries of the social services
(p. 40), Titmuss clearly specified three sectors as its constituents: social
welfare, fiscal welfare and occupational welfare (p. 42).
  Kathleen Slack states that the social services include:

> national insurance, assistance and family allowances, health services, physical
> and mental, education, housing which must be linked with town and country
> planning, maternity and child welfare, care of the deprived and the delinquent
> child and of the adult offender, youth employment, youth work and community
> welfare, welfare of the family, the disabled, aged and the homeless, legal aid,
> advice and information services. (Slack, 1966, p. 13)

Slack indicates a further list of services – private pension or superannu-
ation schemes, industrial or employers' welfare, and fiscal policy in the

form of income tax rebates in respect of dependent children, aged parents or education costs – for which Titmuss makes a strong case for inclusion in the social services:

> on the ground that it is the aim of a service, not the administrative method or the institutional devices employed to achieve the aim, which justifies its being regarded as 'social'. (Slack, 1966, p. 13)

Finally, Slack asserts the need for the study of social administration to include relationships between the content of the subject and cognate disciplines such as social history, psychology, economics and sociology (Slack, 1966, p. 14). Her view is that researchers and students of social administration and social services consider matters such as conceptions of poverty and sentencing policies and practices in the light of different theoretical perspectives (Slack, 1966, pp. 13–14).

Social care

This has come to mean the broad field of services offered to people in need – often assumed to be people in residential and daycare, older people and people with disabilities – by local authority social services departments in England and Wales and social work departments in Scotland, although the latter also are responsible for probation work. As discussed in Chapter 9, in many parts of these countries these departments are being combined with other services. In Northern Ireland, services are delivered through health and social services boards.

Social work

This is a prominent yet intrinsically contested profession. Social workers carry out some of the most demanding tasks of individual and social protection in the whole of society, yet, like the social welfare field in general, are often subjected to vilification in the mass media, as though they, and not the inherently uncertain and problematic situations in which they work, are the problem (Franklin, 1999, 2000). Social work is highly visible in the welfare systems of England, Northern Ireland, Scotland and Wales. The reasons for this are many and complex. Since the Seebohm Report (Seebohm, 1968) and the subsequent Local Authority Social Services Act 1970 which set up social services departments in England and Wales, it has been situated in the personal social services which themselves have been subjected to massive changes in structure, function and organisation. Increasingly, since the mid-1970s, specialist social work has been provided by voluntary agencies, notably in childcare, such as National Children's Homes (NCH), Barnardo's and the National Society for the Prevention of Cruelty to Children (NSPCC). Social work is a troubled and, some would say, troublesome profession. Social work is a political profession, if for no other reason than its close association with the transformation of welfare which has preoccupied politicians for more than half a century since the Second World War.

Social work occupies an ambiguous position in the welfare system, thoughtfully analysed by Geoffrey Pearson (1975). Is it a key agent of social control, from a Marxist perspective, functioning as the iron fist in the velvet glove of welfare? Or is it a potentially subversive empowering agent on behalf of the individual citizen, or a vulnerable or excluded group? Social work, like the welfare state, can be regarded as an activity in terminal decline as other professions encroach on its territory and its practitioners are abused, deskilled and deprofessionalised. Or, it can be regarded as an activity which is subject to transformation as the welfare systems change which provide a major context for its practice, research and theorisation.

How does social policy relate to social work?

The terms 'social work' and 'social policy' carry meanings to do with the way they are approached and the theoretical vantage points or perspectives of the people who study and use them. The study of social policy, like the practice of social work, is inseparable from politics, which means that critical thought and critical practice involve our personal and professional beliefs and values. They affect our ideas about how to define social policy and social work.

We have to acknowledge, also, that other external factors contribute to the social construction of the subjects called social policy and social work. They are not simply a personal matter for the individual. In some ways, while the current study of social policy does not differ significantly from social administration in the 1960s, the world has changed greatly. For instance, the centre of gravity of the study of social policy shifted from the political middle ground of liberalism and Fabianism since the 1960s, to incorporate socialist, feminist and Marxist perspectives from the 1970s. Later, during the Conservative government of 1979 to 1997, Thatcherism was born and the term 'New Right' came into the foreground. Many people shifted towards an acceptance of ideas about the strengths of the market philosophy and the free-market approach, notably sponsored by the right-wing Adam Smith Institute, and away from support for socialism, particularly the more explicitly Marxist and communist forms of socialism.

Different perspectives on politics and welfare policies

It is difficult to create a simple division of something as complex as people's political beliefs and values, expressed in social policies. In practical terms, there are as many sets of beliefs as there are people. Our political beliefs are inseparable from our views about how far the state should meet people's welfare needs. The link between social policy and party politics helps to remind us that the vast range of political affiliations are reduced to two main political parties in England, Labour and Conservative, with the Liberals somewhere between them. From the many attempts by academics over the past 30 years to codify perspectives on social policies, three are selected here, which to some extent mirror what is going on in politics at the time of their publication: George and Wilding, Anderson and Powell.

George and Wilding (1976) wrote before Thatcherism was born, when Labour were in power and Marxism was a critical force. They identify four ideological perspectives on social policies, from the individualism (the state relies on people to look after their own welfare) of the extreme political Right to the full-blooded collectivism (all people can expect, as of right, that the state will meet their needs) of the extreme Left.

Fourteen years later, when the Conservatives had been in power for more than a decade, Communist USSR had collapsed and the Berlin Wall was being dismantled, *Anderson* distinguished three perspectives on social policies in the welfare field and the state: conservative, liberal and social democratic (Anderson, 1990). The *conservative* approach reinforces class and power divisions and inequalities and views intervention by the state as a last resort. It supports traditional family forms and advocates a benefits system buttressing the role of women as mothers rather than as workers outside the home. The *liberal* approach relies on the marketplace as the main bearer of welfare services, supports means testing and private as well as state-funded social insurance.

The *social democratic*, some would say *socialist*, approach supports the principles of universalistic services and equality for citizens. It works towards abolishing inequalities and achieving a high standard of living for all, the total cost of welfare being borne by full employment.

Powell, writing in the year New Labour enters a second term of government, distinguishes the third way of the Blair government from the equality-focused ideals and emphasis on state provision and nation-alisation of the Old Left and the preoccupation with free markets, privatisation, competition and deregulation of the New Right (Powell, 2000, p. 42). He suggests the third way is not new, not coherent and implies it is a pragmatic 'pick-and-mix' of political and policy ideas, borrowing from both Old Left and New Right (Powell, 2000, p. 57) (see Chapter 12).

Social policy provides perspectives on the context in which social work is practised. But the relationship between social work and social policy is far more intimate than the oft-quoted truism that policy pro-vides the context for practice. The reality is that policy infuses practice and practice affects policy in complex and diverse ways. Linked closely with this is a simplistic perception that the major part of social workers' responsibilities is simply the discharge of the law. In support of this, it may be argued that five laws provide the main legal reference points of social work in the new millenium: the Mental Health Act 1983, the Children Act 1989, the National Health Service and Community Care Act 1990, the Criminal Justice and Public Order Act 1994 and the Crime and Disorder Act 1998. Yet the law sets the contours of practice rather than specifying everything social workers do.

Shared territory of social policy and social work

We have seen that although social policy and social work cover distinct territories, they have much in common. They share concepts, draw on many common theories, perspectives and disciplines, use similar language and terminology and occupy neighbouring and overlapping positions in systems of social welfare. Social work is a closer neighbour to social policy than most other disciplines, yet this very proximity makes it more difficult to clarify the relationship between them.

The nature of society is reflected in its social problems and policy is reflected in the nature of social work. Social work has been greatly affected by policy changes, notably in the second half of the twentieth century and the early years of the new millenium. In the 1940s, social work as a generic entity was not even foreshadowed in the children's services set up as part of the inauguration of the welfare state. Fifty years later, although the theoretical and research reference points for social services and social work provision have changed incrementally, the language of policy reflected in service delivery has undergone a sea change. This is exemplified in the key words in the statement that social work demonstrates *diversity of provision* in a *mixed market* which is *contract-based*, the slogan '*quality protects*' informing the practice of *best value* maintained through *competitive tendering*.

Social policy, legislation and social work

Social work is linked with social policy through the legislation which implements policies. The relationship between the law and social work is rightly the subject of debate, the main parameters of which became particularly clear after the publication of *The Law Report* (Ball et al., 1988) which recommended improvements in the teaching of law in social work qualification programmes. Two models representing the polar positions of this debate about the relationship between law and social work are Louis Blom-Cooper's advocacy of legalism and Olive Stevenson's support for the ethical nature of care. This dichotomy highlights the intrinsically contested territory of the seemingly most straightforward aspect of social work – how social workers should practise, in the light of their powers, duties and responsibilities as laid down in legislation.

Legalistic model
The view quoted at the start of this chapter, that social work can be defined purely in terms of the statutory duties of social work agencies, has been criticised for encouraging local authorities to prioritise their statutory work and cut back on other areas, focusing on intervention rather than encouraging client participation and empowerment, leading to procedure-following rather than a service user orientation. It gives the impression that social workers are more powerful than in reality; it promotes the false view that all practice proceeds from the law; it implies that major social problems such as child abuse and delinquency can be abolished simply by passing a law which social workers carry out; and it conceals the constraints on practice and heightens the myth that implementing procedures is good practice.

Ethical duty of care model

Stevenson argues that debates about the quality of law teaching on social work courses arise from more fundamental questions about the nature of social work. She views law as only one component of the mandate of social work to carry out an ethical duty of care, framed by key values and skills deployed by professionals in encouraging client self-determination and in working for change, not only in individuals but in their circumstances (Stevenson, 1998). Braye and Preston-Shoot argue that competence in practice requires a balance between values and the law, as the basis for practice (see Braye and Preston-Shoot, 1990). Carole Smith argues that social work should be more than simply the operation of instrumental rationality. By this she means that there should be space for more than following procedures, scope to achieve what is morally desirable, through the exercise of values such as sensitivity, concern, reassurance, compassion and warmth (Smith, 2001). This corresponds with Ann Brechin's comment that the critical practitioner may be helped by two guiding principles: respecting other people as equals and adopting an open and 'not-knowing' approach (Brechin, 2000, p. 31). These principles of respect for others and uncertainty about knowledge provide a good vantage point from which to survey all the material in the rest of this book.

Chapter summary

This chapter has identified demographic, political and ideological factors affecting the context of social policy. It has examined the difficulties of defining the major concepts affecting welfare policy and provision, including the terms 'social policy' and 'social work'. It has surveyed the main aspects of social policy change with a bearing on social work.

It has justified the necessity for the critical social worker to maintain an up-to-date, informed view of research and commentary in the different areas of social policy which relate to practice.

Further reading

Alcock, P. (1996) *Social Policy in Britain: Themes and Issues*, Macmillan, Basingstoke – now Palgrave

Alcock, P., Erskine, A. and May, M. (eds) (1998) *The Student's Companion to Social Policy*, Blackwell, Oxford

Burden, T., Cooper, C. and Petrie, M. (2000) *Modernising Social Policy: Unravelling New Labour's Welfare Reforms*, Ashgate, Aldershot

Commission on Social Justice (1994) (The Borrie Report) *Social Justice: Strategies for National Renewal: The Report of the Commission on Social Justice*, Vintage, Random House, London

Powell, M. (2000) 'New Labour and the Third Way in the British Welfare State: A New and Distinctive Approach', *Critical Social Policy*, **20**(1): 39–60

Social Exclusion Unit (2000b) *National Strategy for Neighbourhood Renewal: A Framework for Consultation*, The Cabinet Office, London

Part II

Policies

2

Social Security

Social security policies should be considered in the context of significant levels of poverty which persist in society. Child poverty in Britain is three times higher than 20 years ago, and 40 per cent of British children are born into low-income families with unhealthy lifestyles. David Piachaud, professor of social policy at the LSE, observes that

> out of all 13 year olds, 7% are regular smokers. Alcohol consumption among 11–15 year olds more than doubled in the 1990s; one quarter drink every week, averaging the equivalent of over four pints of beer. (Piachaud, 2000, p. 7)

Research on child poverty indicates that children have a disproportionately high chance of experiencing short but repeated periods of poverty which are very difficult to eliminate (Jenkins and Hill, 2000); children's health does not automatically improve simply by giving them more money and government social security policies may not be sufficient to lift the poorest families out of poverty (Gordon et al., 2000). This is partly because the benefits structure offers more to families with fewer children, thereby putting children in larger families more at risk. Also, children in local authority rented accommodation are more likely to suffer deprivation, thus throwing into question the government's linked social security anti-poverty strategies of raising national minimum wages and offering parents more generous in-work benefits.

Social workers face the consequences of poverty on a daily basis, in their work with people. Many members of the public regard social work as largely concerned with relieving people's physical wants. It is common to encounter confusion between the work of social security and social services. While social workers cannot ignore inadequacies in the physical conditions of people's lives, it is an oversimplification to describe social work as wholly concerned with remedying material problems such as lack of money.

The task of trying to guarantee all family members in a given household an adequate level of social security is fraught with dilemmas. One person's welfare may be another person's 'dis-welfare'. In such circumstances, it will be difficult, if not impossible, for welfare agencies to please everybody.

A good deal of legislation used by social workers relates in one way or another to the problems of individual want and social deprivation. The National Assistance Act 1948 enables social services departments to provide residential accommodation for needy people. Section 65 of the Health Services and Public Health Act 1968 provides for financial assistance to voluntary organisations. The Community Care (Direct Payments) Act 1996 concerns payments to people who have negotiated the direct provision of community care services. There is also legislation governing benefits, for which the gatekeepers are professionals outside social work. This includes budgeting and crisis loans from the Social Fund, under the Social Security Act 1986 (s. 167), the Social Security Contributions and Benefits Act 1992 (s. 140) and the Social Fund (Applications) Regulations 1998 (Brayne and Martin, 1999, p. 435). It also includes sources of help through Housing Benefit, under the Social Security Contributions and Benefits Act 1992 (s. 130) and the Housing Benefit (General) Regulations 1987. Further, people with a physical or learning disability may be able to claim Disabled Persons Tax Credit and may be entitled to the Disability Living Allowance for care and mobility needs, under the Social Security Contributions and Benefits Act 1992 (s. 129) and the Disability Working Allowance (General) Regulations 1991 (Brayne and Martin, 1999, p. 434). Incapacity Benefit replaced Invalidity Benefit in 1995. Income Support was often used to top up disability benefits and claimants could apply for help from the Social Fund.

Social workers mediate between people's problems and sources of help from the state. Social workers also operate at the interface between people's individual deprivations and the social problems of poverty. While individuals experience the problems of lack of money, goods and services to meet their needs and the needs of other family members, there is a social dimension to these problems. The practitioner needs to have a critical awareness of those social problems of poverty, when working with individuals.

Policy context

No other social problem preoccupies governments, local politicians and philanthropists as much as addressing the impact on people of having an insufficiency of goods and services to meet their basic needs. But current debates about the social aspects of poverty would be quite foreign to even the most liberal mid-Victorian with a social conscience and a commitment to helping individual poor people. The Victorians would have recognised the term 'pauper', with all the implications of personal failure, moral weakness and inadequacy this carries.

Despite much research into the scale of the problems of poverty, policymakers have failed consistently to arrive at a 'solution' which eradicates poverty. Some critical analysts such as Craig (1998) argue that policies have increasingly obscured the true extent of poverty, suppressing, distorting, manipulating and misrepresenting the collection and presentation of relevant statistics. Evidence abounds of unsympathetic gut responses to social work with poor people, illustrated in uninformed debate in the tabloid press. Many people find it hard to escape the assumption that poor people, especially those in long-term poverty, are somehow less energetic, sensible about budgeting, clean-living, well organised and highly motivated towards work than we are. Do all poor people equally deserve hand-outs from the state, or are some of them scroungers? Are people who sit begging on the pavements really in dire need, or just acting a part? Is poverty a social reality, or merely an excuse for some lazy individuals to avoid pulling their weight in society? The personal and political dimensions of poverty and social security are inescapable and generate difficult choices for professionals making decisions about how best to respond to poor people. Social workers operate at the sharp end of such dilemmas, questions and debates about the realities that poor people face, every time they engage with individuals and families in poverty.

The scale and consequences of poverty

Poverty is not an independent happening or syndrome which strikes people, with its own defining characteristics, its own causes and consequences. Poverty is often brought about by other circumstances which are immense in their effects and catastrophic in their impact. For example, in the post-war recession, in 1920, outdoor relief under the Poor Law cost £5.4 m and unemployment insurance £8.7 m. In 1938, when the Great Depression was at its height and the impact of mass unemployment had been felt for several years, whereas outdoor relief had risen to £19.4 m, unemployment benefit was a massive £51.7 m and non-contributory unemployment allowances a further £41.3 m (Golding and Middleton, 1982, p. 46). Townsend's monumental study of poverty in

Britain in the 1960s and 70s concluded that 28 per cent of the population were

> below or just above the state's standard [measure of poverty] for the year as a whole, but the figure increases to 36 per cent if people who dropped to these levels for at least a short period of the year are added. (Townsend, 1979, p. 895)

Thus, more than a third of the population were in poverty for at least a part of the year and well over a quarter remained constantly in poverty during that period. There was a 'huge scale of unmet need' (Townsend, 1979, p. 891); it was far greater than the government estimates of poor people taking up social security benefits, since

> a higher proportion of those in poverty or on the margins of poverty at any single time are not receiving means-tested benefits than is officially believed. (Townsend, 1979, pp. 891–2)

The level of child poverty, that is, children living in households below half average income, of 4.4 million in 1997, represents an almost threefold increase on the total of 1.4 million in 1968. The Labour government (1997 onwards) was committed to halving child poverty by 2009 and eradicating it by 2019. But the Child Poverty Action Group estimated in 2000 that, at the current level of progress, in 2019 child poverty would only be back to the level of 1979 (Green, 2000, p. 10).

Images of poor people

To the Victorians, pauperism was a condition arising partly or wholly from the inadequacies of the individual, whereas nowadays poverty is held to arise from a range of causes, some of which are social, including the structure of society, the environment and the economy, as well as aspects of employment, housing, social security and other policies.

In the 1970s, there was less sympathy for those who a century earlier were referred to as the 'outcast poor' (Stedman Jones, 1976) or, in less sympathetic contemporary terminology, 'scroungers'. Beggars – from the time of the gangs of 'sturdy beggars', sometimes believed to have terrorised vulnerable people and communities in Elizabethan and Tudor England, to those who beg nowadays on the streets – have traditionally evoked a mixture of sympathetic and rejecting responses.

'Scroungerphobia' is the term used to describe the fear or horror conjured up by scroungers. In 1834, the level of outdoor relief under the Poor Law Amendment Act was set so low, using the so-called principle of less eligibility, as to be below the lowest wage likely to be earned, as a way of discouraging people from voluntarily claiming charity. Nowadays, significant resources are allocated to discovering those who might be falsely claiming entitlement to social security. According to a classic research study, the social security scrounger is a fictionalised folk devil created and sustained by the mass media, rather than a widespread phenomenon (Golding and Middleton, 1982).

What is poverty?

There is no agreed definition of what it means to be poor, and the definition changes through time and according to one's own circumstances. Neither is there a satisfactory set of social policies which can be picked off the shelf, guaranteed to remedy particular problems of poverty. In fact, it can be argued that poverty is a consequence of faults and deficiencies in those very social policies.

Whereas some commentators hold the view that poverty is beyond objective definition, others strive for an objective measure of poverty. To state how much poverty there is in a society, who is poor, how they have become poor and how their poverty is best relieved are matters of opinion subject to argument and controversy, where moral judgements about poor people and their poverty tend to be applied, which are affected by the political persuasion of the commentator.

Despite these inherent problems of specifying the nature and impact of poverty, social investigators have tried constantly to bring evidence of it to the attention of policymakers. Mayhew and Binney (1862) vividly portrayed the lives of poor people, Charles Booth, in keeping with the empirical spirit of researchers of his era, gathered many volumes of statistics on poverty in London (Booth, 1889) and Seebohm Rowntree, over half a century, produced three uniquely detailed surveys of the impact of poverty in York (Rowntree, 1901, 1941; Rowntree and Lavers, 1951). More recently, Townsend's study in the late 1970s is a uniquely comprehensive, contemporary snapshot of poverty. Townsend begins his report with the following definition:

> Individuals, families and groups in the population can be said to be in poverty when they lack the resources to obtain the types of diet, participate in the activities and have the living conditions and amenities which are customary, or are at least widely encouraged or approved, in the societies to which they belong. (Townsend, 1979, p. 31)

Townsend concluded that poverty

> has to be understood not only as an inevitable feature of severe social inequality but also as a particular consequence of actions by the rich to preserve and enhance their wealth and so deny it to others. ... control of wealth and of the institutions created by that wealth, and therefore of the terms under which it may be generated and passed on selectively or for the general good, is therefore central to any policies designed to abolish or alleviate the condition. (Townsend, 1979, p. 893)

Some commentators who discuss the persistence of poverty create the misleading impression that poverty somehow is handed down from one generation to the next. Oscar Lewis wrote a classic study in this vein (Lewis, 1965), arguing that the poorest strata in society have a distinctive culture which tends to perpetuate itself. Although full of detailed illustration and anecdote at the level of the individual and family group, Lewis's work lacks surveys, census data or sociological analysis of the wider society and views the culture of poverty from a judgemental, middle-class position (see summarised critique in Townsend, 1979, pp. 65–70). A related view, espoused by the Secretary of State for Social Services in 1972, was that there is a tendency for deprivation to persist in localities, passed on in disadvantaged families from one generation to the next. Related to this is the idea, familiar among politicians in Britain and the USA from the late 1960s, that there is a cycle of deprivation, which can be broken by motivating individuals and groups of people, providing housing improvements, opportunities for education, enterprise and acquiring new skills for employment. Townsend notes that the way the concept of deprivation was presented reflected the government's intense interest in area deprivation policies. (Educational priority areas, community development and urban aid programmes started in the late 1960s.)

> The concept of area deprivation ... has a close affiliation to a 'sub-culture of poverty'. The discussion in Britain has tended to echo much of the corresponding discussion in the United States. But the assignation of responsibility for the deprivation to the individual and family also has a close affiliation to the sub-culture thesis. (Townsend, 1979, p. 71)

The response, therefore, tends to be

> a mixture of traditional social control and case-work policies. Theoretically, deprivation is treated as being a residual personal or family phenomenon rather than a large-scale structural phenomenon. (Townsend, 1979, p. 71)

Absolute and relative poverty

The distinction between absolute and relative poverty is often made. *Absolute poverty* is usually defined in relation to a view about the minimum level of adequate subsistence. It is often associated with the attempt to justify the view that an absolutely objective measure of poverty can be reached. Critics assert that if the subsistence level is to be meaningful, then poor people below it cannot survive. Defenders of the subsistence concept argue that morbidity and mortality rates reflect the fact that people cannot survive indefinitely below this level.

Relative poverty, in contrast, tends to be defined in more flexible terms which may incorporate the experience of the poor person and can move in comparison with different benchmarks, perhaps representing living standards in different groups or societies. The assumption is invariably that judgements about poverty levels contain a subjective element. For example, spectators of a household in receipt of social security benefits may look through the window and see a family member smoking or buying a can of beer, or watching television, and may regard these as proof of a lack of poverty which therefore cancels entitlement to benefits. But this is a gross value judgement which greatly oversimplifies the nature of poverty. A judgement about relative poverty rests on a comparison between the circumstances of poor people and a notion about the average living standard in the rest of that society, at that time. That standard, of course, varies through history and from society to society.

Even accepting that over the years there has been a great range of conceptions of the poverty of individuals and groups of people, the most restricted definition of poverty – in terms of the number of people with incomes below the level of social assistance benefit to which they are entitled – produces the finding that whereas during the 1960s and 70s poverty and low incomes in the UK may have declined, since the late 1970s poverty has been increasing. The percentage of the population of the UK in poverty, using the above yardstick of income below the level of entitlement to social assistance, increased from 6 to 8 per cent between 1979 and 1992. The percentage of the population living below and just at the level of social assistance in the same period increased from 14 to 24 per cent (George and Wilding, 1999, p. 137).

Wealth and income

The differences between better-off and worse-off people are affected by how much they possess as well as how much they earn. Wealth is much less equally distributed than income. In 1995, the 10 per cent most wealthy people in the UK owned half the wealth of the household sector, whereas only about 8 per cent of the total wealth was owned by half the population (Office for National Statistics, 1999, Table 5.25, pp. 100–1).

In the UK, about a quarter of the total income in the UK in 1995 was earned by about 10 per cent of the population (Office for National Statistics, 1999, p. 101). Although average disposable income in the household has risen dramatically, by 55 per cent from 1971 to 1996, so has the gap between people earning the highest and the lowest incomes (ONS, 1999, Table 5.16, p. 95). People with the lowest earnings include 42 per cent of lone parent families in Great Britain, in the bottom 20 per cent of income distribution (ONS, 1999, Table, 5.17, p. 95).

How far does poverty interact with other social problems?

Research positively correlates poverty with other social problems such as homelessness, long-term sickness and unemployment, underachievement of children at school and the incidence of illness and mental health problems such as depression. The Report of the Commission on Social Justice, inaugurated in 1992 by John Smith and precursor of Labour's social policies before coming to power in 1997, linked problems of poverty with other deficits in the quality of life (Commission on Social Justice, 1994, p. 287).

The higher risk of unemployment and low pay among ethnic minority groups means they are more prone to poverty, relative to the rest of the population (George and Wilding, 1999, p. 142). The Joseph Rowntree Foundation report into income and wealth found that in 1991 over 60 per cent of the total of ethnic minority people lived in neighbourhoods categorised in the worst fifth, in terms of their high rate of unemployment:

> Whereas only 18 per cent of the (white) population was in the poorest fifth of the whole population, more than a third of the non-white population was in the poorest fifth. (Joseph Rowntree Foundation, 1995, p. 28, quoted in George and Wilding, 1999, pp. 142–3)

Among different kinds of household, families with children constitute the largest category of poor people (measured in terms of income at less than 50 per cent of average income after deducting housing costs, in 1994–95), at 39 per cent of the population (George and Wilding, 1999, p. 138). In terms of economic status, families with one or two adults in full-time work constitute the lowest percentage in poverty, while those with the head of the household or spouse over 60 form the highest percentage group, at 23 per cent (George and Wilding, 1999, p. 139).

An impressive research study in the late 1990s has analysed the extent of poverty and social exclusion, relating them to 46 indicators (Howarth et al., 1998). These could be used by governments as benchmarks to assess progress or otherwise in relation to reducing these problems.

Key policy changes and related issues

It is conventional for the first lecture in a sequence on poverty or social security, like a written history of anti-poverty or social security measures, to begin with a stream of legislation to curb pauperism, which runs from the Elizabethan Poor Law to the Poor Law Amendment Act of 1834. But, acknowledging the Local Government Act 1929 which abolished the Poor Law Boards of Guardians and transferred their responsibilities and functions to local authorities, most contemporary policies relate directly to conditions since the 1940s.

While social security provision since the 1940s has been overwhelmingly state provision, other related aspects of welfare services such as pensions and health insurance have witnessed a drift towards the private sector, as those with the means buy these from commercial companies (Burchardt et al., 1999). Bertoud and colleagues suggest that policy responses to poverty can be grouped according to whether they are directed towards the individual in poverty, the area or are national in scope. *Individually focused* policies target particular groups such as older people, disabled people, families including lone parent families, ethnic minorities, women, young people and lower paid workers. *Area-based* anti-poverty policies on the whole arise since the 1960s and include regional economic development, rural employment opportunities, educational priority areas, urban aid, community development projects, inner city programmes and various programmes of urban regeneration. *Nationally based* policies, while similar to those in the previous category, are more targeted towards institutions and systems than towards individuals or groups and involve shifting resources on a macro scale. They include the kinds of institutional reorganisation envisaged by Beveridge, as well as policies intervening in the marketplace such as the provision of subsidised houses through council housing or housing associations and the redistribution of income and resources through systems of taxation and social security (Bertoud et al., 1981, pp. 263–77).

The Beveridge Report (1942) provides the foundation of a more positive approach to state intervention to protect people from poverty, a plan to abolish the five giant evils of want, unemployment, squalor, disease and ignorance. Beveridge made assumptions which would not sustain a social security policy in the twenty-first century: that most males would spend their active adult years in paid employment; that they would be able to pay social insurance contributions to the state; that most women would not join the workforce, but would get married, have children and stay at home to look after them. The reality is that employment patterns have changed dramatically. A significant proportion of men do not stay in full-time employment until retiring age; the numbers of long-term unemployed men has risen; and many women have joined the workforce, part and full time.

From the 1960s there was growing criticism of the failure of the implementation of Beveridge's proposals to eradicate poverty. The phrase 'rediscovery of poverty' dates from the early 1960s. Brian Abel-Smith and Peter Townsend analysed two Ministry of Labour surveys carried out in 1953–54 and 1960. They calculated a poverty line based on rates of national assistance in those years. They found that those in poverty in 1953–54 included 19.6 per cent of households headed by a full-time worker, who, with dependants, amounted to 34.6 per cent of the total number of people in poverty (Abel-Smith and Townsend, 1965). This stimulated an unprecedented debate about how social policy could tackle this apparently intractable and high level of poverty, which had not been touched by the prosperity claimed by the then Conservative government.

Political perspectives on social security

A range of political views can be taken in respect of social security policies. David Green takes one right-wing view, in advocating the abolition of the social security safety net, which he argues discourages the poor from working to help themselves (Green, 2000). On the left-wing are socialists who advocate universal social security as of right to all members of society, throughout raising children, unemployment, sickness, disability and old age. Some left-wing critics advocate extending existing social security benefits and developing a range of measures to redistribute wealth and reduce inequalities in income. A range of positions between these are taken by liberals and leading politicians in the Labour government 1997 onwards, who refuse to adopt universalistic policies of social security and retain means testing for many benefits.

What are the main features of contemporary social security policies?

The definition of 'social security' is difficult, since the term covers a variety of meanings. It is possible, though, to divide social security benefits into contributory, insurance-based social security and noncontributory, means-tested social assistance. Piecemeal developments in social security arrangements since the Second World War have led to an increasingly complex set of legal enactments. John Ditch (1998, p. 274) puts them into one or more of the following five categories: contributory – social insurance, such as retirement pension; means-tested – social assistance, such as Income Support; categorical – neither means nor contribution tested, that is, given regardless of means, such as Child Benefit; occupational – based on employment record/status, such as statutory sick pay; and discretionary – based on rules and judgements, such as payments from the Social Fund, established under the 1986 Social Security Act.

Contributory benefits return to the person who has paid National Insurance contributions, usually, except where self-employed, alongside an employer. These benefits usually are paid on a sliding scale according to how many contributions have been paid. They include retirement pensions and sickness, widow's and unemployment benefits. Some pensions are paid in the form of returns on pension schemes related to particular employment. In addition, employees may claim entitlement to statutory sick pay and maternity benefits. Sick pay may be paid by the employer at a basic minimum, or may exceed this at the discretion of the employer. Income maintenance for lone parents is provided by the Department of Social Security (DSS) which incorporated part of the former Department for Education and Employment in June 2001 and became the Department of Work and Pensions. Claimants are normally required to be available for work unless they are responsible for a child under 16. A number of universal benefits are also available, including free healthcare, and Child Benefit. Income Support (IS) claimants can claim full rent rebates and council tax allowances from the housing benefit department.

Child Benefit was introduced in the Child Benefit Act 1975, which replaced family allowances and tax allowances for children with a new tax-free Child Benefit payable for all children, increased allowances being payable to lone parent families.

Some attempt was made by the Labour government (1974 to 1979) to protect benefits from inflation. The Social Security Act 1975 introduced an earnings-related pensions scheme which aimed to insulate the individual against inflation. By 1980, the entitlement of a claimant for supplementary benefit in real terms was twice that received in 1948 (Fraser, 1984, p. 252). However, there were some major retrograde changes. The Supplementary Benefits Commission was abolished in 1980. Whereas claimants were given more rights through the reduction in discretion which social security staff could exercise, in general they received less through the failure to increase benefits proportionately with inflation. Further, the earnings-related supplement was withdrawn in 1982, which threw more people onto means-tested benefits. In the year between 1980 and 1981 alone, the number of people dependent wholly or in part on supplementary benefit rose from five to eight million. The so-called safety net for the few was becoming a core feature of the social security system for the many (Fraser, 1984, pp. 252–3).

The Labour government (1997 onwards) set out to reduce the liability of the state for significant and increasing levels of welfare payment to vulnerable people without adequate income, such as lone parents and disabled people. The government published its proposals for reforms to welfare policy in the Green Paper (Department of Health, 1998) *New Ambitions for our Country: A New Contract for Welfare*, the aim of which was to reduce the burden of welfare payments on the state, by encouraging as many people as possible back to work. The subsequent Welfare Reform and Pensions Act 1999 was accompanied by the Green Paper (Department of Health, 1999) *A New Contract for Welfare: Partnership in Pensions* and the White Paper (Department of Health, 1999) *A New Contract for Welfare: Children's Rights and Parents' Responsibilities*.

North-south divide: fiction or reality?

In 1854–5, Elizabeth Gaskell wrote an excellent novel about the contrasts between people's experiences of Lancashire and the south of England (Gaskell, 1970) and the Tory, later to become prime minister, Benjamen Disraeli described two nations in Britain, the rich and the poor (Ensor, 1936, p. 30). In the wake of the Depression of the 1930s, George Orwell toured the north of England and found the evils dominating society to be unemployment, poverty, homelessness and lack of social security for sick, disabled and retired people (Orwell, 1967, p. 154).

In the 1980s, Beatrix Campbell used George Orwell's classic book *The Road to Wigan Pier* as her own point of departure in 1982 for a six-month journey through working-class Britain. Revisiting Wigan Pier, she observed that men's oppressive behaviour towards women made their poverty more intense and hard to bear. Gender oppression reinforced class stratification. The spikes (basic sleeping accommodation for 'tramps', homeless travellers and others in similar circumstances) had gone, poverty remained, rooted in sexism and social class stratification (Campbell, 1984, p. 6).

It is true that average gross weekly household incomes in 1996–97, at £321, were lowest in Northeast England closely followed by Northern Ireland at £326, West Midlands at £359, Yorkshire and Humberside at £364 and the Northwest and Merseyside at £377. In contrast, they were highest in Southeast England, at £483 (*Regional Trends* 33, 1998, p. 107). The impact of divisions of age, gender, race and geographical location on social class inequalities between people create double and triple jeopardy, perpetuating inequalities of wealth and income. However, even within areas of relative prosperity, such as the south of England where wealth and higher income are concentrated, other inequalities create hardship. Also, other divisions between north and south appear to have given poorer people in Scotland advantages over those in England, an effect heightened by devolution. In 2001, the Scottish Executive planned to fund long-term health and personal care of older people, whereas in England and Wales healthcare remained free while personal care was means-tested; in Scotland, higher education students paid no tuition fees and school teachers achieved a 21.5 per cent three-year pay increase, in contrast with the situation in England and Wales.

How accurate is it to refer to an underclass in society?

Fear of the potential havoc members of the underclass or residuum could wreak was deeply ingrained in late Victorian society. By the late 1880s, the theory of urban degeneration gained widespread acceptance, inverting Darwin's ideas of natural selection to argue that poor people who migrated into towns and suffered bad housing and working conditions would decline physically and morally and breed a savage and brutalised lower stratum of society, lazy, work-shy and incapable of helping themselves (Stedman Jones, 1976, pp. 286–7). Charles Murray, a century later, argues from a right-wing perspective that a new underclass has emerged. In the 1980s, his work provided the New Right in Britain with evidence to support their arguments. He suggests that there is a causal association between the decline of the family, the growth of illegitimacy, violent crime and unemployment of males of working age (Murray, 1994). His particular targets, therefore, to discourage from an 'unhealthy' dependence on welfare benefits are unemployed people and lone parents, which predominantly means women. His argument is that illegitimacy and the disintegration of the family and its associated moral values contribute to social problems of crime, poverty, social disintegration and, by implication, urban decay. The way to address this, from a New Right perspective, is through confronting the individual. This contrasts with the Social Exclusion Unit set up by the Labour government in 1997 with a view to addressing exclusion as a social problem (see Chapter 8).

Underclass theory resonates with the mid-Victorian belief in self-help and hard work as routes out of pauperism. The assumption is that people should take responsibility for their own misfortunes. The caseworkers of the Charity Organisation Society, founded in 1869, which was the forerunner of modern social work, operated on the belief that time and resources should only be spent on people assessed as being not so far down the social scale as to have lost the capacity to help themselves. They were even below the respectable working class, a 'paupetariat' (Pearson, 1975, p. 174), a residuum (Stedman Jones, 1976, p. 321) or underclass.

Underclass theory can be criticised on the grounds that it distorts the true nature of poverty by focusing on the individual, denies the social dimension of personal hardships, inaccurately represents the realities of poverty and underrepresents its impact on poor people. It also makes value judgements about the virtues of marriage as opposed to cohabitation and lone parenthood. By accepting that there is an underclass, it reifies (makes into a fact) a category or class of people whose diverse circumstances and problems cannot be simplified in that way.

Lone parents

Lone parents have always been a demographic feature of the population. Being an unmarried mother traditionally attracted the scorn and punishment of banishment to a distant relative, incarceration in a mental hospital as a moral imbecile or the workhouse and destitution as an ostracised and stigmatised criminal. Only gradually did the welfare state erode the assumption that women were dependent on men. Unmarried mothers had no financial support from the state until the National Assistance Act 1948, which was rooted in the Public Assistance Board of the Poor Law. Lone fathers remain a neglected minority.

The United Kingdom has one of the highest divorce rates in the EU, about half of marriages breaking up, with 7 out of 10 of the 150,000 couples who divorce having children. Between 1971 and 1996, the number of lone parent families trebled, totalling more than 20 per cent of the total of families with dependent children. A lone parent is a person not living as a married or cohabiting couple, and who lives with one or more children or young people in full-time education. The proportion of lone parent families on state benefits who also received maintenance decreased from a half to less than a quarter, between 1979 and 1989 (George and Wilding, 1999, p. 62). The proportion of lone parent families dependent on social security benefits increased from 44 per cent in the early 1970s to 70 per cent in the mid-1990s (George and Wilding, 1999, p. 61).

Between 1971 and 1995, the proportion of families headed by lone parents increased from about 7 to 22 per cent (Newman and Smith, 1997, p. 25). Lone parents are a legitimate focus of social policy because lone parenthood tends to be associated with poverty, largely evident through their high and, since the late 1980s, increasing rate of dependency on state benefits. Two-thirds of lone parent families depend on state benefits and 80 per cent are on Income Support, costing the government £4 billion in 1989/90 and increasing to £9.1 billion in 1994/95 (Bradshaw, 1998, pp. 264–5). The high level of poverty among lone parent families is reflected in their pattern of housing and home ownership. Whereas four-fifths of married couples with dependent children owned their own homes in 1995–96, more than three-fifths of lone parents with dependent children rented their homes (Newman and Smith, 1997, Table 2.27, p. 45). Possible social policy objectives include enabling lone parents and children to maintain an adequate living standard, and enabling parents to support their children without working if they so wish (Bradshaw, 1998, p. 265).

The social and political construction of lone parenthood incorporates moral judgements. There is a tendency to regard the lone parent as synonymous with the unmarried mother. This discriminates against women by implying that they represent family groups which are somehow incomplete because the man is absent. It also wrongly assumes that lone parents are a homogeneous group of women. Also it does not take account of social divisions of class, age, income, marital status, gender and ethnicity.

The implication is that 'single parent' families are a major cause of individual and social breakdown in society and, consequently, the origins of many contemporary problems of disturbance, depression and criminality can be traced to them. Not surprisingly, governments have focused attention on lone parents in social policy changes in social security.

Paradoxically, Conservative ideology intervened in family life as a moral issue, while maintaining that individualism, self-help, free choice and the marketplace should operate to support lone parents, rather than state benefits. By the 1970s, 45 per cent of lone parents were receiving state benefits, by the 1980s this had increased to 70 per cent (Glendinning and Millar, 1992, p. 151).

Child Support Agency

The Child Support Agency (CSA) was set up under the Child Support Act 1991 (and reformed under the Child Support Act 1995) to try to remedy the above situation. The CSA requires the absent parent to pay towards the costs of supporting the children. The introduction of the CSA was symbolic of the goal of the Conservative government to attack lone parents by pushing the biological parents, notably absent fathers, to take primary responsibility for the support of the child. The consequence was to defer benefits to lone parents who were in a conflictual or otherwise unresolved situation regarding the payment of maintenance by, in most cases, the biological father. This created a backlog of work which the CSA was unable to deal with in time to prevent considerable physical hardship and emotional stress to many lone parents and children.

Social policies concerning lone parenthood followed a broadly similar trajectory under the Labour government of 1997 onwards as its Conservative predecessor. The Blair government set out to reform the Child Support Act, but focused on the alleged failure of the previous Conservative government to reduce the welfare burden on the state and the taxpayer, rather than the shortcomings of the CSA. As a token recognition of the arguments about poverty among lone parents, the Labour government left undeducted from state benefits the first £10 of maintence payments. But lone parents were still subjected to increased government control through the CSA, made more dependent on the absent parent and more dependent on the child/ren for the receipt of benefit, since mothers lost their entitlement to benefit in their own right.

The Child Support, Pensions and Social Security Act 2000 was intended to reform the child support system, by addressing a number of problems besetting the existing system set up in 1993 under the Child Support Acts 1991 and 1995. The new Act aims to increase the 20 per cent of the 1.5 million children registered with the CSA who benefit financially from child support payments; reduce the complexity and consequent delays in assessing liability; and enable families on Income Support, whose benefit hitherto is reduced by an equal amount to maintenance payments, to benefit financially from them.

Implications for social workers

EXAMPLE

Joel is a social worker working in a neighbourhood badly affected by the closure of large factories which employed, part time or full time, most of the adults in the locality. He works closely with local voluntary organisations, welfare rights officers and money and debt management specialists, who advise him and clients when specific problems arise. The large-scale poverty he witnesses brings it home to Joel that he practises at the point where people's individual deprivations overlap with the social problems of poverty.

Joel decides to write a checklist of all the items his critical study of poverty policy has brought to his attention, which are relevant to dealing with the hardships of his individual clients. Here is his list:

- Engage in basic welfare rights work
- Facilitate debt management
- Enable people to develop and use local measures such as credit unions
- Work with voluntary agencies and neighbourhood groups
- Join organisations in the anti-poverty field, such as the Child Poverty Action Group, and continue to develop a critical understanding of poverty and anti-poverty strategies
- Liaise with colleagues to gather ideas. This involves less experienced social workers learning from those who have worked successfully with people most in need
- Involve people in local projects. The advantages are, as Bob Holman notes, that such projects tend to be long term, operate close to needy families, emphasise personal relationships, offer mentoring to help individuals through difficult times and can empower people by involving them in running these projects, as well as sometimes offering people in need a mixture of voluntary and paid jobs (Holman, 2000, p. 22)
- Challenge the scrounger image which bedevils many aspects of social security policy and practice

- Recognise that people are victims of poverty at the same time as offering them the means to empower themselves and overcome the stigma which persists in its attachment to being poor
- Engage in consciousness raising and challenging attitudes and policies in Britain which make it one of the least family friendly countries in Europe by persuading employers, retailers, bus and rail companies, restaurants, pubs and public services to audit and improve services so as to improve social and employment support to parents during pregnancy and childbirth, achieve adequate maternity and paternity leave, balance work and family life, engage in childcare and travel, improve neighbourhood safety and reduce the incidence of traffic accidents
- Contribute to wider anti-poverty, community development and economic self-help initiatives, such as encouraging credit unions.

Chapter summary

This chapter has examined conceptions of poverty and social security. It has surveyed changing anti-poverty and social security policies. It has highlighted the preoccupation with rooting out lazy people and social security scroungers which has played a prominent part in social security policies of both Conservative and Labour governments since 1979. Whereas measures to combat poverty have traditionally been based on assumptions about the fecklessness and failings of individuals, including social work clients, many of the causes of poverty are social in origin and require the redistribution of wealth and income in society.

Further reading

Alcock P. (1997) *Understanding Poverty*, 2nd edn, Macmillan, Basingstoke – now Palgrave
Ditch, J.S. (ed.) (1997) *Poverty and Social Security: Issues and Research*, Englewood Cliffs, NJ, Prentice Hall
Child Poverty Action Group (CPAG) publications, such as:
Oppenheim, C. and Harker, L. (1996) *Poverty: The Facts*, London, CPAG
Walker A. and Walker, C. (1997) *Britain Divided*, London, CPAG

3

Employment

It is quite likely that social work clients will have experienced unemployment, underemployment or work which is unrewarding and low paid. This is because of a massive shift from full-time to part-time working, which meant that by the early 1990s only a third of the British workforce worked a conventional full-time working week (Hewitt, 1993). At the same time, British men, on average, have the longest working hours in the EC, 40 per cent of them in 1990 working an average of more than 46 hours a week (Commission of the European Communities, 1993). Among women, there is a trend towards more unpaid domestic work at home; and in employment, more part-time, relatively lower paid work in absolute terms and relative to men in similar work. This range of unsatisfactory circumstances is not recorded adequately in official statistics. The unemployment statistics tend to record those claiming unemployment benefit, when, according to the International Labour Organisation (ILO), the level of unemployment should total all those seeking a job and available to work, regardless of their social security status.

Understanding such issues is important to social workers. They need to bring to bear on their work with people a critical understanding of employment policies and the consequences for people of being trapped in low-paid work or being unemployed.

Policy context

For many people employed work and its loss have great significance, since they define themselves, and achieve social status, by the employed work they do. It matters to them and to others that they can earn the money they spend on themselves, their families and friends. Clearly, if people cannot find the work they seek, or if they are underemployed, underpaid or out of work, they are likely to suffer. Unemployment also has a social and community dimension. It can reflect economic problems experienced by employers and others in an area where unemployment is high. Mass unemployment has secondary effects on all those individuals, groups, neighbourhoods and sectors of society with whom unemployed people come into contact.

Employed work has different meanings to people in different strata of society. Monetary rewards apart, work varies enormously in the status it confers. Some types of employment, such as hospital consultant, carry high prestige. The situation of people in less desirable, lower paid jobs is more contradictory. If out of work, they may suffer psychologically, becoming depressed and losing motivation, as well as experiencing the deprivations of loss of income. But they still may regard jobs, for example as cleaners or attendants in a sewage plant, with ambivalence. Such work offers none of the rewards of prestige or social advancement open to the successful lawyer or business tycoon. Jobs are a means of rewarding higher achieving people, and confining people at the lower levels, in a stratified society. Renaming dustmen as garbage disposal engineers does not necessarily ensure that they will be able to relate to, say, electrical engineers as equals.

Changing patterns of employment,
underemployment and unemployment

Employment
The proportion of women in the workforce has increased as significantly as the proportion of men has declined. Women are tending to delay having children until they are older, then returning to work more quickly afterwards. Between 1971 and 1997, the proportion of economically active women aged 25 to 44 rose from just over 50 per cent to over 75 per cent. Between 1971 and 1997, the proportion of economically active men aged 45 to 54 fell from 98 to 91 per cent. It is projected that, by 2011, the proportion of all women who are economically active will be 58 per cent compared with 70 per cent of all men (ONS, 1999, Tables 4.3 and 4.4, p. 73). Although the proportion of men in the highest two socioeconomic groups, professional and managerial, has increased between 1975 and 1996 from 5 to 6 per cent and 15 to 22 per cent respectively, the increases from 1 to 2 per cent and 4 to 9 per cent for women still leave them lagging significantly behind men (Thomas et al., 1997, Table 5.6, p. 59).

In spring 1995, almost twice the percentage of white people, 19 per cent, as Pakistani/Bangladeshi people were likely to be managers, and 2.3 per cent of solicitors and less than 2 per cent of police officers were from ethnic minorities (Church and Summerfield, 1996, p. 43). The 14 per cent of Pakistani/Bangladeshi workers were twice as likely to do shift work as the 7 per cent of white people and were twice as likely as white people to be in temporary employment (Church and Summerfield, 1996, p. 44). Across all age groups, people in ethnic minorities suffered higher unemployment than white people (Church and Summerfield, 1996, p. 46). The average earnings of white men were higher than men in any of the ethnic minority groups (Church and Summerfield, 1996, p. 47).

Unemployment
Unemployment remains a serious problem for many developed and developing countries, including Britain. Relatively high rates of unemployment in Britain mirror those in most other European countries, average figures for each decade growing from 338,000 in the 1950s to 459,000 in the 1960s, 976,000 in the 1970s and 2,714,000 in the 1980s (Piachaud, 1997, p. 49).

Britain has suffered repeated economic recessions, invariably accompanied by high unemployment, probably since commentators first started examining the data. Often, such recessions have followed major wars fought overseas, as in 1815 and again in 1918. Some more recent recessions have led to prolonged mass unemployment, as in the 1930s, a period whose hardships are still remembered by many older people. In the late 1970s there was increasing concern about the need to develop policies to combat unemployment, with particular reference to training opportunities for young people (Roberts, 1995, p. 11). Youth employment, especially full-time employment, has declined dramatically since the 1970s. In 1972, the vast majority of the two-thirds of young people who left school at 16 had jobs, compared with only one in ten of school leavers ten years later.

The incidence of unemployment in Britain is by far the highest among semi-skilled and unskilled men, at 16 and 24 per cent respectively, contrasted with 7 and 6 per cent among women and 6 per cent or less among both men and women in professional, managerial and junior non-manual socioeoncomic groups (George and Wilding, 1999, p. 27). Unemployment especially affects disabled people and people from ethnic minorities. It affects some regions where particular employers have dominated the local economy and are now in decline.

Examples are the coal-mining communities of South Wales and Yorkshire, the textile industry of Yorkshire and Lancashire, iron and steel, shipbuilding and sea fishing. In the early 1960s, more than eight million people worked in manufacturing industry in Britain. By the early 1990s, there were four million. Whereas in the USA such dein-dustrialisation has been accompanied by a doubling in output per worker, between 1970 and 1985 in Britain, job losses have been accom-panied by zero growth in industrial output over the same period (Greenhalgh and Gregory, 1997, p. 98). Undoubtedly, long-term unem-ployment, the widespread impact on communities of the loss of major employers and the mass unemployment which follows exacerbate these problems and multiply their impact, not just on the unemployed person, but also on dependants, the neighbourhood and the community.

The level of unemployment, like the level of true crime, is difficult to gauge. The changing basis on which unemployment has been measured points to inherent problems in measuring its true incidence. Difficulties of estimating the motivation of individuals towards types of work they can or cannot obtain contribute to the problematic reliability of related statistics. In the past, measures of the level of unemployment have involved totalling the number of people without work. The shift to regarding the unemployment total as the number of people claiming unemployment benefit underestimates the unemployment total because not everybody who seeks work is claiming benefit, either through lack of eligibility or unwillingness to claim.

Underemployment

The traditional problems of losing one's job are only marginally worse than those of having insufficient, inadequate or unsatisfying work. Underemployment is a contemporary feature of the changing structure of the workforce. More people, especially older people and women, find job opportunities limited to temporary, part-time work, often without security of employment. In the absence of a reasonable level of guaran-teed minimum wage, some people are forced to accept employment at a low hourly or weekly rate which is inadequate and, in any case, may be lower than the level they were employed at previously.

Employers may prefer to draw on a growing workforce of casual labour, as this enables them to trim overheads and maximise profits. When the pool of unemployed labour is relatively large, employers are in a stronger bargaining position and can afford to take for granted the compliance of the workforce.

*Problems associated with employment,
underemployment and unemployment*

Problems of employment
The acceptability of work can be a key determinant of how worthy, confident or depressed people feel. Whereas unemployment has harmful consequences for individuals, their families and other dependents, much employment has negative aspects. Some people work in hazardous occupations, such as sea fishing, or occupations where health risks are unavoidable such as chemical processing, plastics production or mining. Casual and seasonal agricultural work, such as cutting greens in the winter months, can be uncertain, low-paid and create proneness to rheumatism, arthritis of the hands and other chronic conditions. Some work is unsocial, such as night work in supermarkets, early morning and late night office cleaning, hotel and pub work, or residential care. Other work such as caretaking involves long hours. More than five million people in the spring of 1998, about 25 per cent of those in work, habitually worked more than 48 hours per week in their main job (ONS, 1999, Table 4.12, p. 77).

People's health may be affected by prolonged exposure to stressful work. The risks of relatives, including children, suffering indirectly, perhaps through abuse or family violence, are increased by such conditions. Absenteeism from work in Britain in the late 1990s averaged 8.26 days per employee per year (George and Wilding, 1999, p. 39).

Low-paid work is highly correlated with poverty, despite the introduction of social security benefits such as family credit. Many people, especially women, take additional part-time jobs to supplement low wages earned by them or their partner elsewhere. Low-paid, low-status work is often associated with social exclusion.

Problems of unemployment
Most people depend for their living either on their own income from employment, or on the income of somebody else. People may grumble about work, but for most unemployed people any reasonably paid job would be better than chronic unemployment. The work people do often is relied on by them, and by others with whom they interact, as evidence of their respectability and worth. Being without a job often leaves a person with reduced self-respect, and long-term unemployment correlates highly with other social problems such as poverty, health and mental health and other personal problems (Fryer, 1992). It is unsurprising, therefore, that

policies designed to provide employment and reduce unemployment are core aspects of social policy. Being unemployed can create problems for the person without work, psychologically, economically and socially. Its economic consequences may be as serious for other family members, and includes the risk of family break-up (Lampard, 1994, p. 61). People who do not work are likely to be marginalised or even excluded, depending on the extent to which they are able to sustain credible links with the social networks which normally would sustain them if they were in work. Criminal activity (Dickinson, 1994) and drug use (Parker et al., 1988) are also likely to increase. As in the recession and high unemployment of the 1930s, racism may increase, as Husbands found in research 50 years later, positively correlating the growth of unemployment with the growth of the right-wing National Front and racial exclusion (Husbands, 1983). Entire neighbourhoods may be socially and economically devastated by the closure of a factory. Shops and other businesses may be forced to close. The quality of housing may decline. The social and cultural life of a village may be destroyed by the closure of the pit which has provided work for generations of coal miners.

Unemployed people are more likely to experience poverty, because of the lower level of their benefit entitlement and the relatively close surveillance of their activities. Low pay and lack of work are likely to lead to poverty beyond retirement age, because of reduced pension entitlement. Ritchie concludes that in times of unemployment, state benefits rarely offer adequate resources even to meet the most basic needs of clothes, food and heating (Ritchie, 1990).

Furthermore, some would argue that unemployment is creating an underclass of excluded people (Chapters 2 and 8).

The unemployment trap   One result of unemployment is the loss of incentive to work. It is often said that the social security system reduces this incentive still further. The 'unemployment trap' is the term used to refer to the assumed impact on an unemployed breadwinner in a large family, with a high rent, entitled to a relatively large Income Support payment, who could only expect to earn a lower wage when employed. It would be said that there was little incentive for this person to seek work, since this would entail a drop in income. The so-called 'wage-stop' was introduced in the 1960s, following a similar principle to that of 'less eligibility' under the Poor Law Amendment Act 1834. The wage-stop reduced entitlement to benefit to below the expected wage level. The ineffectiveness of this led in the 1970s to means testing of Family Income Supplement (FIS) for workers on low incomes who had dependant children (Alcock, 1997, p. 224).

Young unemployed people Unemployment rates have a particularly close relationship with the level of education a person achieves. People with no qualifications have four times the level of unemployment of people with a higher education qualification (ONS, 1999, Table 4.21, p. 82). On this basis, young unemployed people are particularly vulnerable. Young people's life chances may be adversely affected by the inadequacy of education and shortcomings in the transition from school to work. A report of research by the Paris-based think-tank, the Organisation for Economic Cooperation and Development (OECD), concludes that in only 4 out of the total of 29 OECD member countries – Britain, Hungary, Mexico and Spain – did 20 per cent or more young people drop out of education in less than a year after the end of compulsory schooling. Only Hungary and Portugal, out of 14 countries researched in depth, had as poor a record as Britain in helping young people make the transition from school to work (Atkinson and Elliott, 2000, p. 6).

Paradoxical consequences of changing patterns of
employment and work

The trend towards more fragmented, part-time, temporary job opportunities, and more self-employment, paradoxically creates the potential for greater discrimination and exploitation of the workforce, and greater flexibility for people wanting more time at home with their families, and the opportunity to engage in lifelong learning. The Report of the Commission on Social Justice (1994) initiated by John Smith, then leader of the Labour Party, which informed the employment policies of the Labour government after 1997, stated that

> in the UK, mothers in part-time employment – despite their lower status and lower pay – consistently report higher levels of satisfaction with the balance they can achieve between employment, family and personal leisure. But full-time employment for men and part-time employment for mothers is an unstable and unsatisfactory pattern: the new challenge is to take advantage of increasingly flexible forms of employment to give men as well as women far greater choice as to how they combine employment, family, education, community activities and leisure in different ways and at different stages in their lives.

Key policy changes and related issues

We saw in Chapter 2 how nineteenth-century attempts of governments to relieve individual people's poverty have been compromised by the fear of encouraging idleness among scroungers, a fear which persists into the twenty-first century. The Factory Act 1819 limited the hours of work of children, but it was not until the similar Acts of 1833 and 1844 that measures were built into legislation to require children to spend some time in schools. Primary schooling for all children became compulsory under the Education Act 1870. Legislation in 1891 and 1895 restricted the hours of work further. During the twentieth century, the upper age limit for compulsory schooling increased from 12 to 16.

Increasingly during the twentieth century, policies have been directed at the twin goals of alleviating the impact of unemployment on individuals and intervening in the economy to try to improve the balance between the performance of the economy and the level of unemployment.

Exactly a hundred years after the Poor Law Amendment Act 1834 introduced outdoor relief and the workhouse test so as to ensure that the level of payments was less than the lowest payable wage, in order to discourage 'idleness' by the 'undeserving paupers', the Unemployment Act of 1934 segregated relief against poverty from unemployment insurance. The 1911 National Insurance Act had already provided some restricted recompense for loss of earnings through illness and unemployment, in order to reduce the most drastic consequences for people of losing their jobs. Increasingly from the 1930s, unemployment policy in Britain was influenced by the economic theories of John Maynard Keynes (see below). Sir William Beveridge held the view that the guarantee of decent employment was one part of a broader insurance that the state should provide. Beveridge's reforms led to the National Insurance Act 1946 and the National Assistance Act 1948. Beveridge regarded full employment as desirable, with no more than 500,000 people in 'frictional unemployment', that is, in transition between jobs at any one time (Beveridge, 1944). This remained broadly the case in the relatively full employment of the 1950s and 60s. From the 1970s, the free-market ideas of F A von Hayek (1960) and the monetarist Milton Friedman had an increasing influence over the market-driven policies of the Reagan administration in the USA and the Thatcher government in Britain.

Between the mid-1940s and mid-1970s, Britain enjoyed near-full employment. While governments liked to claim responsibility for this, it is likely that post-war reconstruction, the growing demand for goods and services and industrial development contributed as much to high employment as deliberate manipulation of the economy through economic and social policies. After the oil crisis in the Middle East in late 1973, for nearly a quarter of a century from 1974, Labour (1974–79) and Conservative (1979–97) governments abandoned full employment as a social policy goal.

The Conservative government (1979–97) rejected the Social Chapter of the European Union and refused to accept other employee protection measures such as the restriction of weekly hours of employees through the European Working Time Directive, agreed under the health and safety provisions of the Single Market Act (not the Social Chapter of the Maastricht Treaty) (Hewitt, 1997, p. 87), which set a maximum working week of 48 hours. These failures of Directives and legislative measures to bite in key areas of discrimination indicate that, because of strong antagonism among some politicians and employers, some employment protection measures have limited impact in areas of employment where discrimination is deeply rooted or may be covert rather than overt. Consequently, inequalities remain and are resistant to legislation attempting to eliminate them.

Since the 1970s, when decades of apparently full employment ended, particular attention has been paid to growing levels of youth unemployment and long-term unemployment among adults. The Social Security Act 1988 withdrew the automatic right to benefits from young people aged 16 to 18, thus emphasising and prolonging their economic dependency on adults with parental responsibility or other significant adults, or, where relationships with significant adults had broken down, driving them onto the streets (Roberts, 1995, p. 90).

The incoming Labour government of 1997 onwards, as part of its anti-poverty strategy, reintroduced the minimum wage, a measure of regulation not seen since the 1970s, and set about reshaping welfare provisions to encourage as many people as possible – controversially, lone parents and disabled people claiming Invalidity Benefit (see Chapter 2) – to go to work rather than stay dependent on state benefits. This was partly an attempt to reduce the massive bill for means-tested unemployment benefits which had grown by 300 per cent between 1973–4 and 1995–6 (Glennerster and Hills, 1998a, pp. 2–3).

Attempts have been made to associate policies to combat unemployment with measures aiming to counter social exclusion, reduce discrimination and promote equality. But no government to date has attempted to strengthen anti-discriminatory legislation by combining all forms of age, gender, race and disability discrimination. The submission of the Transport and General Workers Union (TGWU) to the Commission on Social Justice which led to the Borrie Report recommended

> improvements in child benefit, shorter working weeks, a woman's right to an independent income, a national framework for affordable child care and a statutory obligation for single parents to be given priority in housing. (Rubery, 1997, p. 78)

Only limited measure of protection of low-paid workers through the minimum wage was introduced by the Blair government.

What major strategies have been adopted by governments since the 1940s to combat unemployment?

We consider now the six main measures taken since the 1940s to combat unemployment: demand management; nationalisation and economic planning; labour market legislation; taxes and subsidies; benefits and intervention in wages; education and training.

Demand management
The strategy of 'demand management' owed much to the ideas of the economist John Maynard Keynes, who, during the Great Depression of the mid-1930s, put forward the then heretical proposal to stimulate demand in the economy, thereby boosting the demand for goods and services, increasing employment and enabling the economy to expand out of the recession. The brilliance of Keynes's analysis enabled him to rebut the opposing argument that reducing wages would increase employment because it reduced the cost of producing goods and services (Keynes, 1961, p. 261). Sixty years on, a report of the International Labour Organisation (ILO) referred to the role of macroeconomic policy (large-scale policy operating across the economy) in bringing about mass unemployment by deregulating (leaving to their own devices) the financial and capital markets of the world since the 1970s. The result has been that interest rates have risen, investment has been curtailed, many countries have had to follow deflationary monetary and fiscal policies and economic growth has taken place at levels below which full employment can be realised. The ILO argues that there is enough scope in the economies of most European countries wishing to achieve full employment for them to stimulate demand (International Labour Organisation, 1995, quoted in Philpott, 1997, p. 24). But according to Philpott, this policy is not endorsed strongly in the deflationary model of the European Economic and Monetary Union (EMU).

There are three main groups of ideas held by critics of demand management:

- the supply of jobs needs to be increased for demand management to work
- monetarist controls (for example regulating the supply of money in the economy) are necessary to stimulate enterprise and investment

- support for fiscal measures (for example manipulating taxes) is needed to stimulate saving and investment in the job market.

Nationalisation and economic planning
There was ambiguity over whether one major purpose of nationalised industries was to help to maintain full employment in the economy, or whether they should be run on a narrowly commercial basis, with a view to cutting costs and maximising what is often called 'added value' (any surplus revenue once all the costs have been met). Since the early 1960s, there has been a trend towards nationalised industries being run on more commercial lines. Since the Thatcher government of 1979–97, the process of denationalisation has accelerated to the point where the succeeding Labour government did not countenance renationalisation, for example, of the companies which replaced the former British Rail.

National, regional and local planning have tended to suffer problems of conflicting goals, similar to those experienced in nationalised industries. As with nationalised industries, the political dilemma is whether it is the responsibility of governments to use planning as an accompaniment to investment by the state to create jobs, or whether to leave such decisions to the private investor in the marketplace. Given the stake of Labour in state intervention, it is ironic that the Conservative government under Harold Macmillan in the early 1960s was supported by Keynesian economists and the Federation of British Industry (Lowe, 1993, p. 116) in creating the National Economic Development Council (NEDC) for addressing economic problems and planned growth, as well as a number of subsidiary bodies concerned with economic development (often since referred to as 'Neddy' and 'Little Neddies' in the press). The succeeding Labour government under Harold Wilson (1964–70) created the Department of Economic Affairs and the Ministry of Technology. As major industries have been subjected to recession from the 1970s, and mass unemployment has afflicted some localities, this has created policy choices with particular poignancy for those on their receiving end as they are thrown into joblessness.

Economic planning has linked the goal of achieving full employment with other goals, such as improving the housing stock, often through focusing on regional development, targeting run-down urban and rural areas for redevelopment and enhancing the quality of life in the inner cities. Examples include the educational priority area (EPA) and community development project (CDP) initiatives. Enthusiasm among politicians and local government officials for the community action aspects of community work and community development waned during the 1970s. However, programmes giving extra funding to localities targeted as high in social problems continued. The pattern was more to use special funding to supply services which 30 years earlier Beveridge might have argued required core funding by the state to abolish unemployment and want. For example, the Priority Estates Project (PEP) was set up in 1979 and ran for about ten years in locations such as Broadwater Farm Estate in Haringey (Power, 1999, pp. 199–209). More recently, a wealth of schemes have been created, from inner city partnerships to urban aid and urban regeneration programmes.

Labour market legislation
Regulation of employers includes legislation in the spirit of the Treasury White Paper (HM Government, 1944). Employment protection includes tackling discrimination and exclusion and promoting equality. The most significant measures, those designed to abolish restrictive practices, still operate today, as investigations from time to time into price-fixing by major companies demonstrate. The Monopolies Commission was set up in 1948, the Restrictive Trade Practices Court was established in 1956 and the Office of Fair Trading began work in 1973 (Lowe, 1993, pp. 113–14).

Although over the past 150 years in Britain there has been a trend towards legislation governing the conditions of employment, since the 1980s there has been a tendency towards deregulation of some key aspects of employment. For instance, the power of the trade unions has weakened, especially since the confrontation between the Conservative government and the miners during the miners' strike of 1984–85. Legislation has made it easier than formerly to dismiss employees and minimum wage councils have been virtually abolished (George and Wilding, 1999, p. 29). Also, there is a trend towards part-time work, work at unsocial hours and temporary or part-time work which is only supported by temporary contracts and does not carry the contractual security of full-time, permanent work. There have also been initiatives to promote enterprise by equipping unemployed people with the necessary skills to get back to work, either as employees or on a self-employed basis, running their own small business or working in a craft or skilled trade.

Since 1979 there has been a steady erosion of collective pay bargaining and industrial relations procedures, and of the powers of trade unions to take part in these. This has been achieved by a succession of more than half a dozen Acts and by the defeat of trade unions in public and private sector strikes in the 1980s, among which the miners' strike of 1984–85 ranks as the most dramatic confrontation between the governments of either party and the Labour movement since the General Strike of 1926.

Taxes and subsidies

Various tax incentives, weighted towards areas where unemployment was particularly high, were offered also to encourage employers to invest more in plant and machinery.

Benefits and wages

In the wake of Keynesian (see above) attempts to encourage the economy to expand as a way of solving economic problems such as recession and rising unemployment, after the 1940s there were various attempts to develop policies to curb prices and incomes, to try to overcome what were perceived as the dangers of a spiralling increase in wages and prices as demand expanded.

The Blair government's programme of Welfare to Work included the aim of reducing lone parents' dependence on state benefits and inducing them into employment. This was in the face of the reality that it is inadequate childcare provision which inhibits many women, in particular, from this move, rather than lack of motivation (Hewitt, 1997). It did not abolish inequalities arising from the lack of adequate childcare facilities that prevent women entering the workplace on equal terms with men. Sustained lobbying by pressure groups and researchers has led to subsequent policies moving in a more positive direction. For example, childcare support and provision has been enhanced and a Working Families Tax Credit (WFTC), with special regard to childcare, has been introduced.

Welfare to Work programmes have the strength of providing measures of encouragement and support to people who, in principle, want to work. However, they suffer from several weaknesses: they strengthen the punitive, right-wing ideology of self-help rather than state provision of family and child support; they make some people feel under duress to work, thereby running the risk of accepting jobs with poor working conditions and low pay; they make it more likely that lone parents will pass on to their children the values and assumptions – reinforcing support for traditional family forms and discriminating against lone parents – in which these practices are grounded; they strengthen the direct control of people by government regulation of tax and benefit systems; they do not guarantee the alleviation of divisions and inequalities, particularly the harmful effects of poverty on adults and children.

Education, training and enterprise

A range of initiatives have aimed to equip or re-equip the unemployed person for entry or re-entry into employment or self-employment and

The Industrial Training Act 1964 was an early attempt to encourage employers to support better education and training for employees.

The 'New Deal', like 'Welfare to Work' was a term used by the Blair government of 1997 onwards to refer to a new employment initiative. The government developed an Employment Action Plan, partly in response to policy initiatives in the EU, promoting positive strategies for addressing problems of unemployment. This included, as part of the government's Welfare to Work programme, the New Deal for young people aged 18 to 24 and the New Deal for long-term unemployed people of 25 and over. The Labour government's 'workfare' initiatives were consistent with EU requirements of active measures to counter unemployment problems. The aim was to close the gap between the skills and experience of unemployed people and the expectations of employers. The criteria people had to meet to qualify for unemployment benefit were made more stringent. Eligibility depended on having received the Jobseeker's Allowance for six months or more and being prepared to participate actively in seeking work. While the Labour government had reversed the Wages Act of the Thatcher government in 1986, which removed the minimum wage for young people under 21, and introduced the minimum wage, this was set at a relatively low hourly rate and unemployment benefit payments were made conditional on young people accepting available work under the New Deal, even if this was low-paid, relatively low-skilled work. After six months unemployment, young people on benefits had to take part in a Gateway interview, which involved the appointment of a personal supervisor to appraise their qualities, skills, previous training and experience in order to ensure that they obtained paid or voluntary work, or went on to further education or training. Once a young person was working or training in this way, he or she was removed from the list of unemployed people, thereby artificially reducing the unemployment rate.

From 1997, the Blair government did not depart fundamentally from the market-based assumptions of the preceding Conservative government, merely expanding incentives for people wanting to start new businesses and tying unemployment benefits even more closely than hitherto to job seeking and retraining for work, through such initiatives as the New Deal for unemployed people, workfare, and schemes for skill development and retraining.

Labour government policy advocated non-exclusionary employment policies, conditional on participation in the labour market and rejection of long-term unemployment and receipt of benefits. The New Deal on unemployment was strongly influenced by such ideas as 'workfare' in the USA and combined training opportunities – increasingly the receipt of benefits was made dependent on these – with clamping down heavily on unemployed people considered lazy or benefit cheats. The Labour government's Social Exclusion Unit report (SEU, 1998) identified 161,000 young people, 9 per cent of the age group at the end of 1997, as outside education, training and work for long periods after leaving school. Young people not in education, training or work, if they go into employment, are more likely to earn less, have poorer physical health and, if they become parents, experience depression. Nonparticipation at age 16–18 is the strongest predictor of unemployment at 21. The Labour government published the White Paper *Learning to Succeed* (DfEE, 1998) which would offer a universal advice and support service for young people aged 13–19, to target agencies as well as young people in an effort to improve the transition from school to work. The aim was social inclusion: offering all young people access to high-quality learning and accredited achievement by 19; more unity, yet still diversity and choice, of services; recognition of hitherto underacknowledged achievement by young people such as volunteer work; and use of financial and other incentives (noncompulsory) to reduce nonparticipation of 16–18-year-olds in some form of learning.

Implications for social workers

How can social workers use critical insights concerning employment and unemployment policies to improve their practice?

EXAMPLE

Marian is a new social worker, working with Luke, a boy who has just become 17, exactly one year after coming into care when his parents were killed in a car crash. He did exceptionally well at GCSEs but refused to take A levels in the wake of their death. He did have a chronic asthmatic condition when younger, which until two years ago seemed likely to inhibit his mobility so much that he would not be able to secure work, but this improved gradually as he grew older. He found a job last year. However, he lost this job eight weeks ago and seems to have lost all will to seek another. Marian has just found out that he has been pilfering and on talking to Luke realises that he has not received any money since losing work.

The question is what should Marian do? It may be useful to jot down some responses to this question before looking at the follow-up actions described below.

1. Marian meets Luke and with him makes a list of the key features of his situation, paying particular attention to his own experiences, feelings and what ideally he would like to happen next.
2. Marian's and Luke's list includes the following points: Luke's list: fed up because of no money; can't be bothered to look for another job; scared of having another asthma attack; might be chucked out of a job again; what's the point of trying? Marian's list: what put Luke off continuing his education?; he may want to go into higher education and if so he probably needs to pursue A level or GNVQ courses; responsibility for paying Luke's benefits under Children (Leaving Care) Act, Benefits Agency or social services?; role of care staff; reasons why Luke is fed up, loss of job or loss of parents, or both?; what links with careers service?; possibility of access to training and Jobseeker's Allowance; ways of obtaining suitable work.
3. Marian and Luke talk. It emerges that Luke doesn't talk any more to any-one about his grief about his parents' death. The lack of a job seems to have impacted on him psychologically. Marian also speculates what he feels about not continuing his formal education. She arranges for him to meet members of a young people's network and he starts to attend their group meetings and make friends there. Some of them are moving through GCSE and A level courses. His mood becomes noticeably more upbeat over subsequent weeks.
4. Luke refuses to discuss higher education. Marian takes up the question of Luke's entitlement to benefits. It emerges that until he is 18, social services will be responsible for paying Luke's benefits, if he is entitled to the means-tested benefits of Income Support, Housing Benefit and Jobseeker's Allowance. She notes that if Luke's asthma returned, any non-means-tested benefits such as Disability Living Allowance would be paid by the Benefits Agency.
5. Marian is aware that Luke will be leaving care eventually. She meets staff in the residential home and talks to her predecessor social worker, who has moved away from the area, to find out what issues have been dis-cussed at previous reviews. She makes sure Luke has independent access to expert advice on employment, housing, training, benefits and educa-tion. She helps Luke to examine the possibility of further and higher edu-cation, now that he has begun to talk about possibly studying for A levels.

Chapter summary

This chapter has examined the ways governments have drawn on economic theories when developing policies to tackle unemployment.

The widespread consequences of changes in patterns of employment and unemployment have particular implications for social work practice, because of their effects on individuals and families. Prolonged unemployment can be devastating, creating depression and mental health problems, contributing to poverty and being associated with criminal activity.

Further reading

Department for Education and Employment (1999a) *Report of Policy Action Team 1: Jobs for All*, TSO, London

Hewitt, P. (1993) *About Time: The Revolution in Work and Family Life*, IPPR/Rivers Oram, London

Roberts, K. (1995) *Youth and Employment in Modern Britain*, Oxford University Press, Oxford

Social Exclusion Unit (1999) *Bridging the Gap: New Opportunities for 16–18-year-olds not in Education, Employment or Training*, Stationery Office, London

4

Housing

How can housing policy and practice ensure that all people have access to decent housing which meets their needs? Housing policy questions such as this are inseparable from the broader concerns of social policy. The quality of houses that people occupy provides a benchmark for the quality of their lives. Housing is a core aspect of the environment in which people live.

Housing is both a personal matter for the individual and a social issue for the policymaker. Housing deficits and improvements are not just an aspect of the deficiencies or qualities of the individual, but a reflection of social divisions, policies and problems. Deficiencies in housing, depending on the extent to which they are restricted to isolated dwellings or are features of housing in a particular locality, are likely to impact adversely on individuals, families and communities. Thus, housing can be a critical indicator of, and contributor to, other social problems. Housing problems and policies, therefore, are close neighbours to those of the personal social services.

Social workers have much in common with housing officers. Housing and social services both use the law to respond to people's needs. Housing for older people is provided under the National Assistance Act 1948. Homeless people and those threatened with being homeless are dealt with under the Housing Act 1986, which specifies how social services departments and housing departments should work together. The Matrimonial Causes Act 1973 deals with the respective housing and property rights of separating and divorcing couples. Resettlement units for itinerant people are provided under the Supplementary Benefits Act 1976.

Policy context

Over the past two centuries, most industrialised, Western countries have moved from largely rural to predominantly urban concentrations of the population. The industrial city has been a feature of the lives of an increasing proportion of the population since the early nineteenth century. Housing policy has played an increasingly important role in the shaping of industrial and urban Britain since the early nineteenth century. The town has been a particular focus of the ambivalence of people towards the changes associated with industrialisation, symbolising both the best and the worst conditions of human life on earth. This is understandable, since, as the artist Gustave Doré (Doré and Jerrold, 1872) shows in his portrayals of the flamboyant high life as well as the sordid poverty of late Victorian London, the city is a contradiction, a source of great wealth for some people who benefit from its products but utter misery for those who live in its slums or are homeless.

To what extent does the quality of housing make a unique contribution to the quality of people's lives?

People's quality of life depends on their housing meeting their needs. Housing shapes people's lives in immediate physical terms, depending on the extent to which it protects them from the elements, is free of damp and other hazards to health, and allows sufficient space for each person to maintain their lifestyle. Housing, in theory, is flexible in allowing people to choose whether to live singly, in families or adopt other arrangements. It should, in theory, be designed to enable disabled people to live as independently as possible. In practice, physical and financial constraints may militate against such flexibility. Collectively, houses also form neighbourhoods, estates, hamlets, villages, towns and conurbations, which affect quality of life in different ways.

Home ownership can be a major source of wealth; conversely, poor housing represents a key index of poverty. Indices of the nature and quality of housing can be used to gauge a person's status. The location and nature of housing can affect access to friends, shops, leisure, health and social services. Housing interacts with other areas such as transport provision. People without cars living in remote rural areas, or urban areas not served by appropriate or affordable public transport, may be isolated from essential services and those offering a better quality of life.

Between 1971 and 1989, the average size of household in Britain steadily declined from 2.91 to 2.51 people. Since that date, the decline continued, but at a slower rate. By 1996, the average mean size of household was 2.43 people (Thomas et al., 1998, Fig. 2A, p. 11). In 1996, 31 per cent of households consisted of married couples with no children, 10 per cent lone parents with or without children, 7 per cent cohabiting couples with or without children, 3 per cent were other types of household and a massive 27 per cent were one person households (Thomas et al., 1998, Fig. 2B, p. 11).

Ironically, in view of its centrality to the quality of life, and in contrast with other related areas of social policy, most housing provision in Britain traditionally has remained in the private sector. There has been a marked shift, though, during the twentieth century from 1914 when 90 per cent of all housing was in the private rented sector, to 1968 when this figure had declined to 22 per cent (Raynsford, 1989, p. 83). This apart, state intervention has tended to be limited to regulating the private market and on occasions encouraging its operation. Tax subsidies have encouraged many people to borrow sufficient money over long periods of time from specialist financial institutions, such as building societies, to buy their own homes. By 1980, more than 50 per cent of people were owner occupiers, a third lived in rented council houses and a sixth had private landlords (Taylor Gooby, 1996, p. 99). By 1990, the number of council house tenants had declined and the proportion of home owners had increased to more than two-thirds. By the mid-1990s, more than three-quarters of British homes were either owner occupied or rented from private landlords. The total including housing associations was more than four-fifths. This contrasts with areas such as education and health where most provision since the 1940s has been in the public sector (Ginsburg, 1999, p. 223).

Key policy changes and related issues

Housing for the working classes in the nineteenth century was often built quickly and as cheaply as possible, with little regard for their comfort or health. The priority was to maximise the availability of labour, as close to the mushrooming factories as possible. Great conurbations such as Birmingham grew from a few scattered villages in less than a century. Rapid urban growth multiplied human misery. Theories of urban degeneration fed concerns about the threat to respectable society of order breaking down in the slums. Poverty, prostitution, disease and physical disabilities were regarded by Darwinists as an inheritance of a grossly corrupted environment, which could create an underclass – the residuum – of paupers who were beyond help. In mid-Victorian England, social reformers such as Edwin Chadwick put debates about the living environment – notably sanitation and public health – on the agenda of discussions about how to improve the lot of poor people. The

Public Health Act 1848 aimed to address the sanitary problems which, it was beginning to be realised, contributed to devastating and repeated epidemics of cholera and typhoid.

Housing reform was patchy and reflected the Victorian values of respectability and keeping up appearances: smartening up the façades of buildings rather than building first-class housing for all. In similar vein, efforts were made to brighten up the lives of poor people living in appalling conditions, by diverting them with outings to the seaside and countryside. Mass holidays for slum dwellers were made possible by the 'factory fortnight', the growth of seaside resorts, railways and the cheapness of third-class travel.

The utopian drive to create better communities originated in the early nineteenth century with Robert Owen's New Lanark community. The minority of industrialists and philanthropists who designed and built Saltaire and Port Sunlight between Chester and Birkenhead, the Rowntrees' New Earswick housing development in York, Reckitt's village in East Hull and Bourneville in Birmingham set out holistically to cater for the educational, social, physical, employment and spiritual needs of the individual and the community. From the 1930s, the garden city movement led to the creation of new towns such as Welwyn Garden City, Crawley and Milton Keynes.

Meanwhile, many millions of people lived in appalling conditions. Efforts were made to sweep away slums and replace them with respectable housing. The (Torrens) Act of 1868 gave local authorities powers to demolish properties considered unfit for human habitation. Almost a century later, the post-war rebuilding of many towns in Britain affected by the German bombing raids of the Second World War had as one goal the provision of better housing.

In the 1950s, there was a move towards rehousing people from slums in new estates on the outer fringes of cities. Thus, Wythenshawe on the southern fringe of Manchester was created from lifting out part of the population from near the city centre. So-called overspill estates in suburban towns catered for individuals, families and parts of communities from London. However, when social problems arose on those estates, there was an increasing realisation that moving people wholesale did not abolish poverty and the consequences of deprivation.

Poorer people are constrained from exercising free choice about where to live and the more impoverished and overcrowded parts of towns create many persistent social and health problems. Concerns about the health hazards of sulphurous smoke emissions and fog, creating so-called 'smog' in large towns such as London, from the 1950s led to efforts to legislate to create cleaner air, for example by designating 'smokeless zones' where householders could only burn smokeless fuels in their grates and boilers. Debates about traffic congestion and result-ant fumes from petrol and diesel engines in towns led to ring roads being built to carry cars and lorries round towns. Trunk roads and motorways built from the 1950s, the reintroduction of electric trams and other more environmentally friendly transport systems were attempts to relocate traffic on roads which bypassed centres of population and reduced urban pollution.

What major trends in housing policies in the twentieth century are most relevant to the work of the personal social services?

In the twentieth century, housing policy has witnessed the rise of the state as public landlord, a trend towards encouraging home ownership, the subsequent decline of state housing and the growth of diverse forms of private and collective home ownership. The Housing and Town Planning Act 1909 modestly moved local authorities towards providing council housing, although not subsidising it. The Rent Act 1915 came about as a result of protests in many parts of the country about landlords who raised rents in the wake of wartime wage rises. After the First World War, the Housing and Town Planning Act 1919, which introduced government subsidies for council house building, was a partial fulfil-ment of Liberal Prime Minister David Lloyd George's promise to provide 'homes fit for heroes'.

From 1900 to the end of the 1970s, there was a move towards greater regulation of the housing market by the state, while since the 1980s deregulation has prevailed. Social landlords usually are publicly accountable, that is, subject to some form of public regulation and work to some publicly agreed standard of housing and landlord practice. They include public bodies such as local authorities in England, Scotland, Northern Ireland and Wales, privately sponsored but publicly subsidised non-profit housing associations and companies and member-based or resident-controlled cooperative housing schemes (Power, 1999, p. xix).

The Housing Act 1924, the first significant socialist legislation, put council house provision on a more permanent basis. In the 1940s, the failure of Attlee's Labour government to provide sufficient public sec-tor housing for the families of demobbed service personnel after the Second World War contributed to Labour's defeat in 1951. Post-war housing policy and provision is characterised by the growth of mass housing and the further rise of the social landlord. The massive programme of council house building by the Conservative government in the early 1950s played a large part in their re-election in 1955.

Mass housing is a key symbol of the great wave of housing reconstruction which has taken place since the Second World War. Typically, it is publicly sponsored and subsidised, uses mass production industrial construction methods and targets a 'mass' sector of middle- to low-income people who live in urban settings. Bombed sites and land currently occupied by houses considered substandard were subjected to housing clearance and redeveloped, drawing on ideas about town planning and architecture which were popular in that era. New techniques of construction using ferro-concrete, for example, and the use of building techniques and tracked and other vehicles whose prototypes were often created in wartime made possible the rapid construction of large-scale housing developments and the roads and bridges around them. The clearance of slums, however, has been criticised for the destruction of local neighbourhoods and networks of support between people, subsequently rehoused in new developments which cut swathes through traditional working-class districts such as parts of the East End and docklands of London.

The building of high-rise flats in the post-war period was considered at first to provide people with a cleaner and more convenient living environment than living at or near ground level. Later, high rise came to signify not just high-density but high-risk housing.

Housing, planning and regional development

The increasing sophistication of environmental and planning policies has meant a heightened focus in the latter years of the twentieth century on improving the quality of people's living and working environments, viewed strategically and with the aim of preventing rather than remedying social and individual problems. Housing policies have increasingly overlapped into strategies for local and regional development. The new Regional Development Agencies (RDAs) set up by the incoming Labour government of 1997 were intended to develop policies which matched those of local authorities (Local Government Information Unit, 1999a).

Urban deprivation, however, has been recognised for decades as a factor contributing to individual and social problems. The need to improve the quality of existing state/council housing and contribute to 'urban regeneration' was appreciated during the Thatcher government's drive for urban development, but was given a spin reflecting New Right ideology, through its emphasis on enterprise and entrepreneurialism. The Liverpool, Salford and London docklands, for instance, were developed by urban development corporations which transcended the interests of small, local groups, organisations and agencies. Consequently, although representing investment and social improvement on a massive scale, they were criticised for contributing further to the wholesale destruction of neighbourhoods and established networks in urban communities, such as those in the East End of London described by Willmott and Young some thirty years previously (Willmott and Young, 1960).

The Single Regeneration Budget (SRB) was introduced in 1994 in response to criticism that such housing redevelopments lacked coordination between agencies. During the Labour government (1997 onwards), housing policies have begun to link more holistically to policies in other related services such as health, employment and leisure. Health Action Zones are one example of such initiatives. The New Deal for communities represents Labour's central strategy for promoting regeneration. The £800m budget at its 1998 launch was intended to address all the problems of some of the poorest areas of Britain, not only those of housing and other buildings. To attract maximum funding, projects were expected to be underpinned by multi-agency partnerships and community and citizen involvement.

Owner occupation

Between the First and Second World Wars, there was an unprecedented increase in the proportion of owner occupiers, from 10 to 32 per cent. At the same time, the number of owner occupied houses quadrupled, encouraged by more flexible building society loans (Ginsburg, 1999, pp. 232–3). However, the rapid expansion of council housing and the lack of specific inducements to home ownership during the immediate post-war decades did not lead to a continuous expansion in owner occupation. But after the 1970s, house ownership, traditionally a middle- and upper-class phenomenon, spread to the working class in a pronounced way, as the Conservative government's policy of encouraging council house tenants to buy their own homes took effect. During the 1980s, the proportion of owner occupation increased from 54 to 66 per cent. However, during the 1990s, the proportion of owner occupiers hardly changed (Thomas et al., 1998, p. 24). This may be explained partly through the impact of several periods of inflation in house prices.

Growing critical awareness of housing deficits

Alan Murie identifies the mid-1970s as a watershed. By that time,

> it was widely argued that housing problems had been generally solved and what remained were specific, local problems which needed targeted interventions. (Murie, 1998, p. 303)

To some extent, the supply of housing for potential buyers was changing, due to economic factors arising from changes in the supply of, and demand for, housing. Successive inflationary surges in house prices since the early 1970s increased the gap between 'haves' and 'have-nots', as house owners made massive capital gains which, on their main dwelling, were exempted from any taxes, and those without substantial capital or property to trade in were prevented from buying houses. But in another sense, problems of homelessness and poverty associated with living in poor quality housing had always existed, but were highlighted as public awareness, through such dramatic events as Jeremy Sandford's film *Cathy Come Home*, became sensitised to them.

Repossessions

People in the owner occupied housing sector were not exempt from housing problems. Repossessions of houses, usually by building societies and banks loaning money through mortgages, increased dramatically from the 1970s, as mortgagers were affected by unexpected crises such as job loss, compulsory early retirement and in some areas falling house prices. These factors contributed to periods of declining house prices and so-called 'negative equity' (where the price of a house fell below its original purchase price), making it impossible for a house owner to defray expenses by recouping the original outlay on a property. In 1982, there were 33,000 cases of mortgage arrears of more than six months, whereas by 1992, during the economic recession of the early 1990s, there were more than 300,000 such cases (Ginsburg, 1999, p. 240). Shelter estimated that despite the numbers of repossessions falling during 1999, more than 13,500 families and single people still suffered the trauma of losing their home through repossession during the last six months of 1999 (Shelter, Press Release, 26 January 2000).

From the late 1980s, came the first of a number of reductions in tax relief on mortgage interest payments, which, however, only temporarily curtailed the demand for home ownership.

Changes in the social housing sector
The Housing Act 1957 required local authorities to consider housing conditions and assess housing needs in their area, giving them powers to acquire land by compulsory purchase and build and convert houses. By such means, by the 1970s local authority council house provision became a significant part of the housing stock. By the early 1980s, this trend had reversed. The Conservative government of 1970–74 built on Labour's introduction of 'fair rents' and under the Housing Finance Act 1972 brought in the system of 'fair rents' in the council house sector. This attempt to raise council house rents was reversed in 1975 by the Labour government (1974–79) and was followed by the introduction of housing benefit in 1980 by the Conservative Thatcher government.

The Conservative government (1979–97) set out four goals for its housing policy: encouraging private owner occupation; reducing the number of council houses; reviving the private rented sector; and focusing on the most urgent housing problems (Atkinson and Durden, 1994, p. 183). Between 1979 and 1995, the proportion of local authority council houses in the housing stock declined from 31.4 to 18.9 per cent (Ginsburg, 1999, p. 241). Most controversially, the Housing Act 1980 cleared the way for the wholesale privatisation of council housing, by creating the 'right to buy', partly as a means of reducing local authority expenditure, and more than two million homes were purchased by their tenants between 1980 and 1985.

Over the years, the length of waiting lists of people wishing to occupy council housing has become a political issue. The discrepancy between the numbers of empty houses held by local authorities, and the numbers on their waiting lists, has led to efforts to speed the process of new allocations. The first survey of waiting lists in 1949 found more than one and a half million applications, 85 per cent of whom were married couple families, over 60 per cent of whom had children (Green et al., 1997, p. 114). By 1988, the number of people on waiting lists had reduced to 670,000 and by 1995/96 the total was 631,000 (Green et al., 1997, Table 6.1, p. 115).

Housing associations follow the trend of the rest of the social rented sector and tend to cater for poorer people. Housing associations played an increasingly important role from the 1970s, bringing flexibility in home ownership to the housing market. The Housing Act 1974 boosted the funding of housing associations under the Labour government. Rising house prices from the 1970s created difficulties for people of limited means wanting a home. This particularly applied to older people, young couples on low wages and without savings, who wanted to start a family and lone parents. It was a feature of many rural areas which attracted retired people and second-home owners, and parts of the south of England, notably the London area. In 62 per cent of households in housing association accommodation in Britain in 1996, the head of the household was 'economically inactive' (Thomas et al., 1998, p. 36). People with the lowest average gross weekly incomes (£184) lived in the social housing sector, in contrast with people with mortgages (£543). In the late 1990s, lone parent families were the most likely to live in socially provided housing, 53 per cent occupying it as opposed to 16 per cent of other families (Thomas et al., 1998, p. 25).

A person of limited means who met the criteria of the particular housing development owned by the housing association could contract to pay a mixture of rent and mortgage for a house, with part of the proceeds of any profits from its eventual sale being returned to the housing association. Between 1971 and 1996, the percentage of households renting from housing associations on this basis increased fivefold, from 1 to 5 per cent (Thomas et al., 1998, p. 28). This steady expansion in housing association provision was not great enough during the Thatcher government to compensate for the decline in council housing. During the 1980s, the number of new developments started by housing associations averaged about 14,000 annually. Between 1979 and 1994, the previous main activity of housing associations, renovations, declined by 62 per cent (Ginsburg, 1999, p. 241). The Housing Act 1988 provided new financial arrangements for housing associations and initiated housing action trusts in England.

Between 1994 and 1996, housing associations catered for 30 per cent of the total of ethnic minority residents of all types of housing (Thomas et al., 1998, p. 38). Lone parents and their children and people from ethnic minorities, particularly Afro-Caribbean and Bangladeshi people, despite a significant increase in their rate of home ownership, were still much more likely than other groups to occupy social rented housing, that is, council housing and housing association accommodation (Thomas et al., 1998, p. 38). Pakistani and Bangladeshi households were, on average, the largest. At 4.5 persons, they were nearly twice the size of white households, which averaged 2.4 persons (Thomas et al., 1998, p. 13).

The Housing Act 1996 required local authorities to investigate applicants' claims of homelessness, and decide whether they are intentionally or unintentionally homeless. An eligibility test was used to determine whether a person was homeless or threatened with homelessness.

A number of schemes were set up in the 1990s aiming to help people on low incomes gain access to living accommodation in the privately rented sector. Two of the main policies involved grants to voluntary agencies and accommodation registers, boosted by Section 73 funding (under the Housing Act 1985), and schemes setting up special funds to enable potential householders to pay deposit guarantees and rent in advance. Deposit guarantee schemes expanded so rapidly that by the mid-1990s there was a National Forum representing them (Rugg, 1997, p. ix). Evaluation of these access initiatives indicates that they fulfil an important function, reassuring and supporting housing clients, preventing them from risking rooflessness when seeking more suitable and permanent accommodation (Rugg, 1996, pp. xxiii–xxiv). Subsequent policy changes by the Conservative government – notably restricting payments of Housing Benefit to people under 25 – had a negative effect on these access schemes (Rugg, 1997).

A strategic approach to neighbourhood renewal

The main housing policy issues as perceived by the Labour government were summarised in May 2000 in the Housing Green Paper issued by the Department of the Environment, Transport and the Regions. This acknowledged longstanding neglect of the housing stock in Britain, half of which was more than 50 years old. This contributed to widespread housing problems: a backlog of £19b on housing repairs had left many people poorly housed; many run-down housing estates contributed to ill health, crime and poverty; many people, especially older and vulnerable people, could not afford to heat and maintain their homes; most public sector tenants were denied choice about where to live, paid rents not comparable with other comparable homes and, in the case of the most disadvantaged, were often placed in the poorest housing; some, perhaps for reasons of unemployment, could not afford to keep up mortgage payments; and some people were sleeping rough or homeless (DETR, 2000, p. 5).

> There are strong associations between poor housing and poverty, deprivation, crime, educational under-achievement and ill health. People are discriminated against in looking for work or using services because of where they live. Whole neighbourhoods suffer from neglect. (DETR, 2000, p. 5)

The Green Paper advocated measures to improve the standards of service provided by private landlords, supporting sustainable home ownership, supporting local authorities taking a more proactive role in developing a strategic response to needs in their locality in partnership with the private housing sector, consistent with the broader purposes of social, economic and environmental development (DETR, 2000, pp. 10–11).

Reports by the Policy Action Teams (PATs) of the Social Exclusion Unit (SEU) highlighted the need for community self-help, the promotion of local enterprise, neighbourhood management including measures to encourage local leadership, improved housing management, an enhanced role for on-the-spot neighbourhood wardens in reducing crime, enhanced access to local and externally available information, financial shopping facilities and cultural and recreational activities, effective joint working and for a more strategic approach than hitherto to reducing unpopular housing (see Chapter 12 for more details).

Social exclusion: ghettos, 'sink' estates and mass housing
One test of an inclusive society is the openness of more privileged residents to migrants settling from minority, stigmatised populations. Hostility may be displayed towards immigrants, refugees, asylum seekers and people wanting to abolish the segregation of groups seen as 'problems'. Housing policy is one way of achieving this. Anne Power identifies common features of mass housing, that is, publicly subsidised, mass built and associated with deprivation and social exclusion, in her research across five northern European countries (Denmark, France, Germany, England and Ireland) (Power, 1997, p. 397). Some black ethnic minorities are prone to being segregated in this way, as Peter Ratcliffe notes:

> The conventional consensus amongst writers on the UK scene is that the existing spatial patterns involving heavy concentrations in poor (largely pre-1919) terraced housing on the part of Pakistani, and more especially Bangladeshi, households is the combined result of poverty, unemployment and negative housing market effects. These factors, combined with the development of an ethnicised social, economic and religious infrastructure serve to reinforce existing spatial patterns. (Ratcliffe, 2000, p. 174)

They significantly worsen the chance that social workers will succeed in empowering people to counter the effects of stigmatisation. Research indicating that segregating diverse populations into distinct blocks of public and private housing leads to greater fear and resentment encourages optimism that in future residents may prefer to live on mixed tenure estates. But even in streets of mixed housing tenure, only a small minority of residents appeared to belong to an inclusive social group (Jupp, 1999).

Local housing companies

The Labour government (1997 onwards) continued the policy of the Conservatives initiated in 1986, since when the vast majority of local councils have been transferring the housing stock to newly created landlords in the form of local housing companies which include tenants on their management boards. These have taken over the running of about half a million council houses, on estates which often burden local authorities and give off an air of unattractive uniformity and urban neglect.

The Labour government (1997 onwards) acted to reverse some clauses of the Housing Act 1996 and also introduced a number of housing policies to remedy longstanding deficits in housing. These included: acting on the recommendations of the Construction Task Force report and introducing a Quality Mark scheme to improve public and professional confidence in the quality of builders; improving the availability of affordable social housing; improving the effectiveness of housing services delivered by local authorities and social landlords, for instance by adapting the housing role of local authorities to local circumstances so as to meet local needs; using the private finance initiative (PFI) as an umbrella for a pathfinder programme aimed at attracting private investment in local authority social housing; introducing the 'Supporting People' initiative which improves support aimed at increasing the independent living of vulnerable older and disabled people; delivering Housing Benefit more efficiently, through the principles of best value; and expanding the Home Energy Efficiency Scheme to enable older, poorer and disabled people to benefit from insulating and heating improvements.

Central government approaches to quality assurance (see Chapter 9) follow a similar pattern of standard setting and evaluation of performance in the social housing sector as in the related field of personal social services. The Housing Corporation is a UK government agency with responsibility for funding, regulating and facilitating the performance of the social housing sector in England. The Housing Corporation reports annually to parliament and is subject to political scrutiny by a five-yearly Finance, Management and Policy Review commissioned by ministers, is subject to the jurisdiction of the Parliamentary Commissioner for Administration (the Parliamentary Ombudsman) and, if necessary, can be called before the House of Commons Public Accounts

Committee. It is also subject to public scrutiny through the National Audit Office. Housing associations – the major providers of subsidised housing for people, of which there are more than 2,200 – are registered social landlords (RSL) with the Housing Corporation, which evaluates their performance annually against a range of performance indicators, through an Innovation and Good Practice (IGP) grant programme and a guide to good practice. This careful approach to regulating the performance of housing associations in the social housing sector throws into even sharper relief the glaring housing problems elsewhere.

Homelessness
Homelessness may inflict a range of devastating conditions which may cause severe harm, including serious mental health problems (Cooke and Marshall, 1996; Stone, 1997), to individuals, groups, households, families and neighbourhoods. People tend to be driven to leaving home as a desperate measure, rather than becoming homeless from casual choice. Women who leave their partners, 'runaway' children and young people – a high proportion of women and young people who leave home are escaping from abusive situations – asylum seekers, people who are substance abusers, older people may all appreciate the extreme sense of loss and chaos, trauma and isolation, which may result from losing one's home. Homeless people may be offered temporary accommodation, moved to another area and offered housing, squat in empty buildings or sleep rough or on the streets. Access to adequate shelter, food and washing facilities, social security benefits, work, friends and relatives may all be severely restricted by becoming homeless. Women may be particularly traumatised by the loss of home and family including children (Hanmer and Statham, 1999). They may be particularly vulnerable to physical and sexual abuse and, because of inequalities in the employment market, may find it more difficult than men to secure even the most poorly paid and temporary, non-exploitive work to try to retrieve their status as householders. A high proportion of homeless women have been assaulted, raped and abused while in temporary accommodation for homeless people, such as bed and breakfast houses, hotels and hostels (Smith, 1995). Debates about homelessness have become more critical as the perception of homelessness as a category has extended to include those who are inadequately housed. Since the early 1970s, the reduced availability of social, particularly council, housing and increased owner occuption led to social housing being treated as last resort housing for socially excluded people with the most limited housing and social aspirations. Increased demand for social housing has been caused by more family breakdowns,

the expansion of community care, greater numbers of people living alone and the widening gulf between 'haves' and 'have-nots' in society.

The Housing (Homeless Persons) Act 1977 required local authorities to give priority to housing homeless people on the housing waiting list in their local authority of residence. However, a person defined as homeless could be redirected to another local authority where they had a local connection, a principle reminiscent of the Elizabethan Poor Law which directed people to their parish of origin for poor relief. People in debt through rent arrears had to clear their debt before they could become eligible for housing. They then had to compete with other people on the housing list and earn sufficient points to progress up the queue of housing applicants.

The Housing (Homeless Persons) Act 1977 and the Housing Act 1985 provided a safety net for families and vulnerable people, who were not made homeless through any fault of their own. These Acts stimulated local authorities to provide nearly two million affordable homes for homeless people.

Shelter used official statistics to derive estimates that about 400,000 people were officially homeless in England in 1998, about 49,000 families and individuals were placed in temporary accommodation by local authorities – bed and breakfast, hostels or lodgings – and about 78,000 people faced action to repossess their homes (Shelter, 2000b). According to analysis of over 80,000 calls to Shelterline in its first year, the three main reasons for people becoming homeless are criminal violence in the home, financial problems and the lack of a social security safety net for single people (Shelter, 2000a). One particular problem is the vulnerability of young people who have no social security benefits and no legal entitlement to emergency housing in bed and breakfast or hostel accommodation. Many finish up squatting in empty houses and begging on the streets. They are likely to be arrested for trespass or unlicensed begging and are prone to being recruited into prostitution. In contrast, they are often portrayed in the mass media as predators on other people's generosity, rather than as victims of circumstances largely outside their control.

Responses to homelessness, living on the street and begging include theoretical and empirical research. Among a great mass of empirical research, Shelter and Crisis estimated that in 1999 at least 2,500 people, 2,000 in England alone, slept out on the streets on any one night. A quarter of these were between 18 and 25 years old, 6 per cent were over 60, 30 per cent had been in the care of the local authority and between a third and a half were suffering mental health problems (Shelter, Press

Release, 15 November, 1999). A survey of homeless people by Shelter revealed that more than three-quarters had mental health problems and had been discharged from hospital without the security of housing or care services. Many people who had obtained accommodation had problems living independently and ultimately lost their tenancy. Disabled people were often faced with inaccessible accommodation which made basic household tasks impossible. Shelter recommended that local authorities should be required to make sure such people were enabled to put in place comprehensive housing and care plans, including help with their personal care, budgeting and maintaining their tenancy (Shelter, 1999).

Shelter has campaigned for legislation to prevent homelessness rather than offer help only when people reach a crisis, to ensure single people are not excluded from obtaining homes, to avoid homeless people being placed in the worst accommodation and to give homeless people a meaningful say in choosing the type and location of their home, together with the right to a permanent home with the necessary support to rebuild their lives (Shelter, Press Release, 22 February, 1999).

Legislation has tended to address homelessness and street begging in isolation from other social needs, and as though they are problems of the individual person, rather than linked with other aspects of social and economic change. Kennett and Marsh are among those recognising the inadequacy of such a response, instead locating the phenomenon of homelessness in terms of debates about social, economic and policy changes (Kennett and Marsh, 1999). Dean (1999) argues for street begging not to be dismissed as reprehensible, but to be understood in relation to related issues of homelessness and social exclusion, including problems of mental health, sexual exploitation and substance abuse.

Meanwhile, since the early 1990s, the removal of benefits for 16- and 17-year-olds, the implementation of the Housing Act 1989 and imposition of charges for hostel accommodation have combined further to impoverish many vulnerable young people already experiencing severe poverty. So the impact of neo-conservative economic policies in the 1980s and 90s has been to propel more young people into homelessness, begging and, in extreme cases, prostitution, through reducing their ability to support themselves in other ways.

The Labour government set the target of reducing the number of people sleeping rough by two-thirds by 2002 and, ideally, to zero (foreword by the Prime Minister to SEU Report on Rough Sleepers, 1998b). However, it can be argued that targeting rough sleepers in this way accentuates social exclusion and perpetuates right-wing policies, based on the assumption that people become intentionally homeless and that street beggars, for example, are confidence tricksters. The solution to street begging, apparently, is to render less visible and embarrassing the problems of those begging by sweeping them off the streets.

Social support and social control
There is a tension between the roles of housing officials and social workers in supporting people and intervening to protect others in the community. The Labour government introduced antisocial behaviour orders under the Crime and Disorder Act 1998. The purpose of these orders in this connection is to curb anyone over the age of 10 judged to be harassing, alarming or causing distress to others. They run for a minimum of two years, with no maximum, and may be used to curb a person's free access to accommodation in a locality from which, in effect, they are banished.

Asylum seekers   Applications from those seeking political asylum, mainly from Iraq, the former Yugoslavia and nearby countries, grew to more than 78,000 per annum by 2000. Asylum seekers are restricted in access to local authority housing under Section 9 of the Asylum and Immigration Act 1996 and the Housing Act 1996. The situation of asylum seekers is problematic in some parts of Britain, due to antagonism exacerbated by the mass media and misrepresentation of their circumstances and the historical reality of immigration as an important contributory factor in the growth and health of many seemingly indigenous communities. The processing of applications for asylum can be lengthy. During this period, asylum seekers may be imprisoned, confined in conditions resembling imprisonment, or housed in conditions which they experience as stigmatising (see also Chapter 8).

Victims of domestic violence   The Women's Aid movement was a self-help initiative arising from women experiencing criminal violence in the home working together to provide refuges for themselves and other women. Refuges were generally anonymous houses where women and their children could seek protection, emotional support, counselling and advice, while moving towards planning their next moves. Sometimes the refuge offered space to consider police action against a violent male partner, separation or divorce. In general, the refuge offered women an alternative short-term or medium-term home when conditions at home became unbearable.

The Housing (Homeless Persons) Act 1997 provides limited protection for those experiencing criminal violence in the home (see Chapter 6).

Use of temporary accommodation   Since the early 1980s, as a result of the increased tendency by agencies to refer families to temporary accommodation, a staggering increase occurred from that period in households occupying temporary accommodation, from 4,710 households in 1980 to 63,070 in 1992 (Ginsburg, 1999, p. 244). These have often included families which have experienced sudden and unexpected traumas or crises, such as unemployment or family break-up, including diasporas of refugees in the wake of recent wars and other social upheavals. Often, such housing is unsuitable for family life, consisting of bed and breakfast or hostel accommodation, with inadequate space and privacy for family members.

Similarities between housing and social services
There are close connections and some shared territory between housing and social services policy and practice. The functions of housing and social services overlap significantly, not least because of their common focus on the needs of people in the social housing sector. In some local authorities, housing and social services have remained separate departments, while others merged during the 1990s. One local authority in Yorkshire has created a department of Public Protection, Housing and Social Services, with public protection dealing with environmental concerns.

   However, housing officers and social workers exercise different powers under different legislation. Nevertheless, it is worth posing the question: what can social workers draw from housing policy and use to improve their own practice?

Implications for social workers

The following example may help to illustrate how a critical understanding of housing policies may help to improve social work practice.

EXAMPLE

D is a newly qualified social worker, inexperienced in dealing with rent debt, faced with the housing problems of Gloria, a lone parent of four young children who occupies local authority rented accommodation. Gloria is very independent. She has a slight learning disability, can be disorganised in her housekeeping and since getting work has not noticed that her Housing Benefit was overpaid until four months later she has received a visit from the bailiffs. She arrives at D's office early one Monday morning, very distressed but unable to explain what was happening, except that she is terrified of losing her home and having the children taken into care.

What should D do next? It may be useful to make notes on how you would respond before reading further.

1. D calms Gloria, and confirms that she didn't let the bailiffs in. She verifies that the children have gone to school as normal and manages to persuade Gloria to accept a lift to her job, promising to make progress by the time they meet up when she has finished her shift at lunchtime. D consults with colleagues and soon finds out that her local authority landlord has employed bailiffs, in one or two extreme cases, to collect rent arrears at the door. But she still can't understand how the debt has arisen. D receives advice from colleagues on how to proceed and the need for immediate action. One particular colleague offers her a checklist she uses in rent arrears cases and offers to be available on her mobile phone during the day for further consultation. This general checklist is summarised here: getting to know sources of specialist advice on housing law and money management; and finding out the legal stages in debt recovery, from the notice seeking possession to the warrant for possession which precedes eviction. This warrant requires a court order and would need to be suspended by a County Court once debt recovery proceedings reached this late stage.

2. D arranges an immediate meeting with the relevant housing officer and finds out that the local authority has discovered an overpayment of Housing Benefit and has recovered it from Gloria's rent account, leaving her in arrears. She hasn't responded to rent demands. Nobody has visited her or checked to confirm she has received and understood the written notices sent to her. D confirms that the housing officer will be available for follow-up action later in the day.

3. D meets with Gloria at home and, reading the letters and notices which have piled up, works out how the problem has arisen. She works out with Gloria that errors have been made by the local authority in the calculations of Housing Benefit and rent due. She notices the poor state of the upstairs bedrooms, with roof leaks and dampness. Apparently, promised repairs have not taken place.

4. D rings the housing officer and meets with her and Gloria, at Gloria's home. It emerges that Gloria's debt can be challenged by her and she can claim compensation for the delays in repairing the house. By the time the children return from school, all the debt recovery proceedings have been suspended. The next day, D discusses with colleagues how to put housing policy and practice locally on a more positive basis and improve

joint working practices with social services. Later, D puts Gloria in touch with the local tenants' group. It emerges that Gloria knows a neighbour who helps to organise it. Recently, the tenants' group have taken part in training to enable them to gain skills in dealing with their own housing issues. (Capacity building training for residents and housing staff, for example, is provided by the National Tenants Resource Centre at Trafford Hall, tel. 01244 300246.)

5. D knows she hasn't 'solved the problem'. But she is pleased that she has responded in two main ways: starting to deal with Gloria's immediate concerns and starting the process of empowering Gloria to take up wider issues, through networking with other people receiving housing services.

Chapter summary

This chapter has examined the main trends in housing policy, concentrating particularly on those which affect clients of the social services. The policy issues have been emphasised which have implications for improving social workers' practice. Ways in which the critical practitioner can take up implications for changes in policy and practice have been highlighted.

Further reading

Journals: *Housing*; *Housing Review*; *Inside Housing* and (more academic) *Housing Studies*

Green, H., Deacon, K., Iles, N. and Down, D. (1997) *Housing in England 1995/96*, Stationery Office, London

Malpass, P. and Murie, A. (1994) *Housing Policy and Practice*, 4th edn, Macmillan, Basingstoke – now Palgrave.

5

Health and Community Care

Health services are struggling to meet the demands of the public and many are failing the performance criteria of government: excessive length of waiting lists for treatment; variable costs and levels of efficiency; variable standards of treatment in different hospitals; an unacceptable risk of patients becoming infected in hospitals; geographical inequalities in mortality rates; and class inequalities in morbidity (disease and suffering) and mortality rates and the take-up of services (Ham, 1985, pp. 165–83). Community care suffers from different problems but they add up to similar shortcomings in services: a suitable range of facilities is not available to meet the needs of people in all urban and rural areas; care managers finish up prioritising need and determining eligibility for services; rationing occurs to meet available resources rather than to meet all potential assessed needs (Baldock and Ungerson, 1994). Morale among health and social services front-line workers is low, the turnover of staff is higher than desirable, pay and conditions in social care and healthcare professions are not what they should be.

Health and community care services are supplied through a considerable body of legislation. Residential care of older people is provided under the National Assistance Act 1948 and registered under the Registered Homes Act 1980 and Registered Homes Act 1984. Facilities for the employment of disabled people are provided under the Disabled Persons (Employment) Act 1958. Local authorities are required to provide welfare services for long-term sick and disabled people under the Chronically Sick and Disabled Persons Act 1970. Mental health powers in respect of people who are mentally disordered, detained patients and people with mental health problems proceed from the Mental Health Act 1959 and the Mental Health Act 1983. By far the most significant legislation in terms of community services for adults is the NHS and Community Care Act 1990, which provides for the planning and implementation of authority-wide care plans and the assessment of individuals and preparation and carrying out of packages of care services to meet their needs. The needs of carers and the assessment of the level of care they can provide are dealt with under the Carers (Recognition and Services) Act 1995. Discrimination against disabled people is tackled under the Disability Discrimination Act 1995. Direct payments to people arranging their own community care services are made through the Community Care (Direct Payments) Act 1996.

Health and social services require close coordination in the delivery of community care. The organisation of social services may be subsumed under healthcare, or, in some areas, social services departments may be merged with health services. This changes the structure and management of social work, but does not erode the integrity of social working as a distinctive activity. Healthcare remains a need for the entire population. Whereas health has been regarded merely as the absence of disease, increasingly health services adopt more positive, inclusive definitions such as that of the World Health Organization (WHO), full health being:

> a state of complete physical, mental and social well being and not merely the absence of disease or infirmity. (World Health Organization, 1946)

Policy context

Pragmatism rather than idealism has motivated governments to develop health policies ensuring an adequate supply of fit labour for the trenches in two world wars. In the early 1900s, in the aftermath of the Boer War, concerns about the poor quality of recruits to the armed services led to free school meals and free school milk being introduced and under the Children Act 1908 neglect of a child's health by a parent was made an offence.

Towards the end of the twentieth century, critical research studies, scandals about specific failings of nursing, medical and surgical practice and the assumed link with votes on election day motivated the Labour government (1997 onwards) to try to improve what has been dubbed the 'National Illness Service'. There was a move also towards enhancing primary and preventive health and promoting health through health education. Despite this, persistent inequalities in health are reflected in differential risks of disease and premature death for people in different wealth and social class strata of society, identified by the Black Report (Department of Health and Social Security, 1980a). When successive governments failed to ban tobacco advertising absolutely, critics alleged this was partly because they would lose too much government revenue from excise duty on tobacco and cigarette sales and partly because of the enormous global power of tobacco producers.

The balance of power in the coordination of healthcare has shifted from the hospital to the community-based health centre, with the general practitioner (GP) managing the process of assessing the person's healthcare needs and ensuring that they are met.

A range of professionals and para-professionals work together – health visitors, occupational therapists, pharmacists, doctors, domiciliary and social care staff and social workers – sometimes in multidisciplinary teams as in community mental health, in assessing and care planning community care, and sometimes in looser collaborative arrangements in health and community care. In the hospitals, consultants and surgeons – most of whom are male – still wield considerable power, which either may be harnessed to achieving what the patient wants, or may be used to defend traditional power hierarchies and poor practices against complaints. But litigation by dissatisfied patients and advocacy by bodies such as the Patients' Association are signs that inroads are being made into this bastion of professional power by some assertive and empowered people receiving services.

Key policy changes and related issues

The National Health Service (NHS) was set up under the National Health Services Act 1946, a core part of the legislation which inaugurated the welfare state. Although always 'national', the health service has never been totally free of charges. One original aim of the NHS – to extend the principle of access to free services in the interests of preventive healthcare – was to an extent compromised from the outset by the presence of charges for some services such as dentistry, spectacles and home helps (Titmuss, 1976a, pp. 136–8).

Since the Seebohm Report (1968) which led to the establishment of local authority social services departments, health and social services have been subjected to repeated reorganisations, nationally, regionally and locally. In 1968 the Department of Health and Social Security (DHSS) was formed from the merger of the Ministry of Health and the Ministry of Social Security. Continual efforts have been made in the NHS to achieve an improved balance between central government-led, regional, area and local provision. Social services agencies, however titled and organised, are much smaller than health authorities and fulfil the specialist function of meeting the needs of vulnerable and needy people.

After 1945, successive governments became increasingly sympathetic towards shifting the balance of personal social services from residential settings to the community. The publication of *Care in Action* (DHSS, 1981) put community care high on the (1979–97) Conservative government's priorities. In large part, the Conservatives were driven by financial factors linked with cutting back the high, and rising, cost of publicly funded residential care and by economic and political commitment to encouraging enterprise outside the public sector, thus stimulating the growth of the private and voluntary sectors. The momentum for change also came from other quarters. By the mid-1980s, many professionals, academics and critical commentators were advocating policies involving the deliberate displacement of inappropriate residential care, some of which was poor in quality, by high-quality community care. It was hoped this would reduce the segregation, isolation and stigmatisation of people in institutions, which they sometimes lived in for long periods, as a result of professional inertia and the lack of well-thought out community-based planning, rather than for any more positive reason. So, by the late 1980s, the growing demand for further legislation came from the convergence of diverse arguments: the expense to the state for residential provision increased tenfold between 1980 and 1990, to £1000m, due to public funding of private residential and nursing home care through the DHSS; the cost was higher because the numbers of older, dependant people were increasing in absolute terms and relative to other age groups; the Thatcher government was turning away from universal state residential and daycare services and making these services increasingly subject to means testing and private and voluntary provision; local authority resources were under pressure, partly through controls exercised by central government via mechanisms such as rate-capping; existing arrangements were inadequate for joint provision and management of community-based services. Ironically, the availability of funding from the state encouraged older people to go into residential care. At the same time, the lack of public investment discouraged local authorities from developing community care services.

The 1986 Audit Commission Report *Making a Reality of Community Care* criticised the slow implementation of community care. Sir Roy Griffiths, then Secretary of State, was asked in 1986 to report on the future of community care services. His report (Department of Health and

Social Security, 1988) proposed the establishment of a mixed economy of care involving care managers purchasing services from their own staff or from the private and voluntary sectors. But his proposals were judged to involve a heavier local government workload and his recommendations that funding for community care be 'ring-fenced' (that is, the money could only be used for this purpose) conflicted with policy concerned with reducing public spending. The government's response, the White Paper *Caring for People* (Department of Health, 1989), turned away from Griffiths' other ideas but endorsed his proposed creation of a market economy to transform local authority social services departments in England and Wales from near monopoly providers of services into purchasers of services, three-quarters or more of which would be provided from the voluntary and private sectors. Similar proposals were made for the health service in the White Paper *Working for Patients* (Department of Health, 1989), with hospitals becoming self-governing Trusts, GPs becoming fundholders responsible for their own devolved budgets and district health authorities purchasers of services. Subsequently, the NHS and Community Care Act 1990 embodied the principles of these two White Papers.

NHS and Community Care Act 1990

The National Health Service and Community Care Act 1990 (NHSCCA) is one of the handful of most significant laws in the health and social services since the establishment of the welfare state in the 1940s. The Act achieved a sea change in the provision of health and social care services, both feeding into and being influenced by broader social and economic as well as financial changes brought about by the Conservative government during the 1980s. The Act set up internal markets for the purchase, by local authority social services departments and the new NHS Trusts created by the government in the health sector, of services from a range of existing – local agency – and new – private and voluntary sector – providers. The Act required the vast majority of these services to be provided externally, that is, by private and voluntary agencies. It ushered in arrangements for organising, commissioning and delivering community care through a mixed economy of provision through public, private, voluntary and informal care providers, with the local authority social services department shifting from its role as virtual monopoly provider to purchasing the majority of services. The so-called 'contract culture' of health and community care was underpinned strategically by senior managers identifying community needs in their area and publishing a Community Care Plan indicating how they would commission, and, where necessary, develop and contract services to meet the needs of the local population. This contract culture was intended to improve choice for people receiving services. The basis for this was their active involvement in assessment of their needs and the development of a care package under the supervision of a care manager who would ensure its implementation and regular review.

A subsequent backlash against these community care changes came partly from those ideologically opposed to market-style approaches to service provision and partly in the light of evaluative research, such as the £2m five-year Economic and Social Research Council (ESRC) 'Contracts and Competition' programme (Flynn and Williams, 1997). A major shortcoming of these arrangements was also the failure to set in place adequate consultation with people receiving services and their carers or to root the contractual provision of services in empowering principles, using a legalistic or rights-based framework.

The implementation of the NHSCCA was fraught with the problems arising from its inherently contradictory nature and organisational problems resulting from the high level of inter-agency, multiprofessional collaboration that it necessitated (Audit Commission, 1992). On one hand, the advice from the government (Department of Health, 1990) was that the legislation was intended to be liberating, and linked with other measures to improve patients' rights (Department of Health, 1992c), customer choice and involving people receiving services in developing their own needs-led assessments and care plans. On the other hand, the legislation had the potential to be discriminatory, in that the local authority had the power to determine whether particular services or services in a specific locality should be offered. Thus, discrimination was likely in rural areas and for people in minority groups, who lacked the choice of a full range of services.

The arrangements for delivering community care under the NHSCCA had a profound impact on front-line social work staff in social services. Social services in social services departments were increasingly separated into the two client groups of adults and children and families. While middle managers were involved in commissioning and negotiating contracts with providers of services, a significant group of front-line staff became engaged in carrying out the process of care management, going through the sequence of assessing needs and care planning, that is, devising a care package in consultation with people receiving services and their carers, implementing and regularly reviewing it. Many of these tasks were carried out by social services staff in collaboration with other professionals, including community-based nurses, occupational therapists, pharmacists, health visitors and paid and volunteer workers in such fields as disability, mental health and work with older people. Levin and Webb (1997) found that the implementation of the arrangements for community care led to a sharper focus and greater accountability in the work of front-line staff. Resource constraints contributed to gatekeeping and a concentration on short-term crisis work with those in greatest need. Social workers increasingly were removed from direct work with people to administering referrals and care management.

In 2000, changes in health and social care services were announced by the government as the most significant reorganisation since the 1940s (*Social Care News*, 2000):

- a new type of *intermediate care* (see below), increasing people's ability to live independently
- using acute hospital beds more effectively
- measures to improve the health, social and emotional wellbeing of children
- decreasing waiting times for outpatient appointments and operations
- a single assessment process for health and social care
- empowerment of patients through greater information
- greater control over services
- a patients' advocate and patients' forum in every area
- new rights and greater powers for local democratic scrutiny of local health services through local councils
- closer partnership between NHS and social services, including better use of pooled budgets and joint services under the Health Act 1999
- financial incentives to improve joint working
- new care trusts building on strengths of social care and health services and allowing joint commissioning and delivery of primary and community healthcare and social care for older people
- more staff with fairer pay, improved training, wider responsibilities and better working environments
- measures to set national targets for addressing health inequalities and improve cancer screening and treatment and prevention of heart disease, encouragement of healthier diets, resources to improve children's health through the Sure Start programme aimed at a third of children under four who live in poverty, reducing the number of smokers by at least 1.5 million by 2010

- encouraging and rewarding good performance through cash incentives and support for poorer performers through the new Modernisation Agency and grants to reward improved joint working arrangements between health and social services. (Department of Health, 2000d)

The commitment of the Labour government of 2001 onwards to enhancing health services was linked with promoting private funding, through public private partnerships (PPP) and private finance initiatives (PFI), proposals which critics alleged would undermine the goal of better healthcare by introducing the profit motive.

Domiciliary care

A huge and growing sector of community care concerns services to people living in their own homes, who need a range of services involving home visits morning and night, meals on wheels, pharmacological support with taking regular medication. There is little consistency in the quality and patterns of delivery of such services and charging arrangements (see Chapter 10) vary enormously between authorities. The imposition of means-tested charges on people receiving domiciliary services by local authorities (in contrast with European countries such as Denmark where such services are mainly free) (Thompson and Hirst, 1999, pp. 22–3) may put social workers and others involved in assessments and care planning into the position of gatekeeping scarce resources, rather than devising care packages purely on the basis of need.

Intermediate care

This term is used to describe new services, with the emphasis on active rehabilitation, recuperation and prevention, for which health and social services hold joint responsibility. Intermediate care includes a mixture of clinical, therapeutic and social interventions, often short term, geared to helping people to get better and become independent rather than simply caring for them, much of which may be provided through the private sector. An example of intermediate care is work to equip older people in residential care to return and stay in their own homes. The Labour government's projected investment of £900m in intermediate care by 2004 could be regarded as a valuable additional policy which is bound to improve people's quality of life. More critically, it could be viewed as a precarious innovation, reliant on new skills being acquired by an already overstretched health and social care workforce, aimed at increasing the numbers of older people and people at risk being supported by carers at home, away from more expensive long-term care.

Mental health

The expansion of community care in mental health practice has been made possible since the late 1950s (Mental Health Acts 1959 and 1983) by the tremendous growth of the pharmaceutical industry, which has supplied GPs and, through self-prescription in chemists, people themselves with a vast range of drugs and other products which enable them to administer treatments themselves, for example, for depression, without recourse to health service professionals, clinics or hospitals. Financial and organisational factors also have contributed to replacing institutions by community care. Health services are complex to organise and expensive to provide, leading to tensions between levels of desirable provision and resource shortages. One strategy aiming to reduce the high human and financial cost of treating people in institutions such as mental hospitals involves decarcerating them and supporting them in the community. One consequence has been heightened debate about shortcomings in the quality of services, in the wake of a succession of inquiries into deaths as a result of violent attacks by patients discharged from mental hospitals (Ritchie et al., 1994; Blom-Cooper et al., 1995).

People with severe personality disorders
The Mental Health (Patients in the Community) Act 1995 was intended to tighten control over the discharge of people with more serious mental disorders. It introduced a supervised discharge order which made the individual worker, in this case the Community Supervisor, responsible for delivering the service to the client. The Act also introduced a new community treatment order, which gave powers to impose treatment in the community. Critics of this, notably the British Association of Social Workers (BASW, 1995), asserted that it should be reframed as a 'care and treatment' order, was too intrusive a power and should be restricted to particular groups of people, such as those who otherwise would require long-term custodial care.

The Ashworth Inquiry (see Committee of Inquiry, 1992), responding to repeated complaints about conditions in that hospital – one of three special hospitals for containing high-risk patients in top security – recommended the introduction of a new reviewable sentence, in order to protect society against dangerous personality disordered offenders whose offences had not attracted an indefinite sentence. The Inquiry also recommended that small units be developed for small groups of severely personality disordered individuals within existing high-security hospitals and prisons (Fallon et al., 1999).

Risk management

Community mental health practice typically operates within the framework of risk minimisation rather than maximising the potential of the person suffering from mental illness. Assessment of risk is located within the medical model and relies heavily on diagnosis within the disciplines of clinical and forensic psychiatry. Social workers in mental health have to take account of the increasingly multiprofessional practice in such fields as work with mentally disordered offenders and sex offenders. Sections 1, 2 and 3 of the Mental Health Act 1983 define mental illness and specify that people considered a risk to their own safety or that of others should be removed from the community when they do not agree to voluntary treatment. In Scotland, Mental Health Officers (MHOs) exercise compulsory powers under the Mental Health Act 1984. Approved Social Workers (ASWs) carry out such work in England.

Risk management is the pivotal concept on which much practice is based in mental health and community care, being operated by managers involved in gatekeeping and rationing scarce resources. In psychiatry, the concept of risk has been institutionalised in diagnostic and assessment processes. In mental health, risk is used to justify decisions about compulsory detention and the allocation of support services for people with mental health problems or mental health offenders. Risk assessment typically focuses on the potential harm that the person may inflict on themself or others. Despite the great attention paid by the mass media to such cases as the killing of Jonathan Zito by Christopher Clunis (Ritchie et al., 1994), violence is far more likely to be inflicted on relatives and friends, rather than strangers, by people with no history of mental illness. More than 90 per cent of mentally disordered people are not violent. Research continues to confirm a lack of community-based facilities offering substantial support for people, as the study of the work of MHOs in Scotland reveals (Myers, 1999). The Department of Health publication *Still Building Bridges* (1999f) proposes that all mental health services should be located within the framework of the Care Programme Approach (CPA). The proposed mental health legislation advocates that people with mental illnesses should be treated similarly to those with physical illnesses, prioritising informal, home-based treatment, with hospital-based and compulsory treatment a last resort. It would be courageous for policymakers to encourage professionals to balance a risk-taking approach against a risk-minimisation approach. This recognises the potential value to clients, carers and relatives of supporting and enabling the person with mental health problems to live as normal a life as possible.

People with disabilities

Disabled people are affected directly and indirectly by policies and legal enactments. The first legislation directly affecting disabled people was the Disabled Persons (Employment) Act 1944, which established rehabilitation and vocational training centres and imposed on some employers the duty to employ a certain quota of disabled people. Under the 1970 Chronically Sick and Disabled Persons Act, local authorities were expected where practicable to collate a register of people with disabilities and publicise services, but most did not, under this permissive legislation. Other such direct legislation includes the Disabled Persons (Service, Consultation and Representation) Act 1986 and the Disability Discrimination Act (DDA) 1995. Within months of the Disability Rights Commission beginning work in 2000, its chairperson Bert Massie was arguing that the Human Rights Act 1998 provided a more inclusive framework than the DDA against which to argue that any given legislation was discriminatory against disabled people (Revans, 2000, p. 12).

Impairment refers to a physical or psychological condition or disorder, whereas disability indicates the personal and social consequences of impairment for the person. The DDA accepts the damaging consequences of impairment and disability and requires employers to treat people equally, whether or not they are disabled.

The medical or personal tragedy model of disability has a close relationship with concepts of impairment and handicap, located within Western medicine. In contrast, the social model of disability emphasises the concept of disablement as restrictions and disadvantages impacting on a person as a consequence of structures, values, institutions, policies and practices in society which all too often exclude people with impairments and take little account of their needs and requirements. A sociopolitical model of disability has an impact on the professional identity of the worker and the personal identity of the disabled individual.

Criticisms of the medical model of disability underline the fact that medical definitions of disability by and large are created by able-bodied people. Disability civil rights campaigners are among those advocating that it is not the medical impairment which disables the individual but the structural inequality and prejudices of society. Medical and social models of disability exert powerful effects on perceptions of disability and the shaping of policy. But the growth of power by people with disabilities may yet eclipse in importance the challenge of the medical model by the social model of disability and may change the position whereby most services for disabled people are designed, delivered and evaluated by able-bodied people according to principles alien to their lives

(Priestly, 1999). The Community Care (Direct Payments) Act 1996 permits local authorities to give direct cash payments to specified categories of people receiving community care services, including people with disabilities. Receipt of the payments and control of the care package are able to lie with the person with the strongest incentive to make sure that they are appropriately spent and deployed. The payments can contribute to social inclusion by providing opportunities for education, employment, leisure and rehabilitation for people needing community care.

The introduction of direct community care payments is a symbolic act of handing over control to disabled people, often accompanied by other empowering arrangements. For example, the Independent Living Scheme in one local authority, Kingston, gives advice and support to people using direct payments (Hasler, 1999, pp. 6–7). In Scotland, the most wide-ranging consultation for 20 years of services for people with learning difficulties has led to the Scottish Executive taking the views of service users and carers seriously and introducing independent advocacy services as well as the right to direct payments for anyone who wants them (Scottish Executive, 2000).

People with learning disabilities often were hospitalised on a long-term basis in the immediate post-war years. Public and professional awareness of the neglect in this area was raised by complaints by a group of people in a letter to *The Times* on 10 November 1965 which created a wave of public concern. Although most of their allegations against particular hospitals led to no noteworthy official action, complaints about conditions in Ely Hospital, Cardiff were published in the *News of the World* on 20 August 1967. The resulting inquiry report confirmed management failures and cruel and inhumane practices by staff (National Health Service, 1969). The White Paper *Better Services for the Mentally Handicapped* (DHSS, 1971) did not prevent a succession of scandals and inquiry reports over the following dozen years (Adams, 1998a, pp. 114–29), indicating the notable lack of public accountability of these hospitals, the entrenched power of medical staff including consultants, and the persistence of malpractices and imperviousness to change of hospital managements. As the numbers of adults with learning disabilities in long-stay hospitals gradually declined, day services, focused on large, specially built Adult Training Centres (ATCs), remained isolated and stigmatising, a long way from the principles of normalisation (Wolfensberger, 1972) and social role valorisation (Wolfensberger, 1982) advocated by Wolfensberger. The need to develop smaller, more socially inclusive day services and employment schemes with realistic wages for disabled people was recognised by the Department of Health in the late 1990s (Department of Health, 1998a). A government scheme titled Workstep was introduced with the aim of desegregating more than 23,000 disabled people in supported employment, including Remploy, employing more than 10,000 of these in 87 factories, and equipping them to join the mainstream workforce. Supporters of this policy argue that disabled people have the right to work alongside able-bodied people, but critics view it as a way of cutting annual government subsidies of more than £150m to Remploy, Mencap and other bodies employing disabled people (Lindsey, 2001, p. 2).

Older people

Research demonstrates that old people are more likely than the rest of the population to be poor, disabled, badly housed and widowed. There is a cumulative impact, in that an older person experiencing one of these disadvantages is more likely to suffer one or more of the others (Sinclair et al., 1990, p. 367).

The vulnerability of older people to abuse has been recognised as creating additional risks. From the 1980s, the hitherto narrow focus on child abuse was widened by research indicating significant levels of abuse of vulnerable adults. Most research and comment did not challenge the implication of the study by Homer and Gilleard (1975) in which the pathology of the abusing carer was implicit, instead restricting the focus to the carer for the elderly relative (McCreadie, 1991). The more widespread incidence of abuse, for reasons beyond the stress experienced by the carer, has since been acknowledged (Phillipson et al., 1995). Defining abuse more widely, to include active and passive neglect, financial, emotional, sexual as well as physical abuse, promotes a more inclusive view of its true incidence. Adopting a social constructionist theoretical viewpoint makes it possible to appreciate how abuse of older people can occur on a widespread scale, because of the:

> social construction of ageing within Western societies, the politically and economically weak position of older people, the structured dependency enforced upon older people as a group and the negative stereotypes of old age which support and justify their structural inequality. (Hughes, 1995, p. 134)

Partly in belated response to the lack of rigorous selection and suitable training for care staff, the Care Standards Act 2000 created a central list of people judged unsuitable to work with vulnerable adults.

Standards for the residential care of older people were published by the Department of Health Social Services Inspectorate in the mid-1990s, after the NHSCCA. Guidelines for addressing the issue of abuse of older people had already been published (SSI, 1992) and were followed up with more substantial advice (SSI, 1993). Following the White Paper *Modernising Social Services* (Department of Health, 1998a), the Care Standards Act 2000 enhanced protection for vulnerable people, and witnesses of abuse.

Older people with dementia
Medical advances and dietary improvements have contributed to lengthening life expectancies in the relatively better-off countries of the world, including Britain. The incidence of people with dementia grows with the number of older people. Although only about 5 per cent of people over 65 have dementia, the percentage increases to more than 20 per cent of those over 80. From the 1980s, there was an increasing move to avoid moving older people with dementia into hospital wards, instead maintaining them in the community as long as possible, perhaps with brief periods in residential or nursing care to give carers some respite.

While research points to the need for joint working between health and social services professionals to improve early assessment, the findings of research on the outcomes of earlier assessment are somewhat indeterminate. Oakley (1999) suggests that earlier detection of people with dementia enables their community support to be more effective.

Long-term care of older people
A consequence of increased longevity of the population is the growing proportion of people who need long-term care towards the end of their lives. There is ongoing debate about who should pay for continuing and long-term care of older people. Should responsibility for policy on the long-term care of older people lie with health or social services, or be jointly held? Should the resources be provided by the state or the individual, health, social services or some other agency/ies or groups? The 1986 Audit Commission Report *Making a Reality of Community Care* argued that the respective tasks of NHS and local authorities needed clarifying, perhaps by setting up boards for joint working but with separate responsibilities. In the event, the Griffiths Report (Department of Health and Social Security, 1988) and the 1989 White Paper (Department of Health, 1989) rejected this and under the 1990 NHSCCA social services departments were given lead responsibility for assessing people's needs and putting together care packages which, where possible, would enable their needs to be met through the apparently cheaper route of community care, with informal care from relatives rather than professional care wherever possible.

The national charter *Better Care, Higher Standards – Guidance for 2001/02* (Department of Health, 2001) focuses on implementing the Labour government's manifesto commitment to improving services for people needing long-term support and care, with particular emphasis on fulfilling the goals of the Modernising Government initiative, by encouraging local agencies such as health, housing and social services to collaborate, and by addressing the needs of users and carers.

Debates over the provision of continuing or long-term care for older people have become more focused since the report in March 1999 of the Royal Commission on Long Term Care for the Elderly, chaired by Professor Sir Stewart Sutherland (1999). The Sutherland Report advocated that where possible older people should remain in their own homes. If they need residential or nursing home care, they should only pay the cost of board and lodging, the state meeting the costs of care, whether it takes place at home or in the residential setting. Free personal care services for chronically sick and disabled older people, the report stated, would remove a tax on frailty. The Labour government refused to adopt the recommendation of free personal care in England, on the grounds that it would be too expensive. Instead, various funding changes were proposed, the government's argument being that these would make the funding of long-term care much fairer. They included the abolition of payment of the Residential Allowance to new care home residents, the resources being transferred to local councils. In Scotland, the Scottish Parliament's Health and Community Care Committee endorsed the Sutherland Report's recommendation for personal care to be provided free of charge on the basis of assessed need. The Scottish Executive responded as expected to this recommendation (Sutherland, 2001, p. 5), introducing a new system of assessment under which more people would qualify for free health and personal care.

Critics of the government's refusal to provide all personal care free of charge allege that this reinforces discrimination between free health services and charges for personal social services; harms the interests of vulnerable older and chronically disabled people; and demonstrates that the government is prepared to sacrifice the interests of older and poorer people to the voting power of younger, wealthier and healthier people.

Carers: informal care sector

Alongside the public and private sectors is the often unacknowledged but huge informal sector, where unpaid care is provided by relatives, friends and neighbours. Carers are predominantly women, as partners, daughters and sisters. The number of carers is impossible to quantify precisely but lies between five and seven million people in Britain (Department of Health, 1999d). The Audit Commission (2000) found that less than half of carers of people with dementia had been asked if they needed any help. With government policy devoted to reducing the official annual cost of more than £1000m on caring through attendance allowance payments, there is little official incentive to acknowledge the need to offer financial support to carers. However, changing patterns of family life, such as increased financial pressures, growing numbers of lone parents, especially women, and people living alone, are likely to increase the pressures on informal carers. Many carers become the cornerstone of the remaining independence of many older and disabled people, yet their needs remain largely hidden. Legislation only began to recognise the crucial role of carers from the mid-1980s with the Disabled Persons (Services, Consultation and Representation) Act 1986, Schedule 8 of which enabled local authorities to provide support groups and information for carers, and the Carers (Recognition and Services) Act 1995 which explicitly acknowledged the essential role of informal carers to the formal system of community care. Research taking in the perceptions of both carers and people being cared for highlights the complexities of their situations and their different perceptions on needs assessments and service reviews (Williams and Robinson, 2000).

Young carers

It has been known for several years that in Britain, as in other European countries, child carers form a particularly vulnerable group (Becker, 1995). Research into the impact of caring on young people has been scanty. A study of the experiences of 60 young people caring for a parent with a long-term illness or disability (Dearden and Becker, 2000) found that caring often had a significant negative impact on their own education, job prospects, growth to independence and social life.

Implications for social workers

It can be very difficult for the social worker to balance the risks to a client of leaving her or him at home against the loss of independence if a placement in a nursing home is arranged.

EXAMPLE

Colin is working with Mr H, a chronically depressed man in his mid-fifties who has been diagnosed as suffering from a serious medical condition, from which the painful symptoms and loss of mobility could be alleviated if the need for pain management, physiotherapy and occupational therapy services could be assessed. His doctor wants him to go into hospital for a period to enable this to happen. He lives in a rural area on the side of a hill, in the house he was born in, and is terrified that if he goes into hospital he will never come out. The doctor has expressed a preference for having Mr H admitted to a nursing home. He can no longer do his own shopping and there is a real risk to his safety, in the absence of 24-hour personal care.

Should Colin put his efforts into devising a community care package to support Mr H at home, or have him put into a nursing home for his own good?

You may like to reflect critically on your responses to the issues facing Colin before reading further.

1. This question vexes Colin because he feels it is loaded. He wants to empower Mr H and feels resentful on his behalf at the pressure coming from some health professionals to resolve the clear problems of risk, if Mr H stays at home.
2. Colin sets out to win round the views of local healthcare professionals to his view that it is in everyone's interests to work together, in the realistic knowledge that Mr H's condition is likely to deteriorate, but taking into account his wish to retain his independence.
3. This has a surprising outcome, when a concerted effort is made by all the professionals involved to meet Mr H and take on board his anxieties. A number of local neighbours turn up, at Mr H's instigation, who offer a rota of care.
4. A genuinely multiprofessional assessment and community care plan is drawn up. Mr H appears very relieved.
5. The apparently ideal solution is short-lived. Mr H's condition deteriorates rapidly as winter approaches. He suffers a fall in his house and has to be transferred to hospital for emergency treatment.
6. Colin now finds it necessary for him and other professionals to revise their plan. Mr H is forced to accept that he needs full-time nursing care. Some aspects of his day-to-day life have become easier, but in other ways he is struggling to cope with the loss of his familiar surroundings and his mobility, however difficult and restricted these were.

Chapter summary

This chapter has considered the major changes affecting the organisation and delivery of health and community care services since the

1980s. It has examined the major issues arising in respect of the shift towards a mixed economy of provision and a market-based philosophy underpinning the provision of services. It has indicated the major problematic areas for social workers, in particular those arising through collaboration between health and social services. It has highlighted tensions and consequent dilemmas for practice between organisational pressures to minimise risks and follow procedures and the professional goal of empowering people and maximising their quality of life.

Further reading

Allsop, J. (1995) *Health Policy and the NHS*, 2nd edn, Pearson, Harlow

Davies, C., Finlay, L. and Bullman, A. (eds) (2000) *Changing Practice in Health and Social Care*, Open University Press, Buckingham

Payne, M. (1995) *Social Work and Community Care*, Macmillan, Basingstoke – now Palgrave

Symonds, A. and Kelly, A. (eds) (1998) *The Social Construction of Community Care*, Macmillan, Basingstoke – now Palgrave

6

Family and Childcare

Social workers still relate to the Children and Young Persons Acts of 1933, 1963 and 1969 for some aspects of work with children and families, but the bulk of the legislation affecting social work in this area has been consolidated in the Children Act 1989. However, mediation between separating and divorcing couples is dealt with under the Family Law Act 1996, and the Matrimonial Causes Act 1973 deals with the respective housing and property rights of separating and divorcing couples. Maintenance payments are dealt with by the Child Support Agency, which was created and reformed under the Child Support Acts 1991 and 1995 (see Chapter 2), while married couples not undergoing divorce can apply for maintenance orders and lump sum payments under the Domestic Proceedings and Magistrates' Courts Act 1978.

Critical practice involving children and families requires the practitioner to have more than knowledge of how to use the law, important though that is. It necessitates a critical appreciation of the changing nature of the family and ways of interpreting these changes. This chapter examines policy aspects of these changes which bear directly on practice.

Policy context

Families and family forms have undergone rapid change in recent generations, for reasons that are hard to ascertain. Even if it were possible to set aside the strong views that many people hold about the sanctity or otherwise of 'the family' and family values, it would be impossible to develop social policies based on future certainties about what 'typical' families will look like, a generation from now. It is more realistic to plan on the basis that, in the foreseeable future, the character and significance of families in society will continue to change.

Social work intervention in families is a two-edged sword. It may be wielded – as with the compulsory removal from home of a child deemed at risk of harm – with care in mind, but experienced by the individual as painful and detrimental. It may benefit one person and not another. The analogy of the sword is misleading because it implies merely the dualism of the dilemma. Social work intervention more often than not is hedged around with uncertainties and difficulties which, despite the fact that crises may arise suddenly, are often deep-seated and longstanding. Families are complex, problems tend to be multifaceted, decisions tend not to be simple and issues are rarely clearcut. Robert Harris puts it pithily: 'it is impossible to protect a child and not control a family' (Harris, 1995, p. 37).

Lorraine Fox Harding argues that it is invidious to use a term such as 'the family' because

> it contains certain values concerning the worth of a particular type of institution – the married two-parent family form, gender-differentiated, stable through time, and assumptions about social stability which accompany the perception of that form. (Fox Harding, 1996, pp. xi–xii)

Dominant values can be oppressive. Emphasising the 'normality' of the traditional nuclear family has to an extent led successive governments to reinforce a stereotype of the problem-ridden lone parent family. Pat Carlen and Chris Tchaikovsky summarise the assumptions shared by the New Right, those who believe that there is an 'underclass', which symbolises the collapse of the moral health of the nation, and those who want to see single mothers deterred from living off state benefits by punitive welfare and housing policies:

> Basically, the rhetoric goes like this: found in neighbourhoods containing high numbers of fatherless families headed by never-married mothers, the 'underclass' poor are those who, having been reared by permissive mothers and a supportive welfare state, now refuse to work and instead, engage in predatory, violent and society-threatening crime. (Carlen and Tchaikovsky, 1996, p. 208)

Family change is linked with government policy on the family through the medium of politics, and particularly reflects the ideologies of political parties dominating politics and policies at any one time. Despite feminist and radical critiques attacking traditional views about the family as a central institution promoting desirable social values and the roles of husbands and wives as breadwinners and nurturers respectively, social policy since the 1940s, with some notable exceptions, has not departed significantly from these views. The most apparent exceptions include the marked tendency of women to join the workforce, full or part time, the growing numbers of lone parent families and the trend towards same-sex couples (gay or lesbian) wanting to rear children as a family group.

To some extent, how children's socialisation and any associated problems are addressed depends as much on the mindset and societal preoccupations of the day, as on the inherent nature of any of those problems. Many of the changes in parenting styles and the focus of professional intervention in children's lives which have occurred over the past century can be summed up in the statement that whereas in 1900 about 300,000 pauper children in Britain were on outdoor relief, in 2000, about 200,000 children, many alleged to be suffering from attention deficit hyperactivity disorder (ADHD), are being prescribed the behaviour controlling drug methylphenidate (MPH), or ritalin as it is better known. At any one time in 1998/99, about 90,100 children were being looked after by local authority social services departments, mainly through fostering, supervision or spending time in a children's home.

Children's policies and legislation are complex and matters for debate and controversy, reflecting dominant values and norms rather than a consensus in society. Changes in one area tend to have knock-on implications for other areas. Two examples are given here. First, the impact on parental and children's rights of new medical technologies to improve fertility, surrogate parenting and use of stored embryos and sperm, for instance, are profound. Second, the implications of the prime minister's review of adoption from 2000, according to Keith Bilton, include

> the need to reform the law relating to step-parent adoptions, to redefine the status conferred by adoption and to provide a proper basis for services to birth relatives and adult adopted persons. (Bilton, 2000, p. 2)

Key policy changes and related issues

From the early 1960s, the wish to develop policies to prevent the collapse of the family as a bearer of core societal values figured largely in the concerns of both Labour and Conservative politicians.

The ideological emphasis of the New Right of the Conservative (Thatcher and Major) government of 1979–97 was foreshadowed in the Labour government of 1974–79. Key themes evident in children's legislation were individual rights and responsibilities, the upholding of law and order and the primacy of the family as the private domain for nurturing and caring rather than the state having this responsibility. The Adoption Act 1976 marked the shift towards recognition of children and young people as persons with rights. The Children Act 1989 is concerned to emphasise the primacy of meeting the child's needs through adults, professionals and parents, working in partnership and to caution again state intervention unless there is evidence of harm to the child.

Despite the relative increase in marriage and remarriage in comparison with other European countries, in absolute terms marriage is declining. By the mid-1990s the number of people getting married in England and Wales had fallen to its lowest level since 1900 (George and Wilding, 1999, p. 59). Between 1979 and 1996, the proportion of married women aged 18 to 49 dropped from 74 to 57 per cent. Cohabitation seems to be replacing marriage as the preferred pattern, the proportion of cohabiting women aged 18 to 49 increasing from 11 per cent in 1979 to 26 per cent in 1996 (Thomas et al., 1998, Table 12.7, Figure 12B, pp. 200, 204).

The Labour government (1997 onwards) showed a commitment to developing welfare policies which encourage lone parents to work whenever possible. It is hard to avoid the conclusion (see Chapter 2) that this strategy owes more to the impulse to reduce social security spending than to improving the quality of family life. Jack Straw, the Home Secretary, drew attention in a keynote speech to the fact that the proportion of children who live in families where no adult is in paid work trebled from 7 to 21 per cent in the 1980s and early 1990s, an identical increase to the number of families headed by a lone parent (speech by Jack Straw at launch of the Lords and Commons Family and Child Protection Group's Report *Family Matters* on 23 July 1998).

Jack Straw continued:

> In our manifesto we committed ourselves to strengthening family life. We promised to 'uphold family life as the most secure means of bringing up our children. Families are the core of our society. They should teach right from wrong. They should be the first defence against anti-social behaviour. The breakdown of family life damages the fabric of our society.' ... The core of this Government's policy is to provide practical help for parents, through money, time or services, so that parents can better bring up their children.

These statements were consistent with the series of linked measures developed by the Ministerial Group on the Family, chaired by Jack Straw since its inception in 1997, which emphasised the role of the institution of marriage in strengthening family life (Ministerial Group on the Family, 1999, pp. 30–1).

The Ministerial Group on the Family developed five key themes on which the government's family policy should be based:

- better financial support for families ensuring children's needs were met
- strengthened support for marriage and stable relationships between adults (thereby the government acknowledged that adults who were not married could provide high-quality parenting)
- helping families to balance work and home life
- providing enhanced services and support for parents in children's early years
- focusing additional resources on family problems such as criminal violence in the home, juvenile crime and teenage pregnancy.

New Labour's policy of supporting families was based partly on a commitment to women's equality as parents, carers and workers, and partly on keeping the family together by strengthening the support of childcare in the home. The tensions between the multiple roles of women were not resolved by resulting measures, although some improvement had occurred by May 2001 when the second Labour government came into power. By 2000, family support came to mean not only financial help for parents and children but improved support for working parents, through childminding and nurseries. In 2000, there were no less than 82,000 registered childminders, each taking up to three children under five years of age. Between 1990 and 2000, the number of children under five in full-time nurseries increased 300 per cent and the number of daycare nurseries increased from 2,900 to 7,500. A survey of 120 children's information services by the Daycare Trust in February 2001 estimated the cost of childcare for working parents as an average of £6,000 per child per year. The Childcare Commission, after a year-long study, recommended a toddler tax credit to enable working parents either to pay for childcare or to stay at home themselves (Hall, 2001, p. 9). The Labour government's childcare tax credit of up to £70 per week for one child and £105 for two was seen as inadequate to pay weekly bills of up to £200 per child. The statistics were taken to imply that parents either make sacrifices to achieve adequate childcare or are forced to abandon it as too expensive (McVeigh, 2001, p. 12).

Family-based social work, not surprisingly, is the main focus of social work with adults and children. The Children Act 1989 emphasises the principle of working in partnership, between professionals and parents, professionals and children and between agencies (Petrie and James, 1995, p. 315). But one of the key tensions in social work with families involves reconciling the different viewpoints and interests of different family members. Sometimes, conflicts between family members cannot be resolved and agency and social work activity is devoted to enabling those involved to come to terms with such differences.

The Lord Chancellor's Department takes the policy lead in provisions of the Children Act 1989 concerned with family proceedings. The Act governs the work of the social worker acting as guardian *ad litem* (GaL) and reporting officer services. Court welfare services provided by (about 600) family court welfare officers from the probation service were reviewed in 1998 and in 1999 the government decided to establish a unified service, bringing together family court welfare officers, GaLs (about 700–800) and the children's branch of the Official Solicitors Office, dealing with complex High Court proceedings involving children. There were doubts about whether the probation officer and social work components of this service would fit easily together (McCurry, 1999, p. 22).

Childcare and child protection

Whereas those aspects of childcare which touch on child protection are never far from the law and policy, what constitutes 'good enough' or 'excellent' childcare is hardly given equivalent attention. Increasingly, childcare policies and practices in Britain have been overshadowed by the development of child protection responses to child abuse. Nigel Parton regards the late 1980s as a historical moment of shift from an understanding of child abuse as a socio-health problem to a socio-legal focus on child protection (Parton, 1991, p. 146). The multifaceted nature of responses to child abuse is evident in the fact that simultaneously with the child being treated as in need of medical care, the rights of the child were becoming a more prominent concern. The 1991 version of guidance on multi-agency collaboration in child protection procedures was updated in 1999 to meet the requirements of the Children Act 1989 and be consistent with the United Nations Convention on the Rights of the Child and the European Convention of Human Rights.

Public childcare in England and Wales, including childcare by the state, as well as through social services and voluntary childcare organisations such as Barnardo's, the Children's Society (formerly Church of England Children's Society), the National Children's Homes (NCH) and the National Society for the Prevention of Cruelty to Children (NSPCC), has been marked by an increasing emphasis during the twentieth century on reforming legislation intervening in children's lives with a view to promoting their wellbeing. This includes, for example, the Children Act 1908, the Adoption of Children Act 1926, the Children and Young Persons Act 1933, the Children Act 1948, the Children and Young Persons Act 1963, the Children and Young Persons Act 1969 and the Children Act 1989. Undoubtedly, the Second World War (1939–45) scarred the upbringing of many children of that generation, when so many of those who lived in towns were evacuated away from their families and others were subjected to the direct horrors of air raids and the loss of relatives, particularly a generation of young fathers.

By the late 1960s, the large children's homes and approved schools were regarded askance through the critical research of Goffman into total institutions of all kinds (Goffman, 1961), as well as in the wake of specific shocking incidents such as the Carlton Approved School riot (Durand, 1960), which exposed the poor conditions in many childcare establishments.

The 1970s marked a watershed in policy and practice regarding childcare, in at least two major ways. First, the implementation of the 1969 Children and Young Persons Act coincided with the establishment of the generic profession of social work in new social services departments and was also a legislative high-water mark of what might be called the welfare approach to treating problem families and children in the community. Second, by the end of the 1970s, children's rights were becoming more prominent than hitherto and feminism was establishing child abuse along with domestic violence as aspects of patriarchy and oppressive male power. There was growing disquiet over the large number of placements some children experienced, as they moved from foster home to foster home and from one children's home to another. It was felt there was a need to keep such movements and the disruption of caring relationships to a minimum.

Much of the legislation providing the legal framework in England and Wales governing work by a range of statutory and voluntary agencies with children and families needing the personal social services has been brought together under one umbrella – the Children Act 1989. However, a good deal of civil law still relates to other legislation, in the case of adoption for example, including the Education Act 1944, Children Act 1980, Child Abduction Acts 1984 and 1985 and the Child Support Act 1991 (Lyon, 1995, p. 153).

One of the great paradoxes of childcare in Britain since the late 1940s is that, despite a regular catalogue of reforming childcare legislation, there is a continuing incidence of major incidents of child abuse. A significant level of abuse occurs in the very childcare facilities provided by childcare professionals themselves, although it appears that about three-quarters of deaths of children under 16 for nonaccidental injury are brought about by their own parents and relatives (Browne, 1995, p. 43). This suggests that campaigns to persuade children not to trust strangers should be regarded as only addressing a minor part of the problem.

Since the early 1970s, when the inquiry (Secretary of State for Social Services, 1974) into the death of Maria Colwell at the hands of her step-father brought the roles of professionals in child protection into the fore-ground in an unprecedented way, the physical and emotional abuse of children has become a subject of greater public concern than hitherto and child sexual abuse has emerged as a widespread problem. Some aspects of child abuse have become particularly controversial: the question of whether children could be prompted to fantasise or create incidents – so-called 'false memory syndrome' – arose from interviews conducted in the wake of the Cleveland cases; the Orkney case led to a massive professional and public debate about whether satanic abuse was real and a distinguished anthropologist was commissioned to investigate this (La Fontaine, 1994). The mass media coverage of such scandals in childcare sometimes is great enough to transport them across the Atlantic. In the late 1990s, massive media attention focused on the trial in the USA of the English nanny Louise Woodward for the death of the baby in her care. Widespread controversy arose in 2001, when an English couple, the Kilshaws (see Chapter 1) paid a fee in the USA to adopt infant twins, brought them back to England but were later forced to return them, following legal action by the local authority. This highlighted the need for international standards regulating adoption policy and practice.

The great publicity given to the above issues, important though they are, has aligned consideration of the broad field of fulfilling children's rights (Franklin, 1995) and the meeting of children's immediate and long-term needs with child protection. Consequently, many children's services may resemble a fire brigade – prioritising suspected abuse and devoting such marginal resources as remain to other aspects of child-care. Often, the outcry which results from the publicising of abuse and in some cases the death of a child also has the effect of bringing down on social workers, already involved with the family where that child has been killed, charges of professional neglect, negligence or incompe-tence. On most occasions, social workers are accused of intervening insufficiently early to remove children from potentially harmful situations (Blom-Cooper, 1985; London Borough of Lambeth, 1987), although sometimes they are pilloried for being overzealous, as in Cleveland (Butler-Sloss, 1987) and the Orkneys (House of Commons, 1992).

The debate in these circumstances tends to be about how much power social workers and allied professionals should exercise to intervene in families where the parents, or those with parental responsibility, are not judged to be fulfilling their parental responsibilities.

In the wake of the Children Act 1989, policy has shifted towards keeping the family intact and intervening only when families clearly cannot cope, or are not functioning adequately. This, plus the more rigorous scrutiny of evidence required before a case of child abuse is presented in court, leads to some children being left in their abusive relationships at home while sufficient evidence is gathered by social workers.

At the same time, one consequence of the skewing of childcare in social work and social services towards child protection has been the convergence between the roles of police and social workers in investigating suspected cases of abuse (Harris, 1995, p. 31). The links between child protection and the criminal justice system are closer, as a consequence, than between social workers and professional therapists such as family therapists, art and drama therapists and psychotherapists. As Robert Harris also implies, quality may be enshrined in the general principles of childcare as stated in legislation, but this does not ensure that it resides in the quality of practice. Legislation which has the express purpose of protecting children does not always protect. Harris identifies a gap between the rhetoric of childcare and the political complexity of decisionmaking which often governs practice. Whereas 'child welfare is a rule-driven activity', in some parts, notably child protection, 'prescription is impossible, rules are insufficient and … the world seems especially messy and unpredictable' (Harris, 1995, p. 36). The clarity and simplicity of general statements exists only at the level of law and policy.

> The application of law and policy to the individual case is inextricably linked with the moral, practical, strategic and intellectual position and astuteness of the practitioner. (Harris, 1995, p. 36)

The Children Act 1989 moved away from the hitherto widespread belief in good child protection involving minimal involvement by the state and social workers, towards courts taking many decisions formerly taken by social workers (Lane and Walsh, 1995, p. 266). The increasing tendency for children to become victim or bystander witnesses in criminal proceedings has sharpened debates about how to protect them in such stressful and potentially harmful circumstances (Williams, 1995, p. 295).

A succession of inquiry reports into child abuse in residential care contributed to the launch of the three-year 'Quality Protects' programme in England by the Labour government on 21 September 1998. This involved a £375 m new children's services grant to local authorities over the three years. A similar, separately funded programme, 'Children First', was launched in Wales in April 1999. Local government bench-marking in Wales was based on best value principles and had the potential to enable social services departments to contribute to shaping performance indicators in the Performance Assessment Framework of the government (Huber, 2000, p. 20). These programmes aimed to improve the quality – management and consistency of service delivery – of children's services and included four components: objectives for children's services stated in the form of a measurable outcome for children, some of which were associated with precise dates by which local authorities were intended to achieve them; new roles for local councillors in delivering the programme; the requirement for all local authorities to submit a Quality Protects Management Action Plan (MAP) to the Department of Health by 31 January 1999; and a new £375 m grant for children's services. The objectives for children's services included:

- ensuring safe, secure, stable and effective care for all children
- protecting children from neglect and abuse
- enhancing the life chances of children in need and in care in terms of education, healthcare and social care
- enabling young people who leave care to lead successful lives as adults
- meeting the needs of children with disabilities and their families
- improving services through improved assessment
- involving service users and carers actively in planning, decisions and reviews of their services
- protecting children through regulation
- ensuring childcare workers can do their jobs
- maximising the use of resources.

But, as Beatrix Campbell notes sceptically:

> Quality Protects worries as many managers as it enthuses. Will the resources be made available to train and pay foster carers to take on challenging children who currently find their way into children's homes? What would it really take to transform children's homes into locales that are no longer stigmatised by the adult community while functioning as magnets for other disenchanted young people? (Campbell, 1999, p. 14)

And, more critically:

> While Quality Protects may target bad practice, or inappropriate practice in pub-
> lic care, it hardly challenges the adult community about its disposition towards
> children. (Campbell, 1999, p. 14)

For reasons which are not entirely clear, the numbers of children on Child Protection Registers peaked in 1991 at 49,000, then fell by about 25 per cent up to 1993, before levelling out. This followed the implementation of the Children Act 1989. In 1997, neglect was the most common reason for boys and girls being on the Child Protection Register and accounted for about 30 per cent of all cases (ONS, 1999, p. 149).

One indication of the move towards safeguarding the rights of the child was the appointment of a GaL by the court, who acted independently of the local authority in order to safeguard the interests of the child. This role was introduced in adoption proceedings in the Adoption Act 1958, broadened under the Children Act 1989 (Head, 1995, p. 281) and now, along with family court welfare officers, is replaced by child and family reporters and family court advisers.

The marketisation of some aspects of social services has impacted greatly on the provision of childcare services. It could be viewed as unethical for price tags to be placed on childcare provision through contracts which, in effect, reduce children and young people to commodities. In adoption work, for example, fees are paid to individuals and voluntary organisations involved in the lengthy and exhaustive process of social work and family court proceedings, leading to a child being adopted.

Looked after children: residential and daycare, adoption and fostering
From the 1960s, residential childcare was increasingly replaced by attempts to substitute family care through fostering and adoption. In 2000, partly as a gut reaction to the horrors of residential care uncovered by the Waterhouse Report (see below), the Labour government set in motion the prime minister's UK-wide review of adoption. This attempted to increase the speed and effectiveness of lengthy and time-consuming adoption processes, attract, recruit, retain and support more adoptive parents, improve local authority adoption performance, improve the court processes and change the law to put the interests of the child first (Winchester, 2000). In autumn 2000, a new Adoption and Performance Taskforce began work, focusing on eight local councils, encouraging social services departments to regard adoption as a positive, responsible option.

There were still more than 40,000 children in residential childcare in 1971, but the total had declined to less than 7,000 by the late 1990s. There are indications that residential care is more of a last resort than it was. Placements are shorter on average and there are more placements of older children, a significant proportion being above 16, the minimum school-leaving age. The number of new children looked after during 1998/99 fell 5 per cent from the previous year while the number who ceased to be looked after fell by 8 per cent. Consequently, the number of children being looked after by local authorities under the terms of the Children Act 1989 increased by 4 per cent during the year ending 31 March 1999, to a total of 55,300. Of these, 36,100 were looked after in foster placements, an increase of 3 per cent on the previous year. The use of care orders increased by 7 per cent over the year, to a total of 34,100, while the use of voluntary agreements declined (Department of Health, 1999b, p.1).

The review of residential childcare by Sir William Utting (Utting, 1991) identified one weakness as the extremely low proportion of qualified care staff. Almost a decade later, although three-quarters of those running children's homes had a recognised qualification, this applied to less than a quarter of other staff (Hills and Child, 2000). Criticisms that children were housed in institutions, rather than being placed in settings offering a 'home from home', had been made of residential childcare establishments (Millham et al., 1975) since the days of the Home Office approved schools, retitled community homes with education (CHEs) under the Children and Young Persons Act 1969. Twenty years after this Act, most of those large institutions had closed and even the average number of children in the smaller homes had fallen from 10 to 7 (Berridge and Brodie, 1998).

A succession of scandals and inquiry reports was extremely critical of neglect and management weaknesses by the local authorities, failure to monitor conditions in homes and a lack of adequately qualified, experienced and trustworthy staff, which allowed regimes to develop which were abusive to children, sometimes over long periods of time (Kirkwood, 1992; Waterhouse, 2000). Continuing evidence of widespread child abuse in children's homes led to Sir William Utting being commissioned to assess the adequacy of the child protection safeguards introduced by the Children Act 1989 (Utting, 1997). The report of the most comprehensive and large-scale official investigation into child abuse in residential care and foster care was published in 2000 (Waterhouse, 2000). Waterhouse had the status of a judicial inquiry, which, unlike more than a dozen previous inquiries into alleged abuse in childcare in Clwyd, meant that witnesses could be required to give evidence under subpoena powers of the court and the report could be published, with its authors having the legal indemnity usual in a judicial inquiry.

The Labour government broadly accepted (Department of Health, 2000c) the 72 recommendations of the Waterhouse Report (Waterhouse, 2000), which focused on the need to appoint a Children's Complaints Officer in each local authority social services department and upgrade the quality of training and supervision of childcare staff and the operation of child protection procedures. A Children's Rights Commissioner was appointed for Wales, with responsibilities beyond residential childcare to include domiciliary services for disabled children and adoption agencies and services. The government turned down similar proposals for a children's commissioner in England and for children to have the statutory right of access to independent advocates (Martell, 2000, p. 10).

The observation that social services departmental managements neglected their children's homes also came from researchers (Berridge and Brodie, 1998), inquiries into malpractices such as the abusive 'pindown' regime in Staffordshire children's homes (Levy and Kahan, 1991) and the Department of Health itself (Department of Health, 1992b). This neglect included a scandalously low level of educational support for, and achievement by, children in residential care, compared with their peers elsewhere. Three-quarters of young people leave public care with no qualifications, only 35 per cent obtain five or more GCSEs at Grade C or above and less than 19 per cent proceed onto further or higher education (Who Cares Trust, 1999). This has been acknowledged to some extent by the Department of Health (1998a) and the Who Cares Trust is attempting to tackle it through the Right to Read Project, a pilot initiative in five local authorities in association with the National Literacy Association (NLA) and the Paul Hamlyn Foundation. However, the quality of care provided by an establishment depends in part on the culture of the setting rather than external factors alone (Brown et al., 1998).

Positive messages for improving practice in work with children and young people living away from home came from research funded by the Department of Health and brought together in a key series of publications between 1998 and 2000 (Brown, et al., 1998; Bullock et al., 1998; Whitaker et al., 1998; Sinclair and Gibbs, 1998; Wade et al., 1998; Hills and Child, 2000; Farmer and Pollock, 1998).

The attitude that children being looked after by the local authority should not have contact with their natural parents became less important than offering the hope that families ultimately might be reconstituted. Undoubtedly, the work of John Bowlby (1965), which contributed to the widespread view that children separated from their natural parents, particularly mothers, suffered deprivation, played a major part in this shift. But fostering is not a straightforward option for children whose backgrounds are disturbed and disrupted, since they may find it difficult to cope with being cared for in a family household which, nevertheless, is not intended as their permanent family home. Despite the admitted shortcomings of residential childcare, foster care placements break down more often than residential care and this may be due in part to a decrease in the proportion of so-called more straightforward infant adoptions from three-quarters in 1968 to 10 per cent in 1991 (Triseliotis et al., 1997, p. 15); a tendency for excessive numbers of moves between foster parents and residential childcare placements (Jackson and Thomas, 1999); a shortage of suitable adopters and fosterers and of resources devoted to training and supporting them (Berridge, 1997). However, increased resources are now available through the Quality Protects programme and standards for adoption, fostering and 'looked after' children – the unwholesome official terminology for being in the care of the local authority – have been introduced (Department of Health/ Department of Education and Employment and Home Office, 2000).

Children and young people leaving care
The traditional way out of an abusive residential care situation was for a young person to abscond. Often, absconders committed offences and their deprivation was turned into depravation (Millham et al., 1978). The need for support packages for children and young people leaving care was well known (Stein and Carey, 1986). Many piecemeal improvements had been made over a dozen years. The White Papers *Modernising Social Services* (Department of Health, 1998a) and *The Government's Response to the Children's Safeguards Review* (Department of Health, 1998b) committed the government to legislation to strengthen the duties of local authorities to support young people leaving care, at least up to the age of 18. The Children (Leaving Care) Act 2000 gave the local authority the duty to stay in touch with all care leavers qualifying for the new support arrangements, beyond age 21 in some cases. All eligible young people must have a personal adviser to ensure their continued access to support and advice and a 'pathway plan'. The financial arrangements to support them were to be simplified. One aim was to reverse the trend (an increase for 16-year-olds from 33 per cent in 1993 to 46 per cent in 1998) towards more young people leaving care early.

The application of a social exclusion perspective to the life chances of children defined as in need produced four categories of child welfare: young carers, school inclusion, child and adolescent mental health and youth offending. Research indicates that the educational attainment of a child is the single most important indicator of future life chances (Department of Health, 2000b, Chapter 5). The government's programme to support families included setting up the National Family and Parenting Institute, the Sure Start programme and early years initiatives, which began in 2000 with a grant of £500 m.

Teenage pregnancy
A report by the SEU (1999a) on teenage pregnancies identified nearly 90,000 conceptions a year to teenagers across England, but mostly affecting poorer districts and the most vulnerable young people, including those excluded from school and those being looked after by the local authority. Fifteen thousand teenagers a year had abortions, 90 per cent had their babies outside marriage. Teenage parents were more likely than their peers to experience subsequent poverty and unemployment. The SEU report recommended action to halve the rate of teenage conceptions by 2010 and improve the preventive and supportive measures for teenagers and teenage parents, including ensuring that social services prioritise the prevention of teenage pregnancy for looked after children and young people and all Young Offender Institutions provide sex education and parenting classes. A new unit in the Department of Health was set up to coordinate the work.

Implications for social workers

The following example shows how social workers' critical understanding of policies concerning children and families may enable them to improve their practice.

EXAMPLE

Ruth is a social worker working with a mother of five children under 10 years old, who have three different biological fathers. When the mother is depressed, which is every few weeks and is made worse through chronic poverty and poor housing, she loses her ability to parent, turns to alcohol, and at those times her failure to bond with the older two children, both of whom then display behaviour problems, is more apparent. Neighbours have phoned several times reporting shouting in the house.

Should Ruth take action for the children to be looked after by the local authority, thereby protecting their interests?

There are no simple answers to this question. Ruth is faced with genuine unresolvable dilemmas. Here is a summary of some of the issues she faces and the outcomes.

1. Ruth works to enable the mother to build her confidence in her undoubted parenting abilities and to find ways of supporting her through her depressive periods.

2. Ruth realises that her priority is to protect the children, attend to their interests and assess their needs under the Children Act 1989. She isn't confident that local authority care is better for all the children than the care of their mother, at her best. Ruth feels the tension between her interventive role and legal powers and responsibility for counselling, supporting and empowering members of this family. She notes the risks to the children by leaving them with the mother and her sporadically present partners, but views the possibility of neglect as less harmful than splitting the family up by placing the children in long-term foster care or adoption.

3. Ruth hopes to persuade the mother to take part in a local project aiming to support parents and improve their parenting skills. She works to persuade colleagues in the housing department to rehouse the family. She also provides financial assistance which enables the mother to throw away soiled bedding and damaged furniture and smarten the house up.

4. Ruth's risk-taking is justified. Against all odds, the mother's morale improves, her pride in home-building is rewarded by the two older children becoming more positive, relationships within the household improve and the family stays together. The mother has a new partner, who seems to have increased the stability of the household. However, Ruth realises that not all the children feel they have gained from this new partner entering their lives. She knows one person's interests and wishes are almost inevitably going to conflict with another's. However, she remains committed to empowering children, as well as adults, to participate in decisions affecting their childcare. So she asks the children, as she has done before, for their views about the future of their family. From their responses, she judges that on balance the gains for family members as a whole outweigh the losses for some. Also, she feels that the risk of abuse from this partner is far less than if the children had been looked after by the local authority.

Chapter summary

The overwhelming attention by policy has been paid to the preservation of the family, while the major threats to the safety of children come from close relatives within the family, or friends who are close to the family. This ironically presents paradoxes and dilemmas for the practitioner. There is a need to balance the interests of one family member against another. Families need liberating from poverty and children, particularly, need liberating from the consequences of poverty for their life chances. Policies have failed to ensure this in the past. On the basis of past evidence, there is a need to view critically any claims by politicians that family poverty will be abolished in the near future.

Further reading

Fox Harding, L. (1997) *Perspectives in Child Care*, Addison Wesley Longman, Harlow

Franklin, B. (ed.) (1995) *The Handbook of Children's Rights – Comparative Policy and Practice*, Routledge, London

Parton, N. (ed.) (1997) *Child Protection and Family Support – Tensions, Contradictions and Possibilities*, Routledge, London

Stevenson, O. (ed.) (1999) *Child Welfare in the UK*, Oxford, Blackwell

Wilson, K. and James, A. (eds) (1995) *The Child Protection Handbook*, Baillière Tindall, London

7

Youth Justice and Criminal Justice

To judge by the excessive use of custody, youth and criminal justice in the UK remains overpunitive. An unacceptably high number of young offenders continue to be locked up, including some in prison. In the adult sector, an excessive number of minor, including first, offenders are imprisoned. Meanwhile, the number of life sentence prisoners – currently 4,000, the highest total in recorded history – has grown by ten times over the past 30 years, exceeding the total for the rest of Western Europe put together and growing at more than 300 per year. We can expect the equivalent of ten prisons to be catering for more than 7,000 pensioner prisoners serving life or very long sentences, a decade from now. By the criteria used by officials themselves – reconviction rates, cost, cleanliness – prison is not effective.

The average sentence meted out to 15–17-year-old boys increased dramatically from 5.6 to 11.6 months between 1989 and 1997. Increasing numbers of young people receive custodial sentences. Between 1992 and 1998, the number of young people aged 15–17 being given custodial sentences increased by nearly 80 per cent from 3,300 to 5,900 (NACRO, 2000). Between 1997 and 1999, the number of young people aged 18–20 given custodial sentences increased from 17,000 to 18,000 (NACRO, 2001, p. 4). Between 1992 and 1999, the number of 10–17-year-olds convicted or cautioned for an indictable offence fell from 143,000 to 120,400 with a similar decline for those aged 18–21 (NACRO, 2001, p. 2).

Governments tend to justify increasingly punitive policies, especially regarding young people, with reference to the claim that youth crime is rising, particularly crimes associated with sex and violence. However, the total of recorded youth crime, measured by the total of young people aged 10–20 convicted or cautioned for indictable offences decreased

127

by 12 per cent from 247,100 to 217,500 between 1988 and 1998; the numbers of young people aged 10–20 found guilty or cautioned for violent or sexual offences fell by 1 per cent from 30,900 in 1993 to 30,500 in 1998 (NACRO, 2000).

Young people who fail to obtain any graded GCSEs are significantly overrepresented among those coming into the criminal justice system (Office for National Statistics, 1998). The increase in fixed-term and permanent exclusions from school and the lack of provision in many areas for children excluded for a fixed term of up to 45 days, and significant levels of persistent truancy, both correlate highly with offending. A Home Office research study found that half of young women and three-quarters of young men subject to fixed-term exclusions and 63 per cent of young women and 100 per cent of young men permanently excluded were offenders (Graham and Bowling, 1995).

Social factors such as poverty and disadvantage, low family income, poor housing, large family size and inadequate parental supervision make it more likely that a young person will commit offences, as found in the Cambridge Institute of Criminology's long-term research into the criminal careers of young people (West and Farrington, 1997). However, it is difficult to determine which factors operate first in the cycle of offending, the above factors or the failure to achieve qualifications at school, truancy, exclusion from school and unemployment on leaving school (Farrington et al., 1986).

Social work duties in youth justice are placed on the social services department rather than on social workers. Probation officers work with adults under the Probation Services Act 1993 which places responsibility on the individual officer for specific duties, such as offender supervision. They engage in throughcare of offenders sentenced to custody and supervise them after discharge. The National Probation Service, launched in April 2001, replaced more than 50 probation services and had the target of reducing reconviction rates of the 200,000 offenders supervised annually by 5 per cent. Probation officers are involved in programmes to tackle offending behaviour and specialist sex offender treatment programmes. Social workers come into contact with the criminal justice system mostly through work with or in a youth offending team (YOT). Social workers are responsible for fulfilling the responsibilities of local authorities. These mainly concern:

- children appearing in court and needing care, protection or control (Children and Young Persons Act 1933)
- young people needing care, protection or control (Children and Young Persons Act 1963)

- care and treatment of children and young people through court proceedings (Children and Young Persons Act 1969)
- supervision of families and children (Children Act 1989)
- prosecuting a person failing to maintain a spouse or children (National Assistance Act 1948)
- prosecuting a mental health patient for sexual offence/s (Mental Health Act 1959)
- prosecution and after care of detained mental health patients (Mental Health Act 1983). (Brayne and Martin, 1999, pp. 16–18)

These duties bring practitioners into the heart of the criminal justice system, and this in-depth involvement makes it absolutely essential to have a critical grasp of its workings.

Policy context

Changing societal norms

Some areas of criminal justice policy are subject to change as societal norms and legislation change. For example, same-sex relationships between adult males and young people have been affected by changes in the law since the late 1960s yet remain problematic in the sense that, despite equality and anti-discriminatory policies, they are subject to controversy and debate. Lesbian women and gay men were not protected by comparable legislation to the Sex Discrimination Act 1975 or Race Relations Act 1976 (Cosis Brown, 1998). Gay sexual activity was criminalised from the late nineteenth century until the Sexual Offences Act 1967 decriminalised gay sexual activity between consenting adults. The Criminal Justice and Public Order Act 1994 lowered the age of consent for gay men to 18 years. The controversy raised by attempts in 2000 to reform Section 28 of the Local Government Act 1988 indicates how problematic is the social situation of lesbian women and gay men. This is despite the fact that employers are required to apply the same principles of equal opportunity and treatment to their employees as apply to clients, consumers and members of the public. There are proposals to make gay and heterosexual behaviour between adults on an equal basis before the law.

There is also strenuous debate about whether cannabis should be legalised, now that it is no longer subject to police arrest. Drug use is common and increasing. The rate of drug use among 15–16-year-olds is higher in the UK than any other European country.

The problematic legal status of children and young people is reflected in the different ages at which they become 'adult', for different purposes. They can leave school, buy cigarettes (Protection of Children (Tobacco) Act 1986) and fireworks, have certain drinks in a pub, ride a motor cycle unaccompanied to Scotland and marry there at 16. They cannot marry in England or drive a car unaccompanied until they are 17, or vote in a local or general election or buy alcoholic drinks at the off-licence or supermarket (Licensing Act 1964) until they are 18.

Public intolerance of offenders

Social workers and probation officers in the UK work with offenders in a climate of public hostility and intolerance towards adult and young criminals. At the same time, on the positive side, the interests of the victim are taken into consideration much more than they were before the 1990s.

However, widespread punitive and unforgiving public attitudes towards offenders in Britain and USA contrast with the greater tolerance of them in other Western European countries, such as the Netherlands and Scandinavia. Youth justice work suffers from the attitude that young offenders should be punished first and talked to afterwards. Smacking as a parental sanction is still condoned by the government. Traditional disciplinarian approaches to child rearing – whether family-based or residential, for example boarding school – are deeply rooted in the overpunitive and often child-phobic culture of the UK.

Social workers and probation officers are often regarded by the public as too tolerant towards offenders. Intermediate treatment was criticised in the 1970s as playing with young offenders instead of punishing them. More recently, social workers have been criticised for arranging residential courses and what are perceived as 'holidays for criminals'.

Increasing use of custody despite its inadequacies

Prison

Prison remains at the hub of government criminal justice policy. Prison budgets soar, the number of prisons grows. More and more people are needlessly subjected to being locked up in prisons that do not work. Prisons do not reform more than a minority of offenders. Reconviction rates remain so high that any similar commercial organisation judged on reconvictions as key performance indicators would be closed down immediately. Prisons also do not work, in the sense that they are abusive of prisoners' rights to expect reasonable and decent treatment. Prisoners sent to prison *as* punishment invariably are punished in double jeopardy by appalling living conditions which HM Inspectors of Prisons have condemned repeatedly over the past 25 years. A Howard League Commission of Inquiry found unacceptable levels of intimidation, violence and bullying in penal institutions in England and Wales where young people were held on remand and serving sentences (Kennedy, 1995).

Prison is ineffective, too, according to cost–benefit analysts. The costs of the policy of 'three strikes and you're out' for burglars, under the Crime (Sentences) Act 1997, are likely to outweigh the benefits, according to the recently published report by the Prison Reform Trust (1999). Research has largely undermined the justifications for the use of imprisonment. Although keeping a person in prison prevents them offending at that time, a 25 per cent increase in the use of custody would be necessary to generate a 1 per cent change in crime levels (Tarling, 1993, p. 154). In general, incarceration actually can generate more crime, through the magnifying of criminal skills and networks while offenders are together in the criminal culture generated in the institution. Despite the USA using prison between 5 and 8 times the level of most other developed nations, its federal and state prison populations continue to rise and now exceed one million.

In Britain, 53 per cent of all prisoners discharged in 1993 had a further reconviction within two years, and 73 per cent of those discharged in 1987 were reconvicted within seven years (Kershaw and Renshaw, 1997). Of young offenders released from young offender institutions (YOIs), 75 per cent are reconvicted within two years.

It is very difficult to eradicate abusive punishment from institutions and prevent prison regimes themselves being punitive (Adams, 1998c, pp. 99–117). Most women in prison are serving 12 months or less for minor offences including theft and handling stolen goods. Partly because of this, Carlen and Tchaikovsky (1996, p. 216) argue that most women's prisons should be pulled down and only 100 prison places retained. It is hard to find a rational argument against closing 80 per cent of penal institutions and only locking up serious offenders, in view of their known ineffectiveness in reducing criminal behaviour.

Other custodial institutions
Custodial sentences are relatively expensive and ineffective as ways of curbing future offending, particularly repeat custodial sentences for

young people who have been in residential childcare establishments and adult prisoners. The average annual cost of locking up each young offender aged 15–17 in 1998/99 was £26,113 (HM Prison Service, 1999). Political pressures may override the evidence of what is expensive and 'what works', as the actions of home secretaries in the Conservative government of 1979–97 and the Labour government (1997 onwards) demonstrate, in encouraging longer and more custodial sentences.

Research by bodies such as the Howard League for Penal Reform and the Prison Reform Trust and reports on penal institutions by HM Inspectorate of Prisons (set up in 1980) highlight the persistence of injustices and discrimination, including sexism and racism. A disproportionately high percentage (21 per cent) of young people aged 10–20 serving prison sentences on 30 June 1998 were black, South Asian, Chinese or other ethnic minority origin (Commission for Racial Equality, 1992).

In 2001, Labour Home Secretary Jack Straw anticipated that current government policies would cause the prison population to rise to nearly 80,000 by 2007. In contrast, Sir David Ramsbotham, HM Chief Inspector of Prisons, argued for the removal from prisons of all children and young people, pensioners, mentally ill people, asylum seekers and trivial offenders such as shoplifters as well as those imprisoned for drug offences, which would reduce the current prison population from 63,000 to just over 40,000 (Hattenstone, 2001, p. 8). Martin Narey, Director General of the prison service, stated that he would resign unless prison conditions improved. He identified Wormwood Scrubs, Leeds, Wandsworth, Portland and Brixton as 'hellholes', too often regarded as impossible to change (Travis, 2001a, p. 1).

Tougher community penalties

Hand in hand with greater use of custody, both Conservative and Labour governments since the 1980s have introduced measures to strengthen the punitive content of community penalties for offenders. Noncustodial or community-based sanctions for offenders have existed, of course, for many years. The Criminal Justice Act 1948 introduced the conditional discharge and the attendance centre. The Children and Young Persons Act 1969 brought in intermediate treatment and police cautions.

It is commonly recognised that the 1969 Children and Young Persons Act was the high-water mark of the promotion by governments of community sentences as a positive treatment, primarily directed at the welfare of offenders. Thereafter, the need to protect the community, exact retribution from the offender and ensure a deterrent element in the community punishment have all been components in policymaking. First the Conservative, then the Labour governments have been concerned to try to introduce a more stringent and punitive element into noncustodial penalties, notably those supervised by the probation service. The Criminal Justice Act 1972 introduced community service, a purely punitive sanction. The punitive philosophy did not vanish when Labour came into power in 1997. The government's aim of strengthening the punitive element of community punishments for offenders was furthered by the weakening of resistance in the probation service, as Michael Cavadino and James Dignan note (1997, p. 216), through growing managerialist control of officers and the distancing of recruitment from graduation through university-based social work degrees and postgraduate qualifications.

Even though they are more punitive than traditional probation order supervision, most community punishments remain at best an alternative to prison, rather than claiming to replace it (Worrall, 1997, p. 150). More sobering still, community service seems to be an accompaniment to prison and not even an alternative (Oldfield, 1993).

Changes to probation service

Since the 1990s, probation officers' professional base in criminal justice has been eroded, their role has been distanced from the welfare approach, their training has been separated from the professional qualification for social workers and control over their organisation, management and standards of performance has been centralised to an unprecedented extent.

The Criminal Justice and Court Services Act 2000 set up two new services, the National Probation Service for England and Wales and the Children and Family Court Advisory and Support Service, the latter dealing with the work of the former Court Welfare Service traditionally staffed by probation officers.

Since the Dews Report (Dews and Watts, 1995) recommendation that probation officer training be removed from universities and located outside the Diploma in Social Work, there were moves by Conservative and Labour governments, notably through the Home Office, to bring probation staff closer to the prison service and create a seamless custodial and community criminal justice service. The National Association of Probation Officers (NAPO) has raised concerns about the deprofessionalisation of probation work, through the widespread appointment of probation service officers to carry out many of the tasks formerly the responsibility of probation staff holding the Diploma in Social Work or an equivalent professional qualification. The establishment by the Programme Development Unit of the prison psychological service of cognitive-behavioural programmes for offenders in prisons has put psychologists in the position where they can exercise professional supervision over probation officers in the area of face-to-face work with offenders.

Evidence-based and cognitive-behavioural approaches

The move towards an effectiveness approach in the prison service and probation service is linked with a wider shift in the personal social services towards adopting evidence-based practice as a basis for quality assurance. This has several strengths:

- it encourages a reading of relevant research on 'what works' (Hope and Chapman, 1998; McGuire, 1995)
- it creates the impression that practice is based on methods of proven effectiveness
- it promotes greater consistency in standards.

Its weaknesses are:

- it tends to bypass less pragmatic and immediately achievable goals which are less amenable to effectiveness research and/or do not meet the research requirements for a random controlled trial
- it tends to promote the value of psychologically based interventions, such as cognitive-behavioural work
- it does not challenge the simplistic view that we understand what causes offending and can address the diversity of offending behaviour effectively once the correct technique has been identified
- it does not acknowledge sufficiently the complexity of causal mechanisms of offending: individual – genetic, physiological, physical – psychosocial – family, peer – or social – gender, ethnic, social class, geographical, housing, employment. (Webb, 2001, p. 62)

In this connection, Webb warns of the dangers of adopting a simplistic, evidence-based approach to social work, overdependent on natural scientific and experimental research at the expense of qualitative methodologies.

Behavioural theories underpin the expanding programme of reasoning and rehabilitation (R and R) programmes supervised in English prisons by the psychologist-managed Programme Development Unit in the Home Office. R and R programmes attempt to curb criminality by correcting deficiencies in inmates' cognitive processes and perceptions – somewhat ambitious, in the face of the social factors which cause crime. Cognitive skills training or cognitive restructuring has become favoured by the authorities since the 1990s on the basis of research evidence from Canada (see below) that correctional intervention can reduce some categories of offenders' propensity for reconviction.

The growing appeal of cognitive approaches in work with offenders lies largely in its feature of locating the risk indicators or precursors for criminality in the thinking and behavioural and cognitive styles of individuals. This provides a ready justification for interventions aimed at changing the thinking and behaviour of individuals rather than broader goals, such as targeting social and environmental factors, or more flexible social work programmes geared to addressing the assessed needs of individual offenders in achieving cognitive and social competence. These occur in six key areas – self-control, cognitive style, interpersonal problem-solving, social perspective taking, values and critical reasoning (Ross and Fabiano, 1985; Zamble and Porporino, 1988). Cognitive groupwork, thus, is a crude and generalist approach, not designed to respond to individual needs but assuming one treatment plan can meet the needs of all those assessed as in the target group of offenders with cognitive and, it is assumed therefore, behaviour deficits (Porporino, 1995, p. 6). The element of rigidity in the programme does not take account of the individual offender's particular circumstances and the programme by and large does not address social and other factors related to offending, which lie outside the psychological aspects of person's thinking skills. But cognitive-behaviour approaches have built up a huge ideological commitment in the Home Office and it could be argued that they provide the government with its best chance of proving work with offenders can reduce their offending. The successes claimed for such prestructured schemes of cognitive-based work with offenders are large. For example, Porporino quotes research (Robinson, 1995) in Canada, into a precursor of groupwork in UK prisons, combating cognitive deficits:

> in a large-scale and very methodologically rigorous evaluation with Canadian
> federal prison inmates, where there was at least one year of post-release follow-up
> with several thousand cases, it was shown that cognitive skills programming
> reduced the likelihood of recidivism for violent offenders by 18.5%, for
> sex offenders by 39%, and for drug offenders by 29%. (Porporino, 1995, p. 12)

It is naive to expect to be able to transplant cognitive-behavioural programmes from Canada to Britain, without taking due account of the
cultural differences which affect attitudes to offenders in these two
countries. These approaches need using cautiously, in carefully
screened cases where assessment suggests that the person will benefit,
where the worker has access to appropriate professional supervision and
the offender can receive support during and after the programme.

Even an advocate of cognitive approaches such as Porporino observes
that such a strategy will be effective

> only if it is understood and left uncompromised, and only if it is intelligently
> managed and supported in the implementation. (Porporino, 1995, p. 13)

This means that the offenders probably need to be in a custodial setting
which respects and supports them. For the continued effectiveness of
the programme, this supportive and sympathetic attitude to them needs
to continue in the community after their discharge, when they are looking for a job and somewhere to live. The state of British prisons, and
negative attitudes towards offenders by the public at large, make it
unlikely that these conditions will be met.

*Measuring performance in contract culture of
agency and private prisons*

In the early 1980s, the prison department became an agency, the prison
service, as part of the Thatcher government's policy of 'denationalising'
the civil service. At the same time, moves were made to contract out the
running of a few penal establishments. The Blair government of 1997
did not reverse the Conservative government's policy of introducing
privately run custodial institutions (Ascher, 1987). A greater proportion
of British prisons are privately run in 2001 than in any other country in
Western Europe.

From the 1990s, the prison service and probation service adopted
convergent approaches to effective practice. Penal establishments and

the probation service worked to quality standards based on key performance indicators (KPIs). In 1998, Her Majesty's Inspectorate of
Probation (HMIP), the Home Office Probation Unit and the Association
of Chief Officers of Probation (ACOP) supported the distribution to all
probation officers and managers of a Home Office guide to effective
probation practice (Chapman and Hough, 1998). This was an unprecedented attempt to specify what probation officers should do, using
principles of evidence-based practice.

Key policy changes and related issues

Welfare and justice: tensions inherent in policy

Most of the huge volume of criminal justice legislation in the twentieth
century does not affect social workers directly. However, insofar as it
determines the nature, culture, functions and activities of custodial institutions and alternatives to custody and the roles of all professionals in
contact with them – judges, lawyers, police, prison service staff, for
example – it shapes social work practice.

Ambivalence towards children and young people is reflected in the
twin themes of welfare and justice which permeate youth justice legislation and procedures. The so-called welfare principle is inherent
in the Children and Young Persons Acts of 1933, 1963, 1969 and
the Children Act 1989. In contrast, children and young people can
be locked up and subjected to numerous punitive sanctions under
criminal justice legislation such as the Crime and Disorder Act 1998
(see below).

The major thrust of criminal justice policy in Britain since the 1970s
has been towards protecting society and the interests of victims, rather
than attending to the circumstances and needs of the offender. There has
been a tendency towards punitive sentences, that is, custodial rather than
community-based. Or, to put it another way, there has been a move away
from offering the *treatment model*, enshrined in the 1969 Children and
Young Persons Act, based on welfare principles, to disposals based on
the *justice model*.

Advocates of the justice model criticise individualised treatment of
crime as deriving from a misguided view of crime originating in the
pathology of the individual which leads to unfairness and discrimination
in the way offenders are dealt with. The justice model, it is claimed, is
fairer because the offence is attended to through the *due process* of the

law and court proceedings, sentencing following principles of *proportionality* according to the seriousness of the crime.

Justice is an ambiguous ingredient in criminal and youth justice policy and practice. On one hand, it is used by right-wing supporters of more punitive responses to offenders. On the other hand, it is used as the basis for some critical and radical calls for reform. For example, the National Association for Youth Justice (NAYJ) manifesto (2000) advocates improved justice based on reforms to laws on children's rights, for example by raising the age of criminal responsibility to 16, preventing all those under 18 being placed in adult prisons and reversing the legislative trend for younger children to be sentenced to longer custodial sentences.

Policy under the Conservative government 1979–97

Quite exceptionally, Douglas Hurd, who became Home Secretary in 1985, tried to develop criminal justice policies which reduced prison populations. The Green Paper of 1988 (Home Office, 1988) and the White Paper of 1990 (Home Office, 1990) noted the ineffectiveness of prison in crime reduction. He drew on correctional ideas from the USA, legislating 'just deserts' for offenders in the Criminal Justice Act 1991. This attempted to match the punishment to the seriousness of the offence, increase noncustodial sentences and reduce the numbers in prison.

This Act was attacked by politicians and the judiciary as too soft and liberal. The Criminal Justice Act of 1993, passed in the moral panics following the murders of Jamie Bulger and Stephen Lawrence, largely repealed its less punitive measures, giving discretionary powers back to the judiciary and enabling more punitive sanctions to be imposed. John Major started a 'back to basics' initiative that, as he said in his speech to the Conservative Party Conference on 8 October 1993, would 'lead a new campaign to defeat the cancer that is crime'. At the peak of this media-fanned panic, on 7 October 1993, Michael Howard, then Home Secretary, set out the Conservative government's proposals on crime in a 27-point plan to combat what he described as a tidal wave of offending. Michael Howard's philosophy of punishment embodied 'a freely interpreted mix of retributive, deterrent and incapacitative grounds' (Sparks, 1996, p. 76). This ran counter to the direction of criminal justice policy since the mid-1980s. The assertion that 'prison works' was central to this. Since that date, the legitimacy of prison as the central pivot in criminal justice policy has not been challenged by either Conservative or Labour governments. Decarceration and alternatives to prison have only been considered in the context of more harsh and punitive punishments.

Criminal Justice and Public Order Act 1994

The Criminal Justice and Public Order Act 1994 proposed secure training orders for young offenders aged 12–14, who previously had breached a supervision order or who had been convicted of imprisonable offences while on supervision. Curfew orders and electronic monitoring of offenders (known as tagging) also were introduced under this Act.

An Audit Commission report in November 1996 (Audit Commission, 1996) was highly critical of the ineffectiveness of the youth justice system. It concluded that more constructive measures should be developed to address youth crime and prevent further offending, since the youth justice system had failed because young people had not been diverted from the criminal justice system. There was a general recognition among researchers and critical commentators of the continued need to seek significant diversion of offenders from prosecution (Cavadino and Dignan, 1997, pp. 217–18).

Criminal justice under New Labour 1997 onwards

The criminal justice policies of the Labour government 1997 onwards shared with the Conservatives a reliance on custody and on punitive community sanctions. An unprecedented mass of legislation was passed, mostly by the start of Labour's second term in office in June 2001. The policy had four elements:

1. Crime reduction strategy, through every police authority setting challenging targets for reducing vehicle crime, burglary and, in the large metropolitan areas, robbery; a National Crime Reduction Task Force, Regional Crime Reduction Directors and Local Crime and Disorder Partnerships.
2. Increasing penalties for persistent offenders through tougher sentences.
3. Tackling racist crime following the Macpherson Report (Macpherson, 1999), including better definition of racially motivated incidents, a long-term recruitment programme for ethnic minorities into the police and the addition to the statute book of nine new racially aggravated offences.
4. Reducing illegal drug taking.

The positive features of youth and criminal justice policy under Labour include the initiatives to tackle racism; the principle of restorative justice, involving making the offender responsible to the victim; the emphasis on throughcare, involving probation officers planning with offenders throughout the sentence and supervising them after release; and the emphasis on protecting the public and working with offenders to prevent offending.

The negative aspects include the emphasis on punishment in custodial and community sanctions, especially for persistent offenders, such as automatic three-year prison sentences for third-time burglars; the continued prominent role played by the expanded prison system, a feature of Conservative government policy not reversed by Labour; a growing emphasis on preplanned programmes of work with offenders, based on cognitive-behavioural approaches (see discussion above). Goldson and Peters (2000) challenge the punitive element of criminal justice policy which involves locking up increasing numbers of children and young people, at great financial and human cost, recommending instead the use of more just and humane community-based alternatives to custody.

Significant new punitive measures were introduced by the Labour government (1997 onwards) under the Crime and Disorder Act 1998, including antisocial behaviour orders, sex offender orders, parenting orders, child safety orders, local child curfews, police powers to remove truants, drug treatment and testing orders, the final warning scheme, reparation orders (expanding powers in s. 12A(3)(aa) Children and Young Persons Act 1969), action plan orders, the detention and training order, the recall of short-term prisoners and the home detention curfew.

The Crime and Disorder Act of 1998 set up YOTs to provide multi-agency approaches to community problems rather than putting the onus on the police alone, for example, police and local authorities being required to work together to develop anti-crime measures. Electronic tagging of offenders was introduced for adult offenders and in 2000 plans were under way to extend tagging to young offenders committing serious offences. Home detention curfews could be imposed on offenders, with penalties for any breaches.

Section 73 of the Crime and Disorder Act 1998 comprised a new custodial detention and training order for children and young people aged 10–17, introduced on 1 April 2000 and specified as 4, 6, 8, 10, 12, 18 or 24 months, half to be served in detention and half on supervision in the community. It replaced with a single, invariable sentence the secure training order for young offenders aged 12–14 and detention in a YOI for those aged 15–17. It represented a fourfold increase over the six-month maximum custodial penalty previously available to the youth court. It required that a training plan should be devised within five working days of admission, specifying objectives – including those relating to education, health and accommodation – and how they should be achieved and assessed. The supervision of the post-custody period was an integral part of the sentence and involved mandatory meetings with the young person on the day of release and subsequently, home visits at least once a month and supervisory contact twice a week for the first three months and once weekly thereafter, with regular reviews of the training plan.

The Youth Justice and Criminal Evidence Act 1999 introduced a referral order for first-time offenders, supervised by a youth offender panel under the aegis of the YOT. The Powers of Criminal Courts (Sentencing) Act 2000 codified all available sentencing legislation. The Criminal Justice and Police Act 2001 extended child curfews to children under 16 and empowered courts to order secure remands on boys aged 15–16 to prevent them committing further offences. This was expected to increase the demand for secure places.

Pilot YOTs began work in 1998 and all 154 YOTs started work in April 2000 simultaneously with the implementation of detention and training orders under the 1998 Act. Referral orders were anticipated on a pilot basis from June 2000, under the Youth Justice and Criminal Evidence Act and parenting orders, child safety orders, action plan orders, final warning schemes and reparation orders would be available from the same time. Antisocial behaviour orders and detention and training orders (an outcome of amalgamating sentences to young offender institutions and secure training orders) were also introduced. It was intended that their work would be monitored against National Standards for Youth Justice published in April 2000 by the Youth Justice Board (YJB), in terms of the primary goal of preventing offending by children and young people. The final evaluation report published in 2001 acknowledges implementation problems but endorses the positive achievements of strong multi-agency teams in tackling youth offending (Home Office, 2001). This responded to the Quality Protects programme launched by the Secretary of State for Health in September 1998 (see Chapter 1).

Local authorities and social workers were faced with the complex implications of applying Quality Protects (particularly objectives 3 and 4 which relate to improving the life chance benefits from educational opportunities, healthcare and social care and reducing the rate of offending of children in need and looked after children). In particular, this implied working to improve liaison between those responsible for devising and implementing youth justice plans and children's services plans, Quality Protects Management Action Plans, probation and drug action team plans, including health services, police, victim agencies, YOIs and district councils and others responsible for local crime reduction (Bailey and Williams, 2000).

Persistent young offenders
One target of Labour's policy was a minority of young offenders who were alleged to be responsible for waves of multiple offending. This proved largely mythological. The Children's Society researched the situation of children and young people aged 12–14 who were potentially likely to be sent to secure training centres. It examined their circumstances and offences and found crime waves involving them are rare and when they present problems local authorities usually place them in secure provision (Crowley, 1998).

Drug and alcohol use and offending
Drug taking is a particular target of Labour government policy. While many young people may experiment with prohibited substances, most will only take cannabis, will stop of their own accord and will never become involved in other types of offending. The great expense of maintaining dependence on heroin or 'crack' cocaine (upwards of £100 per day) creates strong pressure on those without a regular income to turn to crime. Crack cocaine is a relatively recent phenomenon, not being mentioned in the Misuse of Drugs Act 1971.

The use of drugs by young people is increasing. John Balding's survey notes that at least a third of young people will have tried some illicit drug before they reach 15 and almost half of young males and more than a third of females aged 16–19. Drug taking among 14–15-year-olds has increased about six times since the late 1980s (Balding, 1998). Most drug taking takes place among poorer and less advantaged young people (Marlow and Pearson, 1999). There is apparently a close correlation between illegal drug taking and offending, but whether this is a causal relationship remains unclear. Seventy per cent of young people on supervision were reported to have taken illegal substances (Audit Commission, 1996). The continued criminalisation of cannabis taking in particular, but also other mood-altering drugs such as crack and ecstasy, is held by critics to be responsible for increasing housebreaking and other burglary rates, as addicts try to obtain money to buy drugs. Some critics advocate decriminalising drug taking and making certain drugs available on prescription, to ensure that heroin addicts, for instance, have access to clean supplies of the drug. There is little doubt that, if the taking of cannabis was legalised and registered addicts of heroin and other hard drugs were given access to clean, medically prescribed sources, much of the vast illegal industry associated with other offences of burglary and violence, as drug users try to maintain supplies, would disintegrate and the incidence of recorded criminality would fall significantly. In the meantime, any proposals to decriminalise such drug taking remain controversial and unacceptable to the main political parties.

In the meantime, services responding to young drug users' needs, for instance, should be linked with community services used by young people and clubs and agencies with flexible hours. Research highlighted by the Youth Crime Briefing of NACRO for July 2001 indicates that young people in ethnic minorities are not likely to take up drug services because of distrust of white agencies (Pearson and Patel, 1998), reluctance to admit need (Awaih et al., 1992) and lack of awareness of how drug services could help them (Awaih et al., 1990).

Excessive alcohol consumption correlates positively with offending. A survey of young men aged 17–21 in a YOI found that more than two-fifths of them reported having drunk alcohol at the time they committed the offence (Cookson, 1992).

Of course, research demonstrating correlations between offending and substance abuse does not amount to proof that drinking and drug taking cause crimes. Similar patterns of substance abuse may be present in non-offenders. Nevertheless, the relatively high proportion of young offenders who have taken illegal substances raises the likelihood that YOTs will undertake offending behaviour work to address illegal drug taking and alcohol abuse. This is likely to involve working in partnership with statutory and voluntary agencies working with drug action teams, in particular. The introduction in October 2000 of drug treatment and testing orders (DTTOs) for 16–17-year-olds makes it more likely that social workers will become involved in working with young offenders who are misusing drugs. DTTOs can involve the court imposing compulsory drug testing, and, if the young offender consents, subsequent treatment with regular reviews. Several YJB-funded projects are running, with built-in evaluation, until 2002, to establish whether the drug agencies' widespread practice of harm minimisation helps to reduce offending.

Mentally disordered offenders

People diagnosed as mentally ill who commit homicides have created a public furore in a succession of incidents and inquiries in the 1990s, notably into the death of Georgina Robinson and into the care and treatment of Christopher Clunis who killed Jonathan Zito (Ritchie et al., 1994). In 1991, the Confidential Inquiry into Homicides and Suicides by Mentally Ill People, set up by the Department of Health, identified 34 such deaths over a three-year period (Boyd, 1994; Confidential Inquiry, 1996). Research by the Glasgow University Media Group showed that two-thirds of media references to mental health related to violence, with headline treatment typically of the 'homicidal maniac' type (Philo et al., 1993, cited in Sayce, 1995, p. 129). Significantly, other tragedies in the mental health field do not attract similar attention, notably the approximately one death per week of psychiatric patients, associated with neuroleptic drugs, three to four times the rate of homicides (Sayce, 1995, p. 127). This is evidence of a debate skewed by media and public preoccupations, which risks raising public intolerance of people with mental health problems and focusing policy on controlling them through such measures as supervision registers, rather than responding to the entire continuum of need and the complexities of risk (Sayce, 1995, p. 128).

The task of meeting the needs of mentally disordered offenders may conflict with the requirement that society is protected. The tension is made more pronounced since the trend from the Mental Health Act 1959 for locked wards in the large, often Victorian mental hospitals to be abandoned and mentally disordered people to be treated more and more on an 'open door' basis, and in the community. Many people who have mental health problems finish up remanded or sentenced to imprisonment. There is controversy about whether mentally disordered people who offend should receive different treatment to other offenders. The views of the general public, the police, the victim/s and relatives of victim/s are relevant to this debate, as well as the professional arguments for and against diverting mentally disordered offenders from the criminal justice system. On the whole, a groundswell of professional opinion in the 1990s has supported the argument for maximising the diversion of mentally disordered offenders from the criminal justice system, although the lack of support in the community for those discharged from mental hospitals, who commit serious offences or even murder, has been highlighted in several inquiry reports (Blom-Cooper et al., 1995; Davies et al., 1995; Confidential Inquiry, 1996; Ritchie et al., 1994). The majority of mentally disordered offenders, however, do not fall into this category (Muijen, 1996, p. 151). To the end of meeting their needs, psychiatric/panel court assessment schemes and diversion schemes have been set up, as encouraged by Home Office Circular 66/90 (Home Office, 1990), in more than 60 locations, to develop ways of diverting mentally disordered offenders from the criminal justice system, by multi-agency working. The Care Programme Approach introduced in the 1990s emphasises the collaboration of health and social services in assessing the needs of the person, developing a care package, implementing and reviewing it, with the full involvement of professionals, patient/s, relatives and carers.

Supervision registers were introduced in 1994 (see Vaughn and Badger, 1995). Courts tend only rarely to use the probation order with a condition of psychiatric treatment, which can last six months to three years. The supervision and treatment order under the Criminal Procedure (Insanity and Unfitness to Plead) Act 1991 became operational on 1 January 1992 and is appropriate only for a very small number of people deemed unfit to plead. A guardianship order can be made where the conditions for a hospital order could be met and the nature and degree of mental disorder warrants a person's reception into guardianship.

The need for psychiatric services in mental hospitals and prisons to equate with each other is not likely to be achievable in the foreseeable future. People with mental health problems are not in a powerful position, vis-à-vis professionals, the mass media and the general public, to advocate changes in policies and practices based on their perspective on their circumstances. This imbalance would be helped by strengthening user involvement, independent advocacy for users of mental health services, improved complaints procedures for users, improved training for professionals, health promotion and education work with journalists, as well as an overhaul of mental health policies so as to decrease the emphasis on containing madness and coercion in community care and bring about the treatment of users of mental health services as citizens (Sayce, 1995, pp. 146–7).

Black mentally disordered offenders, and even more so black women, may suffer double or triple jeopardy: being more likely to be apprehended by the police, more likely to receive a custodial sentence and, if regarded as having a mental disorder, more likely to be removed under a place of safety order under the Mental Health Act 1983, to be diagnosed as suffering from schizophrenia or other psychosis and to be given higher doses of medication (Brown, 1990).

There is a tension in government policy between improving the conditions in which some of the most dangerous and disturbed offenders with mental health problems are held and protecting the public. Government policy has created human rights issues on behalf of those offenders. By 2000, the Home Office had put in place measures enabling mentally disordered people to be locked up, who had not committed an offence, were regarded as untreatable for their mental health disorder, and who were considered too dangerous to the public to be left at liberty. Plans were made for the closure of the three former special hospitals and their replacement by a larger number of much smaller secure units catering for people with severe personality disorders as well as mentally disordered offenders. It was anticipated these establishments would be less institutional and more integrated into local mental health provision.

Implications for social workers

Practitioners engaged with work with offenders at different locations in the criminal justice system need to come to grips with the practice implications of the great body of policy and legislative changes since 2000. Here is one example of the range and complexity of issues faced by one social worker.

EXAMPLE

Peter is a youth justice worker in a downtown area, with a group of young offenders displaying a variety of problems.

1. The mother of a girl aged 14 who has committed several offences has herself been sentenced to imprisonment. The rented flat they share may not be available when she is discharged. The girl will be taken into care if negotiations to persuade relatives to offer her suitable accommodation are not successful. Despite indications that the girl goes on drinking binges, Peter manages to obtain the offer of accommodation from a sympathetic and motherly aunt. Peter is aware that some local authorities will not commit themselves to rehousing prisoners on discharge, waiting instead for them to apply for housing as homeless persons (Cavadino and Bell, 1999). Peter will be working jointly with the housing officer to ensure the mother receives housing advice and that their flat is retained for her discharge.

2. A boy at the point of leaving primary school to go to secondary school is getting into trouble and risks being excluded from school. Peter persuades managers to set up a mentoring scheme with local schools, based on Chance, a project in Islington, which will provide the boy with a supportive relationship with a trained, matched adult. Peter also liaises with a project offering targeted help through social work trained school-home support workers, to prevent children judged likely to offend from being excluded from mainstream education.

3. Peter uses as the basis for his future work the guidelines for practitioners in key areas of work in the youth justice system, and the *Manifesto for Youth Justice* published by the National Association for Youth Justice (NAYJ). Among the 18 major aims and principles are the following that Peter finds relevant and useful, paraphrased and summarised here:

- promoting non-discriminatory policies and practices against black, other ethnic minority and disadvantaged children and children in public care
- ensuring the application of child protection legislation
- ensuring the implementation of the UN Convention on the Rights of the Child and the Human Rights Act 1998
- ensuring direct preventive work does not take place with children who have not committed offences or are under the age of criminal responsibility
- providing non-criminalising family support services in preference to child safety orders, antisocial behaviour orders and parenting orders
- clarifying boundaries in multi-agency work
- developing sufficient child welfare and social work expertise to ensure that adequate account is taken of children's development and the impact on them of material and emotional disadvantage
- ensuring consistency and parity, locally and nationally, in decision-making when reprimanding, warning or prosecuting
- minimising the use of powers that result in unnecessary separations between children and their families
- ensuring assessment tools do not harm and that attempts to reduce delays do not compromise quality information gathering and assessment or deny children's rights. (NAYJ, 2000)

In addition, it is important that Peter takes up any mental health problems and drug and alcohol abuse, both of which, he realises, correlate positively with offending in a significant percentage of cases, and, if he is lucky in his area, will be addressed by health resources which have a substantial input to other YOTs of which he knows. Peter also bears in mind that education authorities have an input in the education of school-age children with whom YOTs are working.

Chapter summary

This chapter has surveyed briefly selected aspects of criminal justice and youth justice which affect social work. It would be beyond the scope of this chapter to attempt a comprehensive discussion of the implications for practice of the vast quantity of sentencing provision which has become law since 1998. However, issues of most relevance to practitioners have been examined.

Further reading

Cavadino, M. and Dignan J. (1997) *The Penal System: An Introduction*, 2nd edn, Sage, London

Drakeford, M. and Haines, K. (1998) *Young People and Youth Justice*, Macmillan, London – now Palgrave

Goldson, B. (ed.) (2000) *The New Youth Justice*, Russell House Publishing, Lyme Regis

Haines, K. (1996) *Understanding Modern Juvenile Justice*, Avebury, Aldershot

Matthews, R. (1999) *Doing Time: An Introduction to the Sociology of Imprisonment*, Macmillan, Basingstoke – now Palgrave

Part III

Issues

8

Tackling Divisions and Inequalities

The goal of abolishing discrimination in society and bringing about equality between people has been integral to welfare policy since the establishment of the welfare state. Richard Titmuss, looking back to those days in the 1940s, commented in a lecture in 1964 that:

> built into the public model of social policy in Britain since 1948 there are two major roles or objectives: the redistributive objective and the non-discriminatory objective. To move towards the latter it was believed that a prerequisite was the legal enactment of universal (or comprehensive) systems of national insurance, education, medical care, housing and other direct services. (Titmuss, 1976b, p. 191)

The gap between the political ideal of ending discrimination and reality is apparent. We could argue that Britain's commitment to people's rights and ending discrimination is beyond doubt. But the Human Rights Act 1998, like Britain's anti-discriminatory legislation, offers protection only in certain areas – the right to life, liberty, security, fair trial, free elections and free expression, education, marriage, privacy and family life – but excluding, for example, discrimination on grounds of age, sexual orientation and religion or belief. Ironically, Britain was not represented in Rome in November 2000, the fiftieth anniversary of the signing of the European Convention on Human Rights, when 25 of the member states of the Council of Europe signed Protocol 12 prohibiting all forms of discrimination. Britain refuses to sign, apparently, because the Protocol is too open-ended and general (Palmer, 2000, p. 21). Incidentally, the Human Rights Act affects only England and Northern Ireland, Scotland and Wales having made separate provision in 1998.

Contexts

All societies have some features which are shared by their citizens and which contribute to them being relatively coherent and homogeneous. Inevitably, there will be differences between people, individually and collectively, major divisions and areas of inequality and conflict.

The growing awareness of the reality that social policy and social work take place in the context of divisions and inequalities in society comes about partly through research demonstrating the extent of discrimination, oppression and exclusion on people, individually and in families, groups, organisations and communities. The impact of these is not limited to certain societies but is felt by people in both developed and developing countries. Economic, demographic, social and political factors all affect these inequalities, either exacerbating or modifying their impact on people's lives.

Embedded in everyday perceptions of difference and diversity is the assumption that they present problems to be surmounted. In preference, a goal of anti-discriminatory, equality-based policy and practice should be to move towards celebrating diversity.

Key aspects

Diversity and difference are features of all humanity. The problem is that some people's differences lead to injustice, want and discrimination, some people being in double jeopardy through having more than one difference. For instance, a year after the Immigration and Asylum Act 1999 which focused on the relationship between immigration control and refugee status (Cohen, 2001), researchers estimated that at least 20,000 asylum seekers were disabled; in some cases, when refugee status was granted their situation did not improve. Most were existing at 70 per cent of income support rates; they were not usually eligible for disability benefits; shops stocking their particular diets – for those with diabetes, for example – did not always take vouchers; the interface with local community care practice, under the dispersal policy, was not working (George, 2000, pp. 95–6).

Social division

What is meant by social division? A social division is a way of grouping people which reflects common features of their situation and differences from other social groupings and may rank them in terms of power, exclusion or other measures of inequality. Class is a good example of a way of differentiating groups of people which also ranks them.

Other social divisions which are crucial to social policy and social work are those of gender, age, ethnicity or race and disability, but it is important to other marginalised and excluded groups to keep this list open-ended.

Class
Class is the most obvious social division, although it is a somewhat problematic and changing concept whose definition is difficult. There is a general tendency for class to be associated with the occupation of a person, which leaves partners, carers, unemployed people, children and older people in the same household in the problematic situation of being designated with the social class of the main employee, while people who work in the higher professions are even more advantaged. There are exceptions, since aristocrats tend to be located in the highest class, irrespective of whether they work and part-time workers may be placed below the working class, in an 'underclass' of unemployed people.

There is an important distinction between those divisions such as age which are fixed and those such as social class which are socially constructed and, therefore, subject to debate. It needs to be acknowledged also that, because some divisions are more fundamental or structural features of society, they may be more influential than others, in their consequences for people's lives. But, at the same time, one person's experience, say, of being a black, disabled woman may be far more devastating in a given situation than another's of being an older, working-class person. It is simply not possible to arrive at an undisputed hierarchy of divisions.

The goal of welfare policy might be argued by the Left to be the reduction of class inequalities and enabling people to be upwardly mobile through classes. The idea of social mobility is important, therefore, since it concerns maintaining movement between classes, preferably upwards but, realistically, downwards as well. According to the criterion of reducing class differentials and facilitating upward social mobility, many health and welfare services could be said to have failed. Le Grand (1982) showed how middle-class users benefited most from health and education services; the Black Report (Department of Health and Social Security, 1980a) showed the persistence of social class and geographical inequalities in health provision and people's health, as measured by rates of accidents, morbidity (illness) and mortality.

The underclass   The term 'underclass' is somewhat controversial (see Chapter 2), since its critics say it has been used unfairly by right-wing commentators to refer pejoratively to people who, it is assumed, are inferior to people in higher classes. Charles Murray (1994), for example, is a leading exponent of the right-wing view that the rise of single parent, by which he means lone mother, families is indicative of a moral decline, reflected particularly in the emerging underclass of society. This, he argues, is a key contributory factor in unemployment, crime and irresponsibility, likely to be perpetuated in future marital break-downs in the next generation of children.

Age
The adage that 'you're as young as you feel' unfortunately does not take account of the reality that, in an ageist society, 'you may feel as young as you're treated'. Relative youthfulness or the appearance of being older may lead to a person being discriminated against, in terms of many everyday experiences. It may also affect access to social services and how clients and carers are treated. Age may preclude equal access to some services. For instance, medical and health insurance policies may be age-linked and some expensive treatments and operations in the public sector may be rationed according to age, retirement status, potential for re-employment, prognosis in terms of remaining years of active life and other similar criteria.

Gender
Gender divides at least as fundamentally as age or class. Gender divisions in many societies, most apparent when men exercise power over women, probably predated all other divisions. Less visibly, but no less significant, are historical traditions of discrimination against, and oppression of, women, which are embedded in the structure and culture of society. Despite the pervasiveness of these, in the past and the present, it is only since the 1970s that feminist theory, research and practice have brought gender issues to the forefront of all aspects of the social sciences, social policy and social work. Nowadays, it is recognised that gendered social relationships are embedded in the discipline of social policy itself (Watson and Doyal, 1998) and need acknowledging and tackling in health and welfare services (Doyal, 1998).

Women in leadership roles   Women are some way from achieving equal participation in political leadership and policymaking. By 1995, only 24 women had been elected as heads of state or government, half of these since 1990. In 1994, women represented 5.7 per cent of cabinet ministers compared with 3.3 per cent in 1987 and in 59 countries women held no ministerial positions at all (Corner, 1997, pp. 6–7).

Violence against women One of the most destructive gender-based divisions in society arises from the incidence of male violence towards women. The three long-term goals of Labour government policy in relation to violence against women are both to reduce crimes of violence and the fear of violence, as measured by the British Crime Survey; to enable children to grow up without violence in family life; and to establish good practice involving multi-agency partnerships. These goals were specified in the joint Women's Unit and Home Office document (Home Office, 1999a) *Living Without Fear*. The Labour government commitment to tackling criminal violence against women led to the Home Office assuming the policy lead on violence against women in July 1999, formerly taken by the Women's Unit based at the Cabinet Office. A new Inter-Departmental Group on Domestic Violence and Violence Against Women was set up, replacing and broadening the scope of the original Inter-Departmental Group on Domestic Violence. *Living Without Fear* summarises the serious criminal nature of violence against women and indicates that, since the late 1980s, the number of reported rapes has nearly doubled, often being committed by a person known to the victim. The report exemplifies government policy by identifying a number of preventive strategies, including providing support and protection, bringing perpetrators to justice and creating a number of projects designed to encourage prevention.

Double and triple jeopardy Gender divisions operate independently of, as well as in conjunction with, class, age and other divisions. Thus inequalities on the grounds of gender may be compounded through double or even triple jeopardy, which means, in effect, that more than one factor operates at once. For example, women are particularly prone to being defined as potential carers in community care planning processes. The impact of the caring role on them is likely to be more pronounced where they are also older, disabled and black. Clare Ungerson's research into caring uses empirical data to bridge psychology and social policy. She argues that while some women carers have found their female identity through caring, others bitterly regret their loss of autonomy and identity and feel massively exploited (Ungerson, 1987, p. 149).

Feminist theory, research and practice have raised awareness of gender discrimination as a social reality and have strengthened pressure for legislation to protect women's rights in the home, at work and against sex discrimination in any setting. The Sex Discrimination Act (SDA) 1975 did not abolish sex discrimination. Parents, disabled people and carers continue to experience exclusion from equal opportunities in the labour market through the lack of adequate care provision (Lister, 2000, p. 47).

The increasing proportion of women in the workforce has lessened discrimination against families with children and women at work, mainly in the form of improved preschool provision and improved maternity and paternity leave. But women still experience lower pay than men in equivalent jobs and are discriminated against in promotion and higher appointments in society, especially in health and social services, only 17 per cent of women working as managers in the NHS compared with 26.5 per cent in the workforce as a whole (Equal Opportunities Commission, 1990). George and Wilding draw on findings by the Equal Opportunities Commission (EOC) (1993, pp. 25–32) when they comment that:

> In 1992/93, there was no woman Chief Constable in Britain; only 2 per cent of the top managers were women; only 10 per cent of university professors were women; only 20 per cent of head teachers of secondary schools were women; and, similarly, only 20 per cent of senior executive officers in the civil service were women. (George and Wilding, 1999, p. 141)

Sexuality

The two main divisions in terms of sexuality of most relevance in social work, both of which have a social policy dimension, are sexual activity involving young people and lesbian and gay sexuality.

Sexual activity involving young people is more approved of in some societies than others. In Britain, sexual intercourse involving a young person under 16 is illegal, but in practice, is more likely to be the subject of police investigation and prosecution where one of the parties is over 18. At this age, unlawful sexual intercourse becomes a Schedule One offence, which means that it is subject to the same procedures and serious implications as other sexual offences.

Despite the fact that homosexuality and heterosexuality are both equally approved of in many cultures and societies, in Britain gay and lesbian sexual identity and activity continues to be the subject of debate, controversy and, on occasions, discrimination. Whereas it is illegal to discriminate against a person on grounds of their sex or marital status, discrimination on the basis of sexuality is not illegal:

> It is not unlawful to discriminate against a man because he is gay, or against a woman because she is a lesbian. (Brayne and Martin, 1999, p. 453)

Homophobic attitudes continue to be expressed in double standards relating to homosexual and heterosexual activity. Kissing and embracing in public, for instance, has been illegal for many years for homosexuals, but legal for heterosexuals. Since the late 1980s, section 28 of the Local Government Act 1988 has made it illegal for local authorities and their employees to promote homosexuality or teaching about homosexual relationships as more desirable than heterosexuality. From 1999, the Labour government raised a storm of public and media controversy in the proposal to repeal section 28.

Violence may occur against gay and lesbian people, including so-called 'gay-bashing'. Inhibitions about declaring their sexuality may prevent victims of abuse complaining to the police. Social workers may encounter people who have suppressed anger for many years over abuse.

Public and professional attitudes are often mobilised covertly against gay and lesbian relationships. For example, measures taken to protect people against the risk of HIV/AIDS infection are often targeted at gay males, even though HIV/AIDS is not restricted to the gay population. It is as though moral judgements are being made against gay people for their behaviour and HIV/AIDS is part of the poetic justice they deserve for their deviance (Sontag, 1991, p. 131).

HIV (human immuno-deficiency virus) can take up to a decade to lead, in some cases, to AIDS (acquired immune deficiency syndrome). AIDS, however, is an umbrella term covering a variety of infections and cancers which a person with a damaged immune system may suffer and die from. The virus is not infectious, so cannot be caught through normal everyday contact, but can only be passed on through sexual contact, sharing needles, sharing infected blood, from mother to child before birth or through breast-feeding. HIV/AIDS worldwide affects mainly heterosexual people, although in developed countries gay men, haemophiliacs and injecting drug users were infected first.

People with HIV/AIDS may be treated by employers, insurance companies and even by former friends and acquaintances as though they are afflicted with a disease on a par with an infectious plague. People such as food handlers, whose HIV status poses no risk to consumers and who have no legal obligation to disclose their status, may be subject to exclusion from work on the grounds of other people's sensitivities. Their AIDS illnesses may lead to their employment being terminated in circumstances where other equivalent illnesses may only lead to temporary absence from the workplace.

The law offers no specific legal protection in Britain against direct discrimination on the basis of people's HIV/AIDS status. But specific forms of discrimination, such as the use of medical tests without the person's consent, medical questionnaires and the screening of job applicants who have declared their HIV/AIDS status, could be the subject of legal claims on the basis of indirect discrimination. Indirect and direct discrimination are both unlawful under legislation regarding discrimination against people on the grounds of race and gender. These considerations make it desirable to encourage employers and those responsible for pensions and insurance schemes to include HIV/AIDS status in their equal opportunities policies and statements.

Under the Sex Discrimination Act 1975, for the purposes of sex discrimination, English law recognises only two sexes, men and women, as recorded on birth certificates. Thus:

> the UK was not in violation of the Human Rights Convention for failing to register as father of a child a man who had been female at birth. However, the European Court has ruled that dismissal of a person who changed sex from male to female amounted to sex discrimination against her as a woman. (Brayne and Martin, 1999, p. 453)

Efforts are being made by activists to promote government action which will bring Britain into line with the rest of the EU by establishing equality before the law for gay, lesbian and heterosexual activity and relationships.

Race

Racism is not a short-term problem. For years, black people in Britain have been subjected to unequal treatment by professionals and the state, in most aspects of their lives. Black people are more likely than white people to be poor and unemployed, the trend being particularly marked for Pakistani and Bangladeshi people (Smith et al., 1998, p. 14). Contributory factors include higher than average and relatively increasing unemployment levels resulting from the concentration of black people in inner city areas disproportionately hit by industrial decline; and racism inherent in selecting people for jobs and making them redundant. Also the restructuring of capital on a global basis disproportionately increases poverty among black people (TUC, 1994, 1995b).

Black and working-class people are overrepresented in the penal system whereas black people are underrepresented among staff. A confidential report, following a three-month internal inquiry into the beating to death in 2000 of Zahid Mubarek at Feltham young offenders' institution, concluded that institutional racism existed. Martin Narey, Director General of the prison service, generalised the problem to other parts of the prison system, saying 'It goes beyond institutional racism to blatant malicious pockets of racism' (Dodd, 2001, p. 1). An official report by probation inspectors concluded that the probation service is permeated by racism to 'an unacceptable degree' (Travis, 2000, p. 9).

Criticisms of the limitations of systems for combating discrimination include recognition of the male-dominated judicial system, with overwhelming proportions of white men from public school and Oxbridge backgrounds occupying key positions as barristers and judges. Legal procedures and terminology remain opaque to people from less advantaged positions.

The Race Relations Act 1976 (RRA) made it unlawful to discriminate against people on the grounds of race, in their employment, education and training and in the provision of goods and services to them. It defined race in terms of colour, nationality, ethnic or national origins, but did not include religion. Rastafarians

> are not treated as a racial group because the movement is too recent in origin, so [as late as 1993] it was lawful to refuse a man a job unless he cut his hair ... Gypsies have been accorded the status of a racial group ... although ... discrimination against travellers ... [is not regarded as] illegal, since they represent a mode of life rather than a racial grouping. (Brayne and Martin, 1999, p. 453)

Patriarchal features of countries and cultures where women are subordinated to men lead to double jeopardy for them. Bangladeshi Muslim women, for instance, traditionally have been subjected to violence in the household, but there is also a tradition of oppression and exploitation of women by the state. Race relations legislation, such as the Race Relations Act 1976, has not impacted on discrimination against black women from within their own community. Challenges to women's oppression and failure to gain adequate access to social services and justice agencies such as the police, when subjected to criminal violence in the home, have come more from women themselves as they have achieved economic and social emancipation, and from black community groups and self-help organisations. On the positive side, reforms to divorce laws in Britain have made it easier than hitherto for women to leave oppressive and violent relationships. However, housing policy has not made it easy for black women who are lone parents – many of whom are without adequate educational qualifications and work experience to enable them to find any jobs, let alone employment which does not discriminate against them – to obtain suitable housing.

Contemporary debates in Britain about racial discrimination came to a renewed crisis point in the late 1990s, when the murder of Stephen

Lawrence, a young black man, led to the Macpherson inquiry (Macpherson, 1999) into the conduct of the subsequent murder inquiry. The Labour government introduced measures aiming to improve trust and confidence and combat the institutional racism in the criminal justice system and in the Metropolitan police, identified by the Macpherson inquiry.

Inequality, discrimination and oppression

We can distinguish divisions, which may be positive or negative, from inequalities. Some divisions, such as age and geographical location, are not necessarily associated with inequalities. Others which are often associated with inequalities include gender and race. Divisions such as social class differences are inevitably associated with inequalities, or even oppressiveness.

Alan Carling points out that, while many of the material and social divisions between people are a positive feature of the differences between them, some divisions are associated with injustices which should be rectified (Carling, 1991, p. 1). Critical perspectives on sociology and social policy help to illuminate the nature of such inequalities and point to ways of developing more inclusive services.

The enduring nature of structural and systematic inequalities, which ensure the persistence of discrimination and disadvantage in all their forms, but particularly affect some groups and strata in society, implies that the social worker's responsibilities extend far beyond ensuring that current legislation is complied with in working with people. It also implies that addressing discrimination and inequality is a social and political task and is a proactive requirement.

Direct and indirect discrimination operate at the personal, ideological and institutional levels in society. Direct discrimination involves treating a person less positively on the grounds of age, gender, race, class, nature of ability or disability, religious belief or affiliation, accent and so on. Indirect discrimination involves imposing requirements which it would be more difficult for a person in one of those categories of difference to meet than other people.

The law is a useful weapon in the struggle against discrimination, but is fundamentally restricted because legislation such as the Race Relations Acts of 1965 and 1976 and the Disability Discrimination Act 1995, despite their acknowledgement of the realities of collective forms of discrimination, overwhelmingly focus on the individual rather than protecting the interests of groups and other collectivities. Pressure groups and educational campaigns contribute a good deal. The Visible Women Campaign, challenging race and sex discrimination and hosted by the Commission for Racial Equality (CRE), is one example. In a reference to the requirement that professional qualifying programmes in social work include anti-discriminatory practice, Brayne and Martin observe that 'good practice is way ahead of the minimum that the law requires' (1999, p. 452). However, a local authority is required to adopt and publish a written equal opportunities policy combating sex, race and disability discrimination (Brayne and Martin, 1999, p. 452).

The Treaty of Rome required legislation in England eliminating discrimination on grounds of pay and treatment. Also, complainants may seek access to justice using the additional protection of the European Convention on Human Rights (Brayne and Martin, 1999, pp. 454–5). Legislation to combat discrimination – Sex Discrimination Act 1975, Race Relations Act 1976, Disability Discrimination Act 1995 – has been passed by Labour governments in two main periods, the mid-1970s and mid-1990s. All such legislation addressing direct discrimination tends, by definition, to focus attention on the interaction between two parties rather than taking account of the social inequalities which contribute to discrimination. The group nature of much discrimination, including discrimination in domestic settings, is not addressed by laws focusing on the individual. Neither is indirect discrimination as often a target of legislation and anti-discriminatory practice. One reason for the restricted concentration on direct discrimination is that indirect discrimination is much more difficult to prove in a court of law.

Employment discrimination
The two most obvious and unjust dimensions of employment inequality lie in discrimination against women in the form of unequal access to jobs and unequal pay. In Scotland, for example, despite equal pay legislation, women earn 65 per cent of men's weekly earnings; only 52 per cent of women are economically active compared with 71 per cent of men; 19 per cent of lone mothers are unemployed; and women are segregated in certain occupational skill areas (factsheet on social inclusion by Equal Opportunities Commission, Scotland, http://www.scotland.gov.uk/inclusion/ssin09.htm 18 July 2000). The fact that inequalities persist in the workplace affects not just the situation of individual women, whether in social work practice, management or in politics, but also the quality of decisionmaking in those work settings. Thus, arguments for equal opportunities need to take account of both of these aspects.

The unequal treatment of women who are black and/or disabled compounds the discrimination, creating double or triple jeopardy.

Employment discrimination is tackled to some extent by the Equal Pay Act 1970 and the Sex Discrimination Act 1975. Employment tribunals, formerly industrial tribunals, contribute to the struggle for equal and fair treatment in the workplace. Complainants can be awarded a declaration regarding the rights of the complainant, compensation involving a monetary award, and/or a recommendation specifying an action to be taken to reduce or eliminate the need for the complaint. However, such outcomes apply only to individual complainants and cannot apply to a discriminatory policy or a rule affecting others in an equivalent situation.

Wage inequalities are tackled to some extent through the minimum wage (see Chapter 3). In 1998, the Labour government set up the independent advisory body, the Low Pay Commission (LPC), under the National Minimum Wage Act 1998. The brief of the LPC is to advise the government about the national minimum wage, administered by the DTI. The LPC reported on the level and working of the national minimum wage in May 1998 (Low Pay Commission, 1998), evaluated its introduction and impact early in 2000 (Low Pay Commission, 2000) and is due to report in 2001 on possible increases.

Mental health discrimination
According to large-scale research by MIND, people with mental health problems constitute the most socially excluded group in Britain (MIND, 1999). Mental health survivors testify to the harmful effects of stigmatisation due to various forms of treatment, notably through incarceration in mental hospitals. A continuum exists, however, from that extreme to the no less traumatic labelling experienced by people who may be compulsorily hospitalised for a short period through an isolated psychotic or severely depressive episode and subsequently find themselves discriminated against because it appears on their medical record. In some ways, the invisibility of discrimination on mental health grounds makes it even more insidious because it is less able to be challenged.

Disability discrimination
People with disabilities experience inequalities and discrimination, relative to other groups in society, in their education and work. Their achievements are adversely affected by the fact that schools, colleges and universities are ill-equipped to offer them adequate learning facilities and opportunities. Disabled people suffer higher rates of unemployment

than the rest of the population. When able to obtain work, it tends to be below their capacity and motivation and to offer lower rewards than for equivalent work carried out by their able-bodied peers.

Campaigns by disabled people themselves, buttressed but not displaced by research findings, pressure groups and advocacy, have put disability rights on the social policy and professional agenda. There has been a significant shift from professionals in the personal social services seeking to give people with disabilities the services professionals assess them as needing, to disabled people possessing equal citizenship and having the power to determine the kinds of services they want (Oliver, 1998, p. 261).

Religious discrimination
Religious beliefs have played a prominent part in conflicts at many levels – in the household, in communities and in warfare within and between different states – in societies of all kinds, throughout history. In Northern Ireland there is legislation prohibiting discrimination on the grounds of religion, nevertheless, religious differences have played a major role in years of inter-communal disruption in Ireland and Northern Ireland.

Discrimination against immigrants, asylum seekers and refugees
Of more than 25 million people estimated by the Office of the UN High Commissioner for Refugees (UNHCR) to be displaced by wars and state terrorism, ethnic cleansing and human rights abuses, few ever return home. But the International Institute for Strategic Studies (IISS) estimates that this is the tip of the iceberg, millions more people being made homeless by countries being partitioned, huge development programmes and schemes to depopulate rural areas in order to grab land (Vidal, 1999, p. 19). Like travellers, refugees and people seeking asylum through diasporas and other traumatic dislocations in their lives are likely to encounter discrimination when they arrive in Britain. This is despite the reality that immigrants contribute – socially, politically, culturally and economically – far more than they disturb (Vertovec, 1999). Britain, like most other European countries, is a signatory to the Refugee Convention. This states that if someone is likely to be persecuted they should be allowed a hearing and fair treatment, on arrival to this country. Despite this, since the 1980s, critics of government policy such as human rights lawyers have maintained that the Home Office immigration service has acted illegally so as to detain asylum seekers punitively in the prison system for lengthy periods while their applications, and in many cases their subsequent

appeals, were processed. The 1971 Immigration Act gave immigration officers almost unlimited powers to detain people seeking asylum in the UK. Research by Amnesty (1994) suggested that the average length of detention increased after the Asylum and Immigration Appeals Act 1993. Organisations such as Bail for Immigration Detainees (Bid) and the Refugee Legal Centre (RLC) and civil rights lawyers work to challenge the excessive detention of asylum seekers, many of whom are deeply traumatised by their experiences. Bid works to obtain bail for detainees. The RLC argues that detention for someone who cannot return to their country of origin is illegal under the European Convention on Human Rights (Gould, 2001, p. 7).

Legislation protects Britain's boundaries rather than respecting the interests of asylum seekers. The Asylum and Immigration Act 1996 removed some housing rights (see also Chapter 4) and benefit entitlement from asylum seekers not applying for asylum immediately on arrival in the UK, presumably on the grounds that this would prove they were not genuine. In 2000, the Audit Commission noted that only ten per cent of social services departments in England and Wales had a policy to deal with asylum seekers (Audit Commission, 2000). This followed the voluntary dispersal scheme set up by the Home Office early in 2000, and the implementation of the Immigration and Asylum Act 1999 which made it easier for local authorities to manage asylum seekers by giving them powers to disperse them (Griggs et al., 2000, p. 23), leaving many asylum seekers even more isolated and socially excluded (Bateman, 2000, p. 29).

Refugee children require careful placement to ensure that their class, culture and ethnic background are taken into account as well as the violence they may have experienced and the trauma, isolation and loss they may still be feeling (Dutt, 1999, p. 30). The resources of voluntary organisations such as Refugee Action, the Refugee Council and the Red Cross are often stretched by the need for intensive work with the increasing numbers of people being displaced by social upheavals and armed conflicts in different parts of the world (Wellard, 1999, pp. 8–9).

In 2001, the Labour government began international negotiations to have the applications of asylum seekers processed as near to their country of origin as possible. This procedure was intended to reduce the number of applications to Britain. The number of applications for asylum in Britain in 1999 (76,040) was the highest in Europe, with almost 40 per cent (26,630) being turned down on noncompliance (technical) grounds without the applications being examined (www.homeoffice. gov.uk/rds/pdfs/asy-dec00.pdf, 12 February, 2001). The Refugee Council criticised the great rise in noncompliance refusals since the introduction of a faster procedure in April 2000, as indicating a flaw in the system leading to injustices, most of those refused in this way having failed to obtain legal advice and complete a complex 19-page form in English within 10 working days (Travis, 2001b, p. 9). The system of giving vouchers rather than money to asylum seekers for food may have had the strength of giving them direct access to emergency rations, but it increased the sense they were being stigmatised and heightened the risk of racist attacks (Bateman, 2000, p. 29).

Post-war labour shortages and waves of immigration from the late 1950s, especially from the Indian subcontinent, parts of Africa, notably Uganda, and the West Indies, heightened awareness of deep-seated racism and rejection of black immigrants in particular. They also led to the government developing policies to promote integration and combat racism, demonstrated to a limited extent in the Race Relations Act 1965, prohibiting discrimination in public places.

The British Nationality Act 1981 allowed a spouse to enter Britain and live with the person to whom he or she was married, provided the marriage was deemed to be genuine. The Conservative government introduced the habitual residence test in 1994, to assess a person's immigration status and eligibility for state benefits. According to the TUC, the guidance on how adjudication officers were to distinguish habitual residents, that is, those living in Britain permanently, rather than casual travellers seeking to claim benefits, was too vague, consisting of five factors to be taken into account:

- the intentions of the claimant
- the apparent reason for coming to the UK
- the claimant's employment record
- the length and continuity of residence in another country
- whether the job, home and friends of the claimant were sufficient to indicate that the UK was the centre of interest. (TUC, 1995a)

Critics of these attempts to control so-called illegal immigration provide evidence that they operate in a racist manner, largely discriminating against black people and against other people on grounds of race.

Social exclusion

In 1997, the incoming Labour government initiated a broad swathe of strategies with the aim of trying to transcend discrimination and social exclusion. The Labour government's Social Exclusion Unit describes social exclusion as:

> a shorthand term for what can happen when people or areas suffer from a combi-
> nation of linked problems such as unemployment, poor skills, low incomes, poor
> housing, high crime environments, bad health, poverty and family breakdown.
>   In the past, governments have had policies that tried to deal with each of these
> problems individually, but have been less successful at tackling the complicated
> links between them, or preventing them arising in the first place. (www.cabinet _
> office.gov.uk/seu/index.htm, May 2000)

The Social Exclusion Unit
The government announced the intention to initiate a national anti-poverty and social inclusion strategy, which would apply to both urban and rural communities, monitored by a national civic forum representing all major stakeholders. To this end, one of the government's first actions was to set up the Social Exclusion Unit (SEU) in December 1997, based in the Cabinet Office. The SEU reports directly to the prime minister who steers its work, an indication of how closely it is intended to work with the No. 10 Policy Unit. The SEU's main aim was to help the government improve the coherence and integration of work across departmental boundaries to reduce social exclusion. By 2000, Policy Action Team (PAT) reports on 18 areas covered by the 18 PATs had been published, on key areas of social exclusion (see Chapter 12). These focused on the initial targets of the SEU, namely reducing truancy and school exclusion, eliminating people sleeping rough in towns and cities, developing integrated and sustainable strategies to tackle problems such as unemployment (especially through creating new opportunities for 16–18-year-olds not in education or employment) and crime and drug use on housing estates viewed as the worst. In late 1999, the life of the SEU was extended to 2002.

The government's social exclusion initiative in Scotland was announced on 9 December 1997. Policy and initiatives in Scotland were coordinated by a Scottish Social Inclusion Network (SSIN) formed on 8 May 1998 as a result of responses to a consultation paper *Social Exclusion in Scotland* (Scottish Office, 1998), advocating the need for a more inclusive approach to policy development in this area. The report by the Scottish Office (Scottish Office, 2000) *Social Inclusion: Opening the Door to a Better Scotland* sets out the government's strategy and provides a basis for consideration by the future Scottish parliament.

In June 1999, the Promotion of Social Inclusion (PSI) initiative in Northern Ireland was announced, as part of a broader package of measures aimed at New Targeting Social Need (New TSN) (Northern Ireland Information Service Press Release, 18.7.00). The New TSN initiative was one of the main items in the government White Paper *Partnership for Equality* (Department of Health, 1998c). Social exclusion in Northern Ireland was regarded as resulting

> from the impact on individuals or areas of a combination of linked problems such as poor skills, unemployment, living on a low income, coping with difficult home circumstances, living in poor housing or areas blighted with crime and having difficulty accessing services. (Northern Ireland Information Service Press Release, 18.7.00)

Travellers and people from ethnic minorities were a particular focus for action.

The Labour government advanced proposals to enhance inclusion in the education system through a Special Educational Needs Bill to be introduced in the 2000–1 session of parliament, implementing recommendations of the Disability Rights Task Force regarding schools, post-16 learning and higher education. Labour also promoted the Human Rights Act 1998, which aims to give disabled people the right to education without unfair discrimination.

The SEU reported on the work done across different PATs (see Chapter 12) on minority ethnic communities and social exclusion (SEU, 2000b). The report of PAT 12 found that Afro-Caribbean pupils were, on average, 5 times more likely than other pupils to be excluded from school, rising to 15 times in some inner city areas. This identified several aspects of disproportionate disadvantage for people from ethnic minorities which intersected all aspects of social exclusion. People from ethnic minorities were more likely to:

- live in poor housing in deprived areas
- be unemployed (unemployment rates were 2 to 3 times higher among 16–24-year-olds) and poor
- perform less well at school and be excluded from school
- suffer ill health
- experience racial harassment and racist crime. (DETR, *Minority Ethnic Communities and Social Exclusion* Press Notice, 6 June 2000)

Similar persistent inequalities between ethnic groups were identified by the EOC in Scotland, which also emphasised that gender and sex inequality are common themes in any area of social exclusion. PAT 11, reporting on Schools Plus activities, noted that children from disadvantaged areas fail to achieve their potential within the current educational system, about 24 per cent of students in disadvantaged schools gaining 5 or more GCSEs contrasted with the national average of 46 per cent (DfEE, 2000, p. 19).

The SEU report proposed five broad strategies to address these:

- tackling racial discrimination
- improving services through ethnic monitoring
- targeting specific programmes at the needs of ethnic minorities
- tackling racist crime and harassment
- improving information about these communities. (SEU, 2000a, pp. 8–9)

These statements imply the need for a broad swathe of social policy initiatives. In 2000, the Local Government Association launched its strategic community development initiative, *The New Commitment to Regeneration*, to be evaluated by the Urban Alliance. Other government initiatives aiming to cross-brace with the SEU include rebuilding communities on problem housing estates, Welfare to Work, Employment and Health Action Zones.

Perspectives on social exclusion policies
Levitas (1998) identifies three forms of discourse concerning social exclusion: redistributionist, moral underclass and social integration. The efforts of New Labour to eradicate poverty by focusing on particularly high-profile social problems such as street begging are redistributionist. However, they are not as effective as fundamental changes in social security aimed at eliminating poverty. Moral underclass discourse identifies people's tendency towards becoming dependent on benefits as a weakness dragging them into delinquent and lazy habits. The underclass is treated as an identifiable group of people located outside and, as the term implies, below the remainder of the population. The policies of the Thatcher and Major Conservative governments (1979–97) concentrated on social policies attempting to reduce what was seen as a culture of welfare benefits dependency. The report of PAT 3 *Enterprise and Social Exclusion* (HM Treasury, 2000) was published in 2000 in response to the SEU report on deprived neighbourhoods published in September 1998 (SEU, 1998a). The report advocated promoting enterprise in deprived areas. Patricia Hewitt, former left-winger and member of the CND Committee of One Hundred in the late 1950s and now Minister for Small Business at the DTI, echoed the Thatcher government's

promotion of private entrepreneurship at the launch of the report, with the words:

> I see this report as a contribution not just to the debate on social exlusion but also to the Government's broad agenda for an enterprise society. Enterprise is an outlook, an attitude of mind, that needs to be encouraged right across society, and the proposals here are about one facet of that broader task. (HM Treasury Press Release, *Enterprise – A Vital Force Against Social Exclusion*, 2 November 1999)

Social integration discourse identifies a correlation between people's lack of attachment to the family, work and education and their degree of exclusion. Much discussed phenomena such as the collapse of families, visible in rising rates of separation and divorce (see Chapter 6), and the breakdown of order in schools (to be estimated, it is assumed, through bullying, indiscipline and rates of exclusion and explusion) are held to be symptomatic of a disintegration of the social and moral order in society. The policy responses, therefore, focus on trying to promote people's active citizenship by offering them meaningful and rewarding work and other ways of participating in society. The social policies of the Labour government (1997 onwards) reflect a mixture of moral underclass and social integration discourses, through the tougher responses taken towards people seen as abusing the welfare system, welfare and employment policies based on 'workfare' as practised in the USA, the New Deal (see Chapters 2 and 3) and the stakeholder society (see Chapter 11). The Labour government viewed citizens as maintaining their stake in society by helping themselves and not succumbing to dependency. Citizenship also is a concept which can provide social workers with a framework to develop a critical practice based on inclusiveness, anti-poverty and anti-oppressive policies (Lister, 1997).

From a critical perspective, Jock Young's book, discussing the origins and nature, contradictions and dilemmas of exclusion, makes the point that an inclusive society can be oppressive. This is because it may deny people's values and particular identities and the problematic nature of difference in society (Young, 1999, p. 102).

Anti-discrimination and promoting equality
There is a tendency for legislation to promote a minimum standard rather than an optimum level. For example, section 71 of the Race Relations Act 1976 requires local authorities to make arrangements to eliminate unlawful racial discrimination and promote equality of opportunity. But this does not empower a social worker and client to combat discrimination individually and collectively, at social and political levels.

The CRE and EOC are responsible for working towards eliminating discrimination and promoting equality of opportunity, as well as reviewing the law. The immensity of this task is emphasised by the reality that the nature of discrimination is subtle and not restricted to gross stereotyping of differences between people, or negative labelling and stigmatisation. Inferior and unequal treatment may come about through implicit differentiations which are part of ingrained cultural patterns not recognised by perpetrators, or even victims in some cases, as discriminatory.

The problematic nature of definitions of discrimination is illustrated by the issue of gender reassignment in relation to definitions under the sex discrimination legislation, which identifies only two sexes, male and female, and relies for this on the information contained in a birth certificate.

Also, the Disability Discrimination Act 1995 defines disability in terms of a person's physical or mental impairment having a substantial and long-term adverse effect on a person's ability to carry out normal day-to-day activities. Thus it excludes any consideration of social discrimination which arises from stereotypes and misconceptions rather than being inherent in the impairment of the disabled person. The Disability Discrimination Act, according to one evaluation of early responses by employers and service providers, has had a limited impact. More proactive measures will be necessary to achieve significant change in the direction of actual rather than formal equality for disabled people (Gooding, 2000).

Promoting rights and citizenship

There is a general failure to implement in agency practice the full spirit of European and UN statements on human rights, even though, for example, the Human Rights Act 1998 attempts to incorporate into the law in England and Northern Ireland the principles of the European Convention on Human Rights (Scotland and Wales made their own provisions in 1998). This law sets out rights to life, liberty, security, fair trial, freedom of expression, free elections, privacy, education, marriage and family life. It covers gross abuses such as torture, slavery and forced labour, but not the protection of social, economic and cultural rights tackled by the RRA and SDA. For areas covered by the provisions of the Human Rights Act, citizens no longer have to go to the European Court of Human Rights in Strasbourg. Through the Act, citizens will be able to challenge existing legislation, although this may not be straightforward. For instance, in the field of consumer protection, the Act confers rights on companies as well as consumers and, in theory, companies could use the Act to challenge existing consumer protection legislation on the grounds that it restricts them from exercising their rights against consumers (*Which*, 2000–01, p. 2).

Implications for social workers

The persistence of inequalities and discrimination make it necessary, now as ever, to establish an equality-based perspective (Thompson, 1998, p. 3) on policy and service delivery, but practitioners are likely to encounter barriers, tensions and dilemmas in doing this. Exclusion, as in the circumstances of many refugees, may be hidden and people may live in double or triple jeopardy through having compound problems to cope with. Social workers must exercise vigilance, sensitivity and assertiveness, bringing to bear on individual situations a critical awareness of how people may be excluded or discriminated against. Here is an example.

EXAMPLE

A social worker is making first contact with a Kurdish family of two parents and a child of about ten, living in bed and breakfast accommodation, following a comment by the landlady that the father seems unresponsive and the child has not been seen for a few days. The Benefits Agency have been requiring the father to apply for Jobseeker's Allowance or to sign on for work and the landlady knows he has not done this. She makes a dismissive remark about the apparent lack of motivation of 'these people' to help themselves.

The social worker contacts the local refugee coordinator for the local authority and a worker for a local Kurdish organisation. Using interpreters, because none of the family speaks English, the social worker finds that the child has learning difficulties and could be autistic, but this had not been realised before. He finds the mother is deeply traumatised from being tortured and the father is suffering from major hearing problems, probably through bombs having exploded very close to him. The social worker works with the refugee organisations to ensure that family members receive the benefits to which they are entitled. The father is entitled to help with learning sign language, the mother needs psychological support and counselling and their child's learning difficulties need assessing. The social worker arranges for the family to move to a two-bedroomed rented flat, near other

Kurdish families, with whom they start to communicate more freely. The social worker invites the landlady to attend social events organised by refugee groups and introduces her to some of the issues she must tackle if she is to continue offering accommodation for them, particularly celebrating diversity rather than regarding it as a problem to be surmounted.

Chapter summary

This chapter has dealt with those aspects of divisions and inequalities in society which are most likely to affect social work. It has examined the efforts being made to develop equality-based policy and practice, including the policy initiatives of the Labour government 1997 onwards to tackle social exclusion.

Further reading

Barry, M. and Hallet, C. (1999) *Social Work and Social Exclusion*, Venture Press, Birmingham

Levitas, R. (1998) *The Inclusive Society? Social Exclusion and New Labour*, Macmillan, Basingstoke – now Palgrave: for theoretical perspectives on social exclusion, citizenship and the social policies of New Labour

Lister, R. (1997) *Citizenship: Feminist Perspectives*, Macmillan, London – now Palgrave

Thompson, N. (1998) *Promoting Equality: Challenging Discrimination and Oppression in the Human Services*, Macmillan, London – now Palgrave

9

Organising and Delivering Social Services

We should be sceptical of the argument that the history of the organisation of the social services is one of fairly unimpeded development. Jane Lewis rejects the traditional view that welfare services have moved straightforwardly from the dark ages of the Poor Law to the enlightenment of Beveridge's plans in 1942. She questions the simplistic assumption that the state took on more responsibilities as individualism was replaced by collectivism, as though this inevitably culminated in the wave of legislation in the 1940s which established the welfare state (Lewis, 1999, p. 249).

Policy context

The history of other changes which relate to the birth of the welfare state is exceedingly complex and multifaceted because it relates to social, economic and political changes and multilayered because local, regional and central government were all changing. For example, it had taken almost a century and a half for the system of local government established in 1974 to emerge, although it was to take a further twenty-five years for parliament to pass legislation (Local Government Act 2000) extending the powers of local authorities to enable them to address local problems in partnership with local public, private, voluntary and business organisations with a reasonable degree of autonomy. The Municipal Corporations Act 1835 set up directly elected boroughs to replace the outdated and largely corrupt self-electing corporations which had existed for many centuries. County councils (there were 62 including the London County Council, and 61 county borough councils) were established in England and Wales under the Local Government Act in 1888; and 535 urban district councils, 472 rural district councils and 270 non-county borough councils under the Local Government Act of 1894. The London Government Act 1899 established 28 metropolitan borough councils in London as well as the Corporation of London. In 1963, the London Government Act created the Greater London Council (GLC) and 32 London boroughs. On 1 April 1974, when the Local Government Act 1972 was implemented, the range of authorities comprised the GLC, 47 county councils in England and Wales and 6 metropolitan county councils with 36 metropolitan district councils. On 1 April 1986, under the Local Government Act 1985, the Conservative government abolished the GLC and 6 metropolitan counties and set up a directly elected Inner London Education Authority (ILEA), later abolished by the Education Reform Act 1988. A large number of new unitary councils – responsible for supplying the full range of local authority services – were created under the Local Government Act 1992 and came into existence from 1995. By 2000, there were five different types of local authority – unitary councils, metropolitan districts, London boroughs, and county and district councils. Thus, there were 26 local authorities in Northern Ireland, 32 in Scotland, 22 in Wales and 387 in England, a total of 467, excluding the Isle of Man and the Scilly Isles. In 1998, the Labour government proposed the establishment of a Greater London Assembly with a directly elected mayor and this was implemented in 2000. The setting up of executives including elected mayors formed part of the proposals in the Local Government Act 2000, significantly enhancing the political and financial powers of local authorities to promote the economic, environmental and social well-being of their areas.

Forty-six unitary authorities, the 32 London boroughs and the 36 metropolitan boroughs are single-tier district councils providing all local authority services in their area. The metropolitan district councils in major urban areas include Birmingham, Leeds, Liverpool, Manchester and Newcastle. Non-metropolitan areas of England are two tier, with counties providing most services including education and social services and districts providing other services such as housing.

An implicit bias affects the conventional treatment of the history of social administration, impacting on the view taken of the organisation of local authorities and social services. There is a tendency to examine these from an explicitly or implicitly statutory vantage point. This risks underemphasising the important contributions of the voluntary and informal sectors, underplaying in the process the part played by 'ordinary' people. History is not made only by important people. Power sometimes can be exercised from below. The account of the organisation of social services should not be distorted by only taking into account successive organisations and reorganisations of statutory services. This also applies to the way social services are actually delivered. Jane Lewis reminds us that social services have always been delivered by a combination of state, family, voluntary sector and marketplace providers, with different ones more prominent at different times (Lewis, 1999, p. 249).

The history of the organisation of welfare services in Britain since the Second World War divides into two main periods. Between 1945 and 1975 the welfare state was expanding, while the period from 1975 to 2000 was concerned more with retrenchment (Pierson, 1992). Up to 1975, there were two major periods of reorganisation in the personal social services: from 1945 to 1950 when the welfare state was being set up, and between 1968 and 1974 when local authority and local government reorganisations took place. From the mid-1970s, successive Labour and Conservative governments have been concerned with re-shaping welfare services so as to give the non-statutory – voluntary and private – providers much more prominence.

Changing relationships between central and local government

One of the main ways in which central government exercised tighter controls over local government was through the imposition of ceilings on spending. The local authority grant from central government is based on an estimate of spending needs in the coming year. This is negotiated, but with central government making elements of grants dependent on the meeting of increasingly stringent performance targets.

In 1984, rate-capping was introduced and the traditional system of imposing rates on local householders was reformed several times, a poll tax, community charge and council tax being introduced in succession, the poll tax leading to widespread public protests.

Local authorities have developed imaginative ways of working around shortages of resources: spreading initiatives over a longer period of time; making further payments dependent on the achievement of performance targets; building in a requirement that a project must become self-sufficient in funding terms after a period of several years; increasing the proportion of contracts in the private and not-for-profit or voluntary sectors; making grants on a year-by-year basis; freezing grants; and withholding payments linked to inflation.

Most local authorities comply with central government's requirements of spending cuts in the annual process of bidding for resources and the support grant allocation by central government:

> Others engage in shadow-boxing, using creative accountancy and other methods to avoid having to make cuts or increase local taxes to unacceptable levels, while staying more or less within the confines of the government's policies and grant allocations. A few authorities try to confront the government with 'brinkmanship' strategies, proclaiming that they would not reduce their work-forces or cut their services and in effect daring the government to do its worst. (Elcock, 1993, p. 157)

Styles of management within local authorities were changing. Social workers in local authority social services departments never enjoyed total professional autonomy. They were always accountable to the law and to their line managers. 'Managerialism' is the term used to describe styles of management which put managers in the central role in the organisation. 'New managerialism' (Adams, 1998a, p. 44) is the term used to describe management approaches in the public services which were imported from the private sector in the early 1980s, with decisions based on the criteria of economy, efficiency and effectiveness (Farnham and Horton, 1993b, pp. 237–8). It is probably more accurate to refer to new managerialisms in the plural, since there was not one approach (Adams, 1998a, p. 61). New managerialisms in welfare organisations directly challenged and often undermined the already fragile professionalism of social work.

One key sign of the growing power of new managerialisms was the imposition on probation and social services from the 1980s of measures of achievement by performance indicators and service standards, often incorporated into service agreements and contracts. The aim often was to become more cost-effective and achieve higher standards without increasing resources. Not surprisingly, efforts to achieve this by modernising services, improving quality, introducing computer-based office systems, rather than increasing resources, have not necessarily been accompanied by a lessening in the workload and stress experienced by individual professionals. On the contrary, staffing resources have invariably been subjected to cuts. In the probation service, for example, Home Office statistics indicated a rise of 4 per cent in caseloads during 1998 and predicted a further rise of 2.5 per cent during 1999–2000 (*NAPO News*, October 1999, Issue 113, p. 4). A survey by *Community Care* identified 'unacceptably high' stress levels among over half of local authority staff and 'very high' stress levels among a further 41 per cent (Rickford, 1999, p. 22). A survey by NISW found 62 per cent of staff in

England experiencing stress in the previous year compared with 50 per cent in Scotland and 31 per cent in Northern Ireland (McLean et al., 1999). By 2001, social work vacancy levels in many local authorities had reached 30 per cent.

Key changes and related issues

Organisation and delivery: 1945 to 1974

In the post-war years, general government expenditure (GGE) rose enormously, and part of this expansion was in the public sector of social welfare. Even though the 'national' civil service grew from 387,000 in 1939 to more than one million by 1951, the growth in employees in local government was even more dramatic, from about one million people in the late 1940s to over three million by 1971 (Farnham and Horton, 1993a, pp. 5–7).

Local government was changing in two major ways: first, there was a tendency for local authorities to take on increased duties and powers. This came partly from central government as the complexity, scope and depth of management tasks grew, in the wake of the nationalisation of major industries including coal production, railways, airlines, road haulage, gas and electricity. Partly, it arose from the expansion of housing, education services, the creation of the NHS and the innovation of social services departments, which generated a public sector workforce of about seven million people by 1979 (Farnham and Horton, 1993a, p. 7). The novel feature was that local authorities increasingly were in the business of governing their localities. The term 'local government' began to mean just that.

Second, and largely as a consequence of the above, the diversification of central and local government into new areas of responsibility created pressure towards strengthening the corporate control of services (Elcock, 1993, p. 151). 'Corporate management' was very much in vogue in local government from the early 1970s, if nothing else as a means of addressing the fragmentation of local authority services, perceived in official reports at the time (Maud Report, 1967; Bains Report, 1972) to need better coordination (Elcock, 1993, p. 151). Local authorities appointed chief executives from the 1970s and relied increasingly on managerial concepts and practices imported from commerce and industry. Financial control assumed greater importance than previously, senior management teams were created across departments and covering an entire local authority.

Between 1945 and 1975, from at least two points of view, local government was in decline: it lost responsibility for delivering gas, electricity, national assistance, hospital services, residual health and water services; and its financial dependence on central government grew as its income from central government grew from 30 to 45 per cent. In the personal social services, local government dependence is best illustrated by the fact that after 1970 all appointments to the post of director of social services had to be approved by the DHSS (Lowe, 1993, p. 88). Paradoxically, the power of local government waned as its income and expenditure trebled in real terms and increased in absolute terms as a proportion of the gross domestic product (GDP) of the country (Lowe, 1993, p. 88). Local authority councils exercised existing powers in areas such as education, where the provision of schools and youth services was largely a matter for local government.

The uniquely powerful situation of local government in the organisation and delivery of social services from the early 1970s was ensured by two separate but related processes of government-initiated reports and their implementation.

First, in the personal social services, the implementation of the Seebohm Report (1968) led to a considerable enhancement of the responsibilities and powers of local authorities, through the setting up of a unified social services department in each local authority. Seebohm's recommended structural changes in the organisation and delivery of social services were implemented in the 1970 Local Authority Social Services Act, which combined the hitherto separate childcare, welfare and mental health services in a single generic social services department in each local authority.

Second, the impact of the Seebohm innovation was increased by the almost simultaneous deliberations of the Redcliffe-Maud Royal Commission (Redcliffe-Maud, 1969). This recommended creating 58 unitary local authorities, each intended to be no less than 250,000 people and responsible for all the services in their area. The exceptions were Birmingham, Liverpool and Manchester where services were split between two tiers of government. But the Conservative government of Edward Heath rejected these proposals, insofar as they would have destroyed county councils where there was strong support for the Conservatives. The resulting Local Government Act 1972, implemented in 1974, was a political compromise. It reduced the number and increased the size of local authorities, but hung onto the two-tier structure by retaining county councils. This perpetuated traditional rivalries and divisions between services. Lowe notes, for example, that responsibility for personal social services and housing continued to be divided between county and district councils in the 47 non-metropolitan counties of England and Wales (Lowe, 1993, p. 90).

Organisation and delivery: 1974 to 2001

The main obvious influences on the way that the personal social services were organised and delivered from the 1970s were the Seebohm Report, the creation of social services departments and the changes brought about by the Conservatives under Margaret Thatcher, who came to power in May 1979. But some of the policies developed by the Conservatives after 1979 were foreshadowed by the preceding Labour government of 1974 to 1979. The first of these irrevocably changed the identity and image of what social workers and social services departments did, while under the Conservatives the size of the public sector, and the way it and the voluntary and private sectors were organised, changed greatly.

Despite attempts by some local authority managers during the 1970s to take measures to find out more about the views and expectations held by the public about their services, most local authorities followed fairly traditional, often bureaucratic practices. During the 'winter of discontent' of 1978–79, social workers in some cities such as Leeds joined many other public service workers in strikes and other demonstrations of widespread discontent with the Labour government. Striking and other demonstrating social workers tended to link their individual concerns with the wider issues of high unemployment, poverty, local authority budget cuts and declining quality in social services.

Marketisation of health and social services

From the time of the incoming Conservative government of 1979, there was a tendency for central government to enhance the contribution made to the provision of personal social services by agencies in the voluntary sector. From the late 1980s, the Thatcher government brought about a shift in the roles of local authorities from providers to commissioners, contractors and purchasers of services. This was in the wider context of the government's strategy of reducing the size of the public sector and undermining the power of trade unions.

The Local Government, Planning and Land Act 1980 forced local authorities to sell off council houses to sitting tenants, at significant discounts. It also empowered them to put out services to competitive tender (Elcock, 1993, p. 159). The later introduction of compulsory competitive tendering (CCT) (Local Government Act 1988) facilitated the operation of market forces in the supply and demand for workers and strengthened managerial control over the level of pay and working conditions of employees (Farnham, 1993, p. 121). Some local authorities established Direct Service Organisations (DSO) to carry out the tendering process on behalf of the staff of that authority.

The establishment of the contract culture under the NHS and Community Care Act 1990 meant the replacement of the virtual monopoly of state provision by a mixed economy, a quasi-market, of health and personal social services, delivered through a much more evenly balanced range of providers than formerly, through public, private, voluntary and informal sectors. The setting up of internal markets in social services departments – notably under the NHS and Community Care Act 1990 – for the purchase of services for clients, which were formerly provided by the department, forced local authorities to sell off many facilities to voluntary and private agencies, from whom the social services department subsequently bought similar services. These changes in the ways services were organised and delivered had major implications for the style of management in the local authority, for professionals, people receiving the services and members of the public who want a stake in local services.

Private as well as voluntary agencies and organisations played an increasing role in provision, in such areas as daycare, nurseries and playgroups. Childminding, traditionally located in the informal sector, was subject to increasing regulation. A repeated pattern was for scandals over failings in services to arise in particular localities and inquiry reports to highlight shortcomings in mechanisms for quality assurance. The inquiry report into abuses of children in nurseries in Newcastle (Barker et al., 1998) is typical.

By 1991, the public sector workforce had fallen from its peak of 7.5 million employees to about 6 million, of which about 3 million were in the local authorities (Farnham, 1993, p. 100). In contrast, the local authority workforce (full and part time) of the social services grew steadily throughout the period. In 1961, there were 170,000 workers in social services, increasing to 272,000 by 1974, 368,000 by 1984 and 414,000 by 1991 (Farnham, 1993, p. 102). The total full-time equivalent workforce in the public sector of the social services workforce showed a more steady increase, from 235,000 in 1979 to 288,000 with a slight reduction to 287,000 in 1991 (Farnham, 1993, p. 103).

The Conservative government restricted the autonomy of local government by reorganisation, financial controls and changes in the delivery of services through CCT, contracting out and marketisation.

Reorganisation of local government

Just before the Labour government swept into power in the general election of May 1997, the Conservative government had fulfilled its aim of restructuring local government into single-tier unitary authorities. One aim of the reorganisation was to create councils small and local enough for people to identify as their own, accessible and responsive to local communities. Size mattered, and the issue of participation.

The second wave of reorganisation of local government took place early in April 1997. It created 13 new unitary local authorities in England, Scotland and Wales, in addition to the 67 new unitary authorities created in 1996 and the further 19 due to emerge in 1998 (Craig and Manthorpe, 1999b).

Devolution

The Labour government's main policies affecting social welfare were linked with the intention to devolve powers to Northern Ireland, Wales and Scotland and enhance the participation of citizens in local and national government. Ironically, this stated commitment to enhancing citizen empowerment and participation was employed through a style of governance more tightly controlled from Westminster than that of the previous Conservative government.

The devolution of power to Northern Ireland, the national assembly for Wales and the Scottish parliament marks a significant move towards democracy. It offers the opportunity to break away from the pattern of domination of the four countries by primary legislation framed in Westminster and in one sense brings central and local government closer to each other. In another sense, though, it complicates that relationship by interposing a further stage of government – in Wales, Scotland and Northern Ireland at any rate – between Westminster and the local authority. The issue of developing meaningful government is complicated by the simultaneous impact of local government reorganisation. In Wales, for example, before the 1996 reorganisation the 8 counties had coterminous boundaries with the local health authorities. Now, there are 22 local authorities and 5 health authorities.

While it is too early to evaluate the impact of devolution, several features stand out. First, the relationship between Westminster and the devolved Scottish parliament and Welsh assembly has been somewhat tense. Labour has found it traumatic, perhaps, to devolve power. Second, the governing of the Welsh assembly by a minority contrasts with the coalition government in Scotland and two overwhelming Labour majorities in Westminster. Third, it will take some time before

Welsh and Scottish ministers develop a distinctive agenda, not simply derived from London (Taylor, 2000, p. 14). Fourth, the trend towards structural change in social work and social care has accelerated in Scotland, with an increasing number of authorities opting for integrated departments, with social work, housing, leisure, education and other services being managed together (McKay, 2000a, p. 12). Fifth, moves to integrate social work services with other services has proceeded in the context of no single ministerial brief being allocated to social work in the Scottish Executive (McKay, 2000b, p. 24).

Quality assurance
In 2000, the Social Care Group of the DH – one of the three key areas of responsibility in the DH alongside the NHS Executive and the Public Health Group – is for improving the quality, reliability and efficiency of the social services in England. It has six branches or subdivisions concerned with policy and training, children's services (two branches, one concerned with Quality Protects), community care, disablity and mental illness and care standards. These support government ministers and communicate policy to people inside and outside government.

Governments since the 1970s have attended to professionals' requests for more resources with the stringent response that failures in health and social services quality are primarily a consequence of shortcomings in the management and deployment of existing resources. Despite this, concerns continue to be expressed in many areas of practice about resource and staff shortages in health and social services. Associated with this, for instance, it can be asked how lawful, ethical and professionally sound it is for social services staff to screen assessments over the telephone in the key area of community care, only offering full assessments to those judged to be at significant risk of harm (Clements, 1999, p. 28). In July 2000, the DH published the results of the response to the June 1999 set of performance indicators. These showed a twofold variation in death from all causes, in deaths from all circulatory disease and from suicide and accidents, between the worst and best health authorities. There were nearly five times as many people on waiting lists in the worst performing health authorities as in the best (NHS Executive, 16 July 2000, Press Release *NHS Performance Indicators:* http://www.doh.gov.uk/nhsperformanceindicators).

The Care Standards Act 2000 was implemented under Labour's second government. Its purpose is to address failings in quality including the many shortcomings in social services for adults and children revealed in dozens of scandals and inquiries since the early 1970s. It has established a national register of qualified staff through a separate council in Wales,

Scotland, Northern Ireland and England, to register more than a million care workers and 50,000 social workers on an incremental basis as their qualifications are judged adequate. It introduces a parallel measure to the Protection of Children Act 1999, which dealt with people unsuitable for working with children, to exclude from the national register people unsuitable for working with adults. It covers statutory, private and voluntary health and social care, including more than 30,000 establishments providing social services for about half a million adults and children, such as long-term nursing and social care for older people and people with disabilities and residential, daycare, adoption, fostering and childminding services for children. It will set up the National Care Standards Commission (NCSC) in 2002 as an independent watchdog to regulate health and social services organisations, agencies and establishments of all types. The Commission, with a majority of lay members, has powers to inspect conditions in the full range of services to people in need. Ofsted, a government body replacing Her Majesty's Inspectors of Schools, responsible for inspecting schools under the Education (Schools) Act 1992, with strong interventive powers to insist on remedial special measures under the School Inspections Act 1996, sections 3(1), 10 and 14, is responsible for inspecting daycare and childminding. A separate division within the Commission is responsible for healthcare, inspection being centralised rather than being located in the inspection units of 100 health authorities in England and 5 in Wales.

The 8th Annual Report of the Chief Inspector of the SSI confirmed the government's intention

> to modernise local government (and) bring new political and decision making structures together with a new duty to achieve Best Value across all services. (Department of Health, 1999b, p. 5)

Two of the main means of achieving this were to be first, the continued pattern of inspections, both by the SSI alone and through joint reviews of social services with the Audit Commission; second, the Performance Assessment Framework (PAF) already introduced to assess key aspects of social services performance throughout the country. The Best Value Performance Indicators for social services were cross-referenced by the DH with the performance indicators listed in the personal social services PAF and cover the following areas:

National Priorities and Strategic Objectives

- stability of placements of children looked after
- educational qualifications of children looked after

Cost and Efficiency

- costs of services for children looked after
- cost of intensive social care for adults

Effectiveness of Service Delivery and Outcomes

- intensive homecare
- older people (aged 65 and over) helped to live at home

Quality of Service for Users and Carers

- clients receiving a review
- percentage of items of equipment costing less than £1000 delivered within 3 weeks
- users/carers who said they got help quickly
- percentage of people receiving a statement of their needs and how they will be met

Fair Access

- assessments per head of population
- users/carers who said that matters relating to race, culture or religion were noted
- relative spend on Family Support. (Department of Health, 2000b, p. 1)

These are the benchmarks by which quality of services will be evaluated in the future.

Implications for social workers

Social workers have been particularly affected by three main organisational changes since the early 1990s:

1. The creation of internal markets, locating most social workers either on the purchasing or the providing sides of the equation of managing and delivering social services.
2. Growing managerialist control of the professional area of social work.
3. The requirement that practice is quality assured to ensure 'best value' is measured against published standards of service.

Chapter summary

This chapter has examined the main changes affecting the organisation and delivery of services since the 1940s. It has highlighted some particular themes which currently are relevant to the practice of social work.

Further reading

Cutler, T. and Waine, B. (1994) *Managing the Welfare State*, Berg, Oxford
Lowe, R. (1993) *The Welfare State in Britain Since 1945*, Macmillan, Basingstoke – now Palgrave
Mullender, A. and Perrott, S. (1998) 'Social Work and Organisations' in, R. Adams, L. Dominelli and M. Payne (eds) *Social Work: Themes, Issues and Critical Debates*, pp. 67–77, Macmillan, Basingstoke – now Palgrave
Payne, M. (2000) *Teamwork in Multiprofessional Care*, Macmillan, Basingstoke – now Palgrave

10

Financing Social Services

The issue of finance affects social work at two points: at the strategic level of resourcing services and at the tactical level where the agency and the practitioner are charging the client for services. This chapter deals with each of these two aspects in turn.

Contexts

Some of the most dramatic consequences of changing social policies for people receiving social services are in the area of finance. Since the early 1990s, many people have been paying for services hitherto provided free of charge and other charges have increased as a result of new arrangements for financial assessment. Bradley and Manthorpe (1997) quite correctly locate the necessity for social workers to come to grips with issues of finance in the contextual pressures created by economic and demographic trends and currently identified social problems, as well as factors within social work such as its nature as a profession and the reshaping and reconceptualising of care since the NHS and Community Care Act 1990.

However, finance not only affects the micro aspects of practice but also macro issues concerning policy on the funding of services. Questions of the funding of services have impacted on welfare policies for several decades, in Britain and in other developed countries.

Perspectives on financing services

Arguments about whether services should be supplied through the public or private sectors, or through a mixture of providers including voluntary and informal provision, relate to political, economic and social

186

perspectives and theories which are based on fundamentally different assumptions. Arguments by advocates of different approaches frequently appear to be based on independent evidence, but start from ideological assumptions reflecting a commitment either to public or private provision, with all that entails. The debate is by no means limited to Britain or Western Europe, as is illustrated by Donahue's examination of the relative merits of public and private garbage collection in the USA (Donahue, 1989, pp. 60–8).

The New Right: laissez-faire

At one extreme, classical economic theory, sometimes called laissez-faire because it assumes that the system of supply and demand can be left to its own self-regulatory devices, advocates letting people who want a service make their own arrangements, choosing a supplier who, presumably, offers it at the most competitive price.

In the 1980s, New Right ideas and practices were exchanged freely across the Atlantic between the Thatcher and Reagan governments. Von Hayek (1960), the right-wing economist, provided justifications for arguments used by Republicans and 'neo-conservatives' in the USA that spending more was not necessarily effective, that the so-called 'war on poverty' and the 'great society' programmes of the 1960s had failed (Mishra, 1984, p. 31). Similar arguments were used in Britain by neo-conservatives to show that promoting economic growth through higher spending had not achieved the claimed benefits (Mishra, 1984, p. 32). The New Right argument flourished under Thatcherism, targeting inflation and using monetarism (cutting back the supply of money in the economy through cutting government, that is, public, borrowing and spending and manipulating rates of interest for borrowers and investors) to try to reduce inflation. The second stage, in theory, was to cut taxes so as to encourage enterprise and business initiative, thus creating wealth through market forces, demand and supply being stimulated and the economy recovering its health. (See Chapter 3 for further discussion of relationships between economic theories and welfare policy.)

Collectivism

Towards the other extreme, there is a variety of socialist and Marxist perspectives. Basically, they share the view that the only way to ensure that all people who need a service get access to it is to provide it through the state and in the process subsidise those who cannot afford to pay.

Marxists and neo-Marxists revived the analysis of the crisis of capitalism during the 1970s, as the economic difficulties of many Western economies in the face of their own recessions, exacerbated by the sudden increase in Middle Eastern oil prices, became apparent. Marxist analysis shares the neo-conservatism pessimism about the plight of welfare provision under capitalism, but for different reasons. Whereas New Right commentators would say the state cannot afford these services, Marxists would add that the capitalist state is failing through the crisis brought about by its own internal contradictions and conflicts. The state and public expenditure continue to grow, but cannot be afforded. A breakdown of social order will be inevitable as the crisis deepens and the working classes become more frustrated with the exploitive activities of capitalists who are becoming ever richer at their expense. Social conflicts such as mass urban riots are one sign of this crisis erupting. From another perspective, of course, it could be argued that, whereas in France and Russia there have been major revolutions, in Britain smaller scale riots are a means of venting frustrations, which therefore never accumulate sufficient pressure to become universal, mass uprisings.

New Labour and the third way
On the wide continuum between these extremes lie advocates of mixed models of service provision and payment. Soon after the Labour landslide victory in the general election of 1997, the arguments of New Labour about a 'third way', between the extremes of Conservatives and the so-called 'extreme' Left, were being worked out in practice. The New Right attack on the perceived excessive cost of social welfare was taken over, in effect, by Labour and incorporated in the view that the way forward was by means of partnership between the public sector and private and voluntary sectors, in the market economy revitalised by enterprise.

Key aspects

Resourcing services

Local authority finances
In most local authorities, social services are responsible for the largest amount of revenue spending, after education services. Within the budgets of social services departments, the largest single item of expenditure is residential and domiciliary services for elderly people. In the late 1980s, as Beverley Hughes notes, community care for older people was an obvious target area for increasing the control of finances and resources, through the introduction of market principles (Hughes, 1995, p. 3).

Arrangements for financing personal social services provision have been affected by three major developments: privatisation, notably through the introduction of contracting out and competitive tendering; the marketisation of the provision and purchase of services; and the use of financial auditing as a contributor to procedures for quality assurance.

Economic factors

Governments have been beset with problems of financing welfare services for many years, far longer than a superficial retrospective view from 2000 would suggest. Conventional wisdom has it that between 1945 and the mid-1970s, the welfare state expanded, and from the mid-1970s it was in crisis. This crisis could be seen as having two linked aspects. The first was a shortage of cash and the second was an acute problem of high unemployment. The 1974–79 Labour government in 1975 faced a shortage of money in the economy plus a total of unemployed people of just under one million. In the budget of April 1975, it was decided not to increase public spending or to reflate the economy and generate new job opportunities. By this decision, Labour turned away from one of the fundamental principles of the Beveridge Report (1942) that the social security system – guaranteeing people security of income – should coexist with, and buttress, the positive benefits of gainful employment (Lowe, 1993, p. 1). The shortage of ready money in the economy was linked with this problem of rising unemployment and became a running sore in the sides of subsequent Conservative (1979–97) and Labour (1997 onwards) governments. The task was to find ways of continuing to finance the high and growing number of people eligible for social security payments, when the productive workforce, relative to the number of unemployed and other dependent young and older people, was in decline.

But the problem of financing welfare services has been a problem since before the 1970s. In 1968, Vic George, in his classic analysis of social security, observed that

> the recent failure of the economy to grow at a rate parallel to the growth of rising expectations and public expenditure has highlighted once again the role of the state in social provision. (George, 1968, p. 235)

A decade before that, there were public debates about the extent to which the fiscal and tax policies of government should encourage people to make private provision for their own social security benefits and pensions (Seldon, 1960, quoted in George, 1968, p. 236). In what Brian Abel-Smith calls the most influential essay Richard Titmuss ever wrote

(1976a p. iii), Titmuss refers to the continual tension, since the 1920s, between trying to arrive at social policies and social services which guarantee subsistence for people in times of want, and the task of devising equitable taxation and other systems to pay for them (Titmuss, 1976a, pp. 49–53).

So it is no surprise that the major issues regarding which welfare services should be provided generally have been framed, even since before the establishment of the welfare state, in the form of questions about how they should be paid for. It is important to bear in mind the distance that Britain and other Western European countries have moved away from this notion of the state as the sole guarantor of welfare benefit, since the early 1970s. This has huge implications for questions about who pays for services, and who we believe *should* pay, and, consequently, at what points, and how, to charge for these services. Interaction between politicians in the EU and the USA has contributed to the development of plural means of funding welfare services, and the declining emphasis on the state as sole or even major provider of some services.

Demographic factors

Chapter 1 dealt with the major demographic changes affecting social policy. It is worth emphasising here those which particularly affect the financing of services. The main shift is from social workers before the 1980s working mainly with children perceived as 'in trouble' or 'at risk' in the terms of the Children and Young Persons Act 1969, to working with an increasing proportion of older clients, people with disabilities and people with mental health problems at home and in community settings. The increasing proportion of people surviving into their eighties and nineties also leads to greater workloads with this age group of significantly older people, who often have more pronounced problems associated with health, mobility and dependence on others.

However, while some adults who are clients of the social services are relatively poor, a significant proportion are home owners who have savings and occupational or other private pensions. While the typical profile of clients of the social services can vary considerably, in terms of social class, ethnicity and affluence, from district to district, within a locality there are often marked differentials, which complicate decisions about the allocation and, perhaps, gatekeeping and rationing of resources.

Financial auditing as a contributor to quality assurance

One tension is between the management and professional social work agendas inherent in frameworks for performance. Another is between accountabilities in respect of finance and with regard to professional services. Michael Power (1997) argues that the enormous expansion of many kinds of audits – of money, service delivery, technology and management – in England, Northern Ireland, Scotland, Wales and the USA have undeniable benefits but may have costs which are less often acknowledged.

A key feature of the process of financial audit, which enhances the element of control by an external body (such as the Audit Commission, see Adams, 1998a, pp. 55–7), is the employment of experts who are deployed in teams to carry out inspections of particular authorities and services. It is intimidating for managers with relatively scanty financial expertise to be on the receiving end of such activities, even though the auditor may not have the relevant knowledge of the specific services (Power, 1997, p. 78).

Community care: curbing revenue expenditure

Since the 1960s, one major justification for developing community care, for example in mental health, has been the potential benefits through savings in expenditure on hospital provision. The development of drugs which can curb symptoms of conditions such as schizophrenia made this possible and the trend was encouraged by legislation such as the Mental Health Acts of 1959 and 1983. The long-term savings have been considerable. Between 1991–92 and 1996–97, the number of long-stay hospital beds for people with a mental illness declined by almost 50 per cent, from over 29,000 to less than 15,000 (Office for National Statistics, 1999, Table 8.13, p. 142).

It is not surprising, given the general thrust towards cost-saving in community care, that books about its cost aspects tend to be driven by this dominant view. Thus, Taylor and Vigars start from the premise that

> demand, through the raising of assumptions and standards of care, is infinite: resources are finite, in terms of what a society is prepared to spend, or can spend without substituting decline for growth. One can make a good case for saying that we spend much less on care than we should do ... getting value for money is as important to the relief of suffering as the provision of care itself. (Taylor and Vigars, 1993, p. 57)

One consequence of local authorities responding to budgetary pressures in the contract culture is that costs are driven down at the expense of quality, according to research into services for older and disabled people (Unwin, 2001).

Community care: markets and quasi-markets
Under the NHS and Community Care Act 1990, the model of purchase
of services was intended to mirror the market for the supply of goods in
a free economy, with the proviso that it was subject to management by
the authority, whether jointly with others such as the health service, or
alone as the social services or other departments. Thus, this market for
the supply of welfare services was termed a 'quasi-market'.

One consequence of the introduction of quasi-markets in the personal
social services was the necessity for systems of financial management to
be in place which met government requirements and guidelines. Such
systems need to operate at two levels, setting up and managing contracts
for the purchase of services in blocks, such as for a group of clients or
service users, and the purchase of services to fulfil an individual care
package for a single client.

The generation of multiple contracts at these different levels makes
it necessary for social services departments to develop systems for
monitoring spending and to ensure that cash flows throughout the financial year keep pace with available budgets. It also makes necessary the
provision of channels of communication with service providers and
individual users of services and, where appropriate, their carers. The
diversity of service providers by no means ensures an enhancement of
services. On the contrary, it may lead to 'uncertainties in supply, variation
in quality and high monitoring costs' (Mares, 1996, p. 47).

In some areas, budgets have been devolved to staff responsible
for assessing people's needs, managing care and creating care packages.
Thus, departments, teams or, in some cases, groups of clients, such as
people with disabilities, are designated as cost centres, that is, as holding their own budgets. This policy of devolving budgets is consistent
with government policy in other areas such as making school governors
and head teachers responsible for the local management of schools
and hence for school budgets. At the same time, where resources are
limited and no ongoing negotiation of extra funds is permitted, such a
system, in effect, forces staff into the position of identifying their costs,
rationing resources and prioritising which clients' needs should be met,
rather than focusing on assessing needs and relying on funds being
drawn from elsewhere to meet the identified needs.

This illustrates one way in which, rather than management losing
control of devolved budgets, through the enhancement of local financial
responsibility, managements use delegation of financial controls
to increase control over local policies and practices. Finance is a convenient focus for the political demand for greater accountability by local

managers and practitioners in social services (Power, 1997). It is relatively easy for central government to use financial controls as a means of controlling services, where it ties grant-giving to the achievement of specified goals by particular means. For example, since the 1980s, government-wide management exercises exist, such as the Financial Management Initiative and the Rayner Scrutinies (Ascher, 1987, p. 169). Financial control is also maintained through linking central government funding of local authorities with the allocation of grants for specified services.

Privatisation: *contracting out and competitive tendering*

Part of the motivation for the Conservative government introducing privatisation into public services in the 1980s was to cut costs, but another motive was undoubtedly a reflection of the ideological commitment to undermining the power base of independent management in the public services. In the health service, for example, during the 1980s a number of privatisation initiatives took place in the name of improving financial viability, including raising the proportion of pay beds, closing down hospitals considered uneconomic and selling off other residential health facilities (Ascher, 1987, p. 169). One consequence of these was to reduce the monopoly of managers in the public sector over provision.

Arrangements for the financial appraisal of competing bids for contracts have tended to be complex since the early days of compulsory competitive tendering (CCT), in view of the variety of factors needing consideration in appraising the relative merits of bids (Ascher, 1987, pp. 150–2).

Contracts are not a neutral item in the market economy. Their economic theory is based on a recognition of their limitations, in terms of what a contract can enforce. The kinds of outcomes of using a contract vary according to the nature of the contract itself. The criteria to judge whether or not it has achieved its objectives are crucial. It is almost inevitable that at least one of the criteria will be expressed in economic or financial terms. Quite apart from the financial requirement that the contract should deliver at or below the quoted price, economic efficiency is widely used to refer to

> the purchaser getting as far down its list of priorities as possible for a given level of reward to the providing organization (and the people who work for it). (Barker et al., 1997, p. 83)

In community care, managers generally are responsible for selecting a potential provider and negotiating a service agreement about what services will be paid for and provided. The award of a contract and its subsequent monitoring and reviewing are ongoing management responsibilities (Mares, 1996, p. 44).

Charging for services

Approaches to charging people for services

National and local governments constantly seek ways of recouping from people the costs of governing and supplying services. Taxation is the most obvious way to do this. Tax may be direct – charged to the individual like taxation of a wage, salary or pension – or indirect – like value added tax (VAT) charged to the producer of goods or services and added to their cost at the point of purchase. Taxation may be progressive, that is, levied at an increasingly high rate as income increases, like income tax, or regressive, including flat-rate charges such as VAT, which means people pay the same regardless of their income or wealth. Those who believe that one function of the taxation system should be to reduce inequalities of income and wealth often support progressive taxation. The regressive nature of individual flat-rate charges is crudely alleviated by rebates which may be means-tested, made part of all-in payments in rented accommodation or linked with receipt of other social security benefits. Domestic rates were replaced with the poll tax under the Local Government Finance Act 1988, which was the subject of mass protests and subsequently replaced with the council tax under the Local Government Finance Act 1992. Charging for community care services such as meals on wheels and home helps takes place on a haphazard basis. This leads to unevenness in charging practices, which is in itself a form of discrimination. The Labour government's intention to standardise charges for domiciliary services will have a direct impact on local budgets and funding of related services.

The issue of how far individual recipients of services should pay their real cost, or any charge at all, predates the creation of the welfare state and has always generated debate and controversy. Notably, practices differ between agencies and between different local authorities. Whereas an older person would not pay for services provided through the NHS, such services as domiciliary care provided by the social services department could be subject to charges. But the level of charges would vary considerably from authority to authority. Additionally, although assessment of the person's needs and financial assessment are linked, practice varies considerably between local authorities. In some, assessment of needs and financial assessment are integrated activities, while in others social work staff assess needs and non-social work staff make a separate financial assessment (Bradley and Manthorpe, 1997, p. 48). The complexity and variety of methods of assessing charges to clients and carers can be added to a tendency for continual changes in these methods. Bradley and Manthorpe (1997, p. 12) illustrate this from a survey of five different areas of England and Wales by Chetwynd and Ritchie (1996), which found that each had a different way of calculating charges and each had changed this at least once in the previous three years.

Paying for services: from means testing to financial assessment
The term 'means test' traditionally has associations with stigma in the history of welfare services in Britain, which is at least as old as the Poor Law Amendment Act of 1834 with the workhouse test, based on the principle of less eligibility before outdoor relief could be granted. The aim was to set the level of benefit below the lowest wage an able-bodied person could earn, in order to discourage scroungers.

In the 1990s, the aim of financial assessment in community care is to assess how much the person receiving services should pay towards their cost. Those administering financial assessments of individuals might claim the aim is to ensure that all a person's outgoings are recorded and all available benefits are claimed. However:

> financial assessment is double-edged. On the one hand, users may find out from the assessment process that they can get a higher level of existing benefit ... [or] income from pension or insurance schemes. On the other hand, they may be asked to put this additional income towards paying for services. (Mares, 1996, p. 129)

Further, the process of assessment involves completing a form, which for older people is reminiscent of means testing for eligibility for national assistance and other benefits. The form asks questions which some regard as invading their privacy, concerning all forms of savings and income from pensions and other sources. It is hard to reconcile the claimed goal of meeting as much of the client's unmet need as possible with the agency requirement that the maximum contribution by the person receiving the service be offset against the full cost of the care package. After all, the resultant net cost has to be aggregated with the net cost of other care packages into a gross annual budget which is limited, with the implication that the services provided have to be prioritised and rationed, according to national or local guidelines. As Penny

Mares puts it:

> Budget constraints mean that front-line workers have to plan care packages
> by balancing 'What is required?' with 'What is achievable?' You may be asked by
> the budget-holder to identify those care needs which it is 'essential' to meet and
> those which are 'desirable'. (Mares, 1996, p. 126)

Dealing with debt

There has been a huge increase since the 1980s in the debt burden of individuals and families. Some of the problems of debt that poorer people
experience are brought about by their inability to meet living expenses
from benefits. In some parts of the country – London, Edinburgh and
towns in the south of England – the cost of renting and purchasing living
accommodation has soared. At the same time, finance companies, banks
and building societies are increasingly willing to offer people loans.

Government departments, local authorities and private individuals
pursue debtors in different ways in different localities. Debt recovery
procedures may involve the employment of bailiffs, or private companies
specialising in collecting money. Social workers are likely to be involved
with clients whose other problems lead them into debt.

An example of a positive strategy for dealing with the financial exclusion of debt improves people's circumstances by redistributing actual
cash. The Debt Redemption Initiative (DRI) in Ely receives referrals
from specialists such as the money advice workers in the local Citizen's
Advice Bureau, buys people's debts off them and owes the money for
them while they repay the DRI. A condition of such a loan is that they
must join the local credit union (Drakeford and Sachdev, 2001).

Appointees to deal with people's finances

The context of assessment lies in policy and management issues which are
often beyond the ability of the practitioner to influence. People receiving
services and their carers tend to experience even more keenly than practitioners the disempowering impact of charging policies being beyond their
control and anger and frustration at the way escalating charges may take
little or no account of their ability to pay (Chetwynd and Ritchie, 1996,
p. 16). The complexity of charging policies and practices may increase the
risk of people receiving services being subjected to financial abuse.

A person's money may be dealt with on their behalf by a relative or
friend taking out power of attorney through a solicitor, where the person's
mental capacity is regarded as sufficiently impaired. However, it is more
common for the appointee procedure to be operated, through the Benefits
Agency, for the managing of a person's social security assets and income.

Several aspects of such procedures are problematic. Criteria for making the judgement about the point when a person is no longer capable of managing finances are not specified sufficiently rigorously. Consequently, there is scope for different judgements to be made by different professionals, even though the circumstances may be similar. Policy and practice vary in different localities regarding a person taking powers to deal with personal finances on behalf of an individual. Langan and Means surveyed 27 local authorities and found considerable differences between them in respect of procedures for working with people, where another person is appointed to manage the finances of a client with dementia (Langan and Means, 1996).

The procedure described by Bradley and Manthorpe (1997, pp. 64–5), whereby a person applies to the Benefits Agency, under Regulation 33 of the Social Security (Claims and Payments) Regulations 1987, to manage the financial affairs of a person felt to be no longer able to do this, appears too loose and subject to the vagaries of personality and other factors, rather than operating purely on the basis of objective factors.

More subtle factors operate to complicate the practice of working with a person not deemed capable of managing his or her finances. There is a tension between the social work principle of empowering the person and the appointee system, which involves the removal of powers and choices from the person. Sometimes, the person is living in a private residential setting and the officer in charge becomes the appointee. Or the local authority may become the appointee and charge the person for administering this service. It is arguable that, in such circumstances, another independent person – possibly one with a role similar to that of the former guardian *ad litem* in childcare – should be appointed to ensure that the person's best interests are pursued.

Implications for social workers

EXAMPLE

Samira is the social worker for Mrs J, an older woman in the early stages of dementia living in a nursing home, and her daughter Ms P, who is physically disabled, lives at home, has various community care services and is experiencing difficulties with rent arrears. Mrs J says her daughter is trying to get her hands on her money. The daughter says she needs power of attorney because her mother can't be trusted to look after her money.

How should Samira approach this situation?

1. There is a need to find out how the nursing home deals with the tension between residents' rights and the need to ensure that their financial affairs are managed. There is also a need to clarify how the local authority approaches funding community care services. Samira is aware that different approaches to these policies impact differently on practice. She knows different assessment and means-testing procedures in neighbouring local authorities lead to different amounts being charged for community care services. Professional work with a person aiming to meet needs and maximise the quality of life may not be fulfilled or may actually conflict with financing policies, procedures and practice decisions carried out on a pragmatic, functional or cost-driven basis.

2. Samira starts with Ms P's rent arrears and other debt problems. She contacts the landlord, in this case the local authority, and finds out that the problem is not serious yet, but could be if a summons is issued. She works out a debt management programme with Ms P, a financial adviser and a welfare rights expert. Ms P admits, now the pressure is off, she was worrying about her mother's money with her own, rather than with her mother's, interests in mind. Samira offers the comment to Ms P that if she applied for a move two miles to the neighbouring local authority, the bill for her domiciliary care services would be reduced significantly. Ms P opts to stay where she is.

3. Samira is aware of ongoing problems created for Ms P by the fact that questions of their financial commitments and the assessment of her needs are dealt with by non-social work staff. Samira's view is that the assessment of need is complex and includes aspects of risk assessment, which imply a level of subjective judgement impacting on areas such as a person's finances; so financial assessment cannot be segregated from the social work assessment of need as a whole. Samira discusses the unfairness of the variations in charging policies between local authorities with a welfare rights specialist, who uses Ms P's case as the basis for a test case and a complaint to the ombudsman. It emerges there is some discretion in the system and Ms P's charges are reduced on the basis that she cannot afford them.

4. Samira realises that while Mrs J may be unable to control her personal finances in the future, at present it would violate her rights to remove this control from her. It is agreed with staff in the nursing home that Mrs J should be in a position to decide how her money is spent.

Chapter summary

This chapter has reviewed policy and practice aspects of the financing of, and charging for, services by local authorities. The implications for practice of the differences in policy and practice in different authorities emerge as having serious implications for those receiving services and their carers.

Further reading

Bradley, G. and Manthorpe, J. (1997) *Dilemmas of Financial Assessment*, Venture Press, Birmingham

Chetwynd, M. and Ritchie, J. (1996) *The Cost of Care: The Impact of Charging Policy on the Lives of Disabled People,* Joseph Rowntree Foundation, York

Langan J. and Means R. (1996) 'Financial Management and Elderly People with Dementia in the UK: As Much a Question of Confusion as Abuse?' *Ageing and Society*, (16): 287–314

Rowe, J., Davies, K., Baburaj, V. and Sinha, R. (1993) 'F.A.D.E. The Financial Affairs of Dementing Elders and Who is the Attorney?' *Journal of Elder Abuse and Neglect*, **5**(2): 73–9

National Audit Office (1994) *Looking After the Financial Affairs of People with Mental Incapacity*, National Audit Office, London

11

Who Controls Social Services?

Social workers are responsible for working with people so as to empower them to take control over their lives. This is intrinsically contradictory, though, because it implies that the empowering professionals are in control. Many initiatives aiming to give people choice and power are compromised in a similar way. It is important for practitioners to explore these and other similar problems and paradoxes raised by efforts to advance practice in this area. This chapter examines the issues affecting the practitioner engaged in increasing the control of services by people receiving those services and their carers.

Contexts and key aspects

Who does control key decisions about the nature and delivery of personal social services? More crucially, who *should* shape decisions about these services: politicians, civil servants, professionals, or those receiving the services? A number of debates and dilemmas arise in practice, when people in power try to implement their vision of empowerment for those who, in formal terms at any rate, are historically relatively powerless. The formal goal of strengthening democratic control, and the links between the public and the council serving it, may be inconsistent with delivering best value, that is, quality, but cheaper, services (Rickford, 2000). The Local Government Information Unit, commenting on the Labour government's modernisation programme for social services, identified a tension between the setting of standards and performance indicators by central government and the aim of giving local authorities discretion to respond to local people (Local Government Information Unit, 1999).

New labour and the stakeholder society: paradoxes of power

Tony Blair, Prime Minister in the 1997 and 2001 Labour governments, promoted the idea that social exclusion would be addressed by the Labour government, through social policies which were aimed at social integration and the elimination of the dependency culture (Levitas, 1998) which had contributed to the costs of welfare benefits rising to unacceptably high levels. The notion of the citizen as having a valid and meaningful stake in society is central to these policies. This means being empowered to take part in local government and exercising choices about exercising rights, duties and responsibilities. A further element in Labour government policy is the notion of the stakeholder society. This accepts that a variety of people and interests need representing in decisionmaking. The previous Conservative government had acknowledged already the distinctive circumstances and needs of carers alongside service users in receiving community care services. The Carers (Recognition and Services) Act 1995 gave carers the right to their own assessment of needs.

A further important shift away from professionals monopolising the power has come through the disability movement. The points of comparison and contrast between the medical and social models of disability have been examined in the literature (Oliver, 1990). It is important to recognise the additional perspective brought to this area of practice by disabled people themselves. The passage of the Welfare Reform Bill – introducing means-tested benefits for disabled people and abolishing incapacity benefit as hitherto known – through parliament in 1999 was marked by protests from groups associated with disability, among many others. The significance of such actions is in demonstrating the extent to which people receiving services, in certain sectors, have taken control.

However, it is difficult to envisage the aspirations of all stakeholders in a particular area of social policy being met. In circumstances where people are moving from dependence to independence, one person's empowerment is likely to lead to another person's disempowerment. In circumstances such as families and neighbourhoods, consensus between all people is unlikely, so no policy, practice decision or initiative is going to please or satisfy everyone.

A further complication involves the contradictions inherent in Labour government aspirations to achieve major reforms in the operation of local government. The Labour government set out its aim that community leadership should lie at the heart of the role of modern local authorities, in the White Paper *Modern Local Government: In Touch with the People* (Department of the Environment, Transport and the Regions, 1998). The

White Paper proposes that local authorities should have freedom and corresponding extended powers to work with the range of statutory, private and voluntary organisations and groups to generate local solutions to local problems.

At one level, empowering citizens to participate in the stakeholder society raises no complications. But the White Paper (Department of the Environment, Transport and the Regions, 1998) puts local government officials and professionals in the position of power, when it states that

> community leadership is at the heart of the role of modern local government. Councils are the organisations best placed to take a comprehensive overview of the needs and priorities of their local areas and communities and lead the work to meet those needs and priorities in the round ... Concerted action at local and national level is needed to address issues such as sustainable development, social exclusion, crime, education and training. (DETR, 1998, paras 8.1–2)

Further, the statement that central government needs to take strong concerted action with local government makes it even less straightforward for the citizen, however empowered, to make a meaningful contribution as a stakeholder.

Local participation: perspectives on empowerment

Empowerment is a term largely associated with practices, in the absence of a worked-out body of theoretical positions, discourses, approaches, methods, or practices. Politicans, civil servants, managers of public services and professionals in local government, including social workers, have responsibilities for personal social services. The Labour government (1997 onwards) stated in the White Paper *Modern Local Government: In Touch with the People* (DETR, 1998) that local authorities should have community leadership at their heart and this implies citizens having a dynamic interest in active participation. People receiving these services, their carers and other friends and relatives also have an interest in the nature of those services. The National Care Standards Commission set up under the Care Standards Act 2000 requires service users to participate actively and this encourages the view that policymakers are committed to user empowerment. The question is whether these interests can be anything more than the right to make views known, or in some circumstances to be consulted before policy decisions are made.

Much of the social work literature employs a truncated or taken-for-granted concept of empowerment to refer to procedures for involving people, consulting them, rather than achieving transformational changes in the personal, organisational, social and political domains through their participation. The notion of user involvement is largely confined to health and care services (Adams, 1997). In schools, for instance, pupil participation in the running of schools continues to be minimal, as was traditionally the case (Adams, 1991, p. 213). Prisoners' attempts in Britain and the USA to gain more involvement in the running of prisons have not succeeded (Adams, 1994). The acid test of rhetoric by the authorities is whether users who start to make vociferous collective demands are heeded. It is much easier to offer a say to compliant, manipulable clients who do not ask awkward questions about shortcomings in services. Self-advocacy remains marginal to social services, except in what are regarded widely as specialist problem areas of disability and mental health, which paradoxically reinforces their difference and exclusion from the mainstream. Otherwise, progress towards empowering service users who engage in protests has been modest (Adams, 1998b).

Much of the literature on empowerment in social work is neutered, classless, depoliticised, ablist and ageist in its implications. The empowerment literature tends to represent activity on a linear continuum, from individual to collective activity, or from self to other. Thus, it replicates features of the very features of dominant realities which should be challenged in the furtherance of empowerment. One useful approach which avoids these difficulties is that of Clarke and Stewart, who identify three models of empowerment:

1. The person as customer exercising individual choice in the marketplace of services.
2. The person as citizen with legally defined civil and political rights.
3. The community as a focus for new democratic structures and processes. (Clarke and Stewart, 1992, p. 22)

This is helpful, because it provides a framework in terms of which a range of possible initiatives, including those referred to above, can be viewed critically. The customer and citizen are both viewed as people with freedom to make decisions and choices, but these are given to them by the authorities who wield broader powers. This is a realistic portrayal of the situation in most local circumstances. Responsibilities are exercised by people 'on licence', as it were, from the real holders of power. In the personal social services, for instance, disability groups would be able to negotiate directly with the potential providers of services, rather than having their demands and needs channelled through professionals and agencies.

The third model is somewhat different. It takes the community as the focus and offers the possibility of empowering people independently of existing local government structures. Hirst offers some practical thoughts about how what he calls associative democracy would achieve the ideal of people becoming empowered 'from below', 'limiting the scope of state administration, without diminishing social provision' (Hirst, 1994, p. 12). His ideas revive the principles of the self-regulating communities advocated by Robert Owen in the social experiment of New Lanark and Pierre-Joseph Proudhon's notion of a decentralised, federated state rooted in cooperative production by local artisans in a mutualist economy (Adams, 1996b, p. 221). Hirst does not detail how to fill the gap between concepts and existing structures and political processes. However, his redefinition of politics is useful because it includes the notion of a variety of organisations involved in political action, some of which will be locally based, while others reflect shared interests by service users on a wider geographical basis (Cochrane, 1996, p. 205).

Citizen empowerment by policymakers or professionals is inherently paradoxical and ultimately condescending. However, we should not underestimate the power of people who empower themselves and make their own views and experiences known. For example, disabled people and people with mental health problems, through the group Survivors Speak Out, increasingly have taken power for themselves. Legislation provides legitimate space for this to impact on local government. The Local Government Act 1999 introduced the principle of 'best value', increasing the accountability of local authorities by requiring: more clearly stated objectives; specific criteria for measuring performance and outcomes; the involvement of citizens in the community – *including people receiving services* – in assessing the quality of services; and efficiency in using resources.

Changing ideas about empowerment

Empowerment strategies develop in the context of a variety of different perspectives and theoretical constructs, which may not be made manifest, but which nevertheless embody assumptions informing actions.

First there is a vast range of radical positions from which action may be undertaken: feminist, Marxist and other socialist positions and other radical viewpoints. Second, there are a number of participative approaches which may be linked, more or less explicitly, with social democratic and liberal positions. Third, in the health and personal social services fields at any rate, there are some organisations and groups aligned with the focus on a particular category of client or service user, such as the Patients'

Association, a range of organisations in what has been called the disability movement, self-advocacy groups such as Survivors Speak Out and voluntary organisations such as MIND. These tend to draw on a variety of perspectives associated with personal rights and social justice.

There is a notable lack in the the UK of a forum giving all contributors to the personal social services an equal stake in debates about the ideas and practices of empowerment. Empowerment has emerged as a widespread preoccupation of professionals in the health and social services in the UK since the 1980s, with significant support from professional bodies such as CCETSW and, ironically, in areas such as community care, from the Department of Health in its official guidance on practice (see DH/SSI, 1991a, for instance). These developments have occurred largely in the absence of a theoretically grounded literature, or arenas for political, policy, professional and public debates about the concepts and practices which are regarded as empowering and disempowering. Ideas of empowering people and improving their participation have been espoused by government ministers and civil servants, professionals in the Department of Health and Social Services Inspectorate, senior managers in social services and social work departments, practitioners in social work and probation work and other professionals in allied areas. But there has been little involvement by people receiving services, or their carers, in the development of these ideas. They have been colonised by officials preparing guidance, in consultation with professionals in higher education, with some involvement of clients, service users and carers, and by researchers and commentators in higher education in their own right.

Some of these contributions claim links with, or even roots in, the experiences and perspectives of people receiving services (Beresford and Croft, 1993; Croft and Beresford, 1995), while others do not. While in fields such as disability, some notable contributions have been made by disabled people who are also academics, researchers, teachers and writers, there is a key question about whether the discourse of professionals or disabled people is, or needs to be, uppermost.

In a ground-breaking book, in terms of its methodology as well as its content, the sociologist Thomas Mathiesen reflects critically on his work with the Scandinavian prisoners' rights movement (1974). He notes that threats to the purposes, or even the existence, of collective protests by prisoners come not only directly from the authorities at the point of direct confrontation, but also through outflanking by the authorities, once the full extent of the demands from the prisoners are known. This is a major reason why he emphasises 'the unfinished', the necessity for the manifesto of the prisoners to remain essentially incomplete.

Changing conceptions of citizenship: what do we call the clients?

Many attempts have been made to clarify what the role of the citizen should be in particular political regimes. It is important to recognise that the ideas informing practice are not immovable, but are socially constructed. The concept of citizenship changes as people using it change their perspectives. Ruth Lister explores the questions and dilemmas as to which rights to attach to the status of citizen. Should paid work count, unpaid housework, mothering (Lister, 1997, pp. 178–82)?

Likewise, the notion of the person receiving social work and social services is not rooted in a concept of what that person essentially is. This is not just playing with words. One indication of the lack of consensus about the identity of the individual member of the public is the multiplicity of terms used to describe this person, especially when receiving services. Evidence of the problematic concept of empowerment in the health and social services is the lack of a satisfactory word to use, in English at any rate, to refer to the receiver of services, notably in the light of the fact, presumably, that they may be empowered, as they are in contact with these very services. This is indicative of the complexities in the status of the person receiving services. In the UK, terms such as 'client' which were considered acceptable and unproblematic have been dislodged from their central position, apparently without any critical questioning by professional bodies, by such terms as 'user' and 'service user'. At the same time, such terms as 'consumer' and 'customer' have begun to be used by some agencies. In some circumstances, the words 'citizen' or 'stakeholder' may be applied.

People can be offended by being referred to with a term they consider inappropriate or demeaning. Some regard 'client' as implying therapy or treatment is received. Others argue that the term 'consumer' carries the implication of receiving goods and services rather than determining their nature. The term 'user' may imply passivity and, to some people, an association with uses and abuses of substances.

Reflexivity and empowerment

Empowerment is a reflexive process which operates holistically to affect the empowered person and others with whom they interact. Reflexivity is a term which refers to the process of monitoring one's own feelings and actions in a dialogic way, and creatively using the interaction between self and external realities to sustain or even transform social relations. To the extent that empowerment associated with protest involves social movements from below, it provides a means of challenging impositions from above (Adams, 1991). Of course, reflexive activity does not escape the ambiguities which are inherent in other areas. Thus, it may contribute to such impositions, and the containing of personal and social conflicts, or to radicalising and transformational activity (Cox, 1997, p. 15). Reflexivity is a powerful methodology, however, since it provides a means of self-reflection on this dichotomous position, bringing together the domains of the self, the group, the organisation and the community (Adams, 1996b).

Transforming policies and practice

While theoretical perspectives deployed in the literature and practice of empowerment include a diversity of Marxist, radical, feminist, anarchist and ecological perspectives, they share a concern with what we might call transformational politics, policies and practices. Lena Dominelli has argued with increasing force (Dominelli and McLeod, 1989; Dominelli, 1997) for an approach to anti-oppressive practice which recognises diversity and is not driven by a single theoretical approach. In any given situation, of course, it will be useful to know whether such a strategy is informed by idealism or pragmatism and necessity. Further, beyond and behind diversity and the fragmentation emphasised by postmodern perspectives lie persistent and pervasive divisions and inequalities, exemplified in the gendered, ageist, disablist and class-based nature of much of the literature in the fields of empowerment and protest. For example, Auckland notes that the campaign opposing the extension to the M11 motorway north of London would have been more successful if more attention had been paid to women's suggestions of alternative strategies of protest and also, practically, to the need for blankets and food (Auckland, 1997, p. 10). Again, Auckland comments that groups and communities may be empowered through protest, but in reality such empowerment is differentially distributed through a particular group or community (Auckland, 1997, p. 11).

Examples of initiatives

After coming to power in 1997, the Labour government promoted the involvement of adults and children in local government, through the publication of a guide, suggesting ways of involving children and young people in decisionmaking and the delivery of local services. The guide gave examples of more than 50 such schemes (Willow, 1997).

In Redditch, neighbourhood groups were introduced as a means of improving consultation and feedback to Redditch Borough Council. People were enabled to demonstrate civic leadership through involvement of members of the local community in the development of the community plans of the local council (Local Government Information Unit, 1997a). In the London Borough of Newham, focus groups were used by the council as a powerful means of extending consultation (Local Government Information Unit, 1998). Citizens' Panels were set up by councils in Bradford, Eastleigh, Halton, Kirkless, Southampton and York, as a means of enhancing consultation with individuals, groups and organisations (Local Government Information Unit, 1997b). 'Capacity building' was the term used to describe equipping people in local communities with the training, skills and resources to develop their potential to play a more active and meaningful part in the process of urban regeneration (Local Government Information Unit, 1997c).

Councils are required by the Local Government Act 2000 to consult local people before adopting a model of local government from different options: a mayor who chooses a cabinet, Westminster-style; a 'political' mayor working alongside a powerful council manager or chief executive; and a streamlined structure of existing committees. The mayor may be chosen by the councillors or directly elected by the people. Voters can force councils to hold a referendum on choosing a mayor, by submitting a petition signed by 5 per cent of the electorate. Councils must furnish central government with democratic reform plans, demonstrating how local people have been consulted and will be encouraged to stay involved. Standing conferences, citizen panels, local links shops and stalls where all council services can be accessed and local fora are typical means of attempting this. Particular efforts are made to get young people involved, through school-based events and conferences on democratic themes of particular interest to them.

Involving people in assuring the quality of services they receive

The most obvious way of evaluating how far people receiving services are participating in an empowered way is by assessing the extent of the contributions made directly by users to the shaping, delivering and quality assurance of their services. In these areas, the practice of developing greater client or service user involvement in practice is not straightforward. The further the practitioner goes towards that goal, the more hurdles and dilemmas are likely to be encountered.

If we take the role of the client in quality assurance as an example, the most difficult area for client involvement happens, paradoxically, to be the most vital from the client's point of view, that of commenting critically on mistakes, problems and shortcomings of services. There are four key areas on which the practitioner should focus in this connection: whistleblowing by the client; complaints by individuals or groups; contributions to independent inquiry reports; and protests or other direct action.

Whistleblowing

The Labour government is keen to encourage whistleblowing and endorses the Nolan Committee's (Nolan, 1995) support for whistleblowing as a means of widening accountability in public life. Various organisations, such as the Institute of Employment Rights and Public Concern at Work, have campaigned with some success for the protection of whistleblowers through increasing their legal rights. The British Association of Social Workers has published guidance for staff who wish to take action to end exploitation of clients and alert management and colleagues to the circumstances (BASW, 1997).

The caution is that a survey of all English social services departments found that in 1999 only a third had a corporate policy in place on whistleblowing and in four-fifths of the cases where corporate policies had been developed the initiative had come from other departments (Holihead, 2000, p. 20). A further caution is that contracts between purchasers and providers in the health and social services sector sometimes build in confidentiality clauses. This can complicate the situation, where the practitioner and the client are aware of shortcomings in service delivery which are not being tackled, despite attempts to achieve progress through legitimate channels in the organisation.

Complaints

The Citizen's Charter and other similar charters attempt to strengthen people's rights to complain and gain their entitlements to particular services. Some local authorities have pursued the goal of enhancing people's rights as consumers of services, offering people opportunities to take part in consultations and state their wishes as part of the decisionmaking process (Elcock, 1993, p. 168). Others have decentralised provision of social services, for example, by locating teams of social workers and other social services staff, such as those delivering community care, in local neighbourhoods (Hadley and Hatch, 1981). Consumerism and decentralisation are seen by some critics as side-stepping crucial issues concerning citizen participation (Beresford and Croft, 1993). They are viewed as tokenistic in the sense that they can be implemented without affecting the existing power of managers and professionals over the nature and delivery of services.

Complaints procedures have been the subject of detailed scrutiny by policymakers, politicians, managers and professionals over the past decade. The NHS and Community Care Act 1990 required every social services department to have a complaints procedure. Staged complaints procedures were introduced following the Children Act 1989, from informal complaints settled without formal procedures to more formal processes and review by a complaints panel with an independent chair. Guidance was issued by the government for social services departments in general (DH/SSI, 1991b) and for staff having first contact with customers, notably receptionists and telephonists (DH/SSI, 1991c). Organisations such as the National Consumer Council published detailed guidance on the practical issues associated with setting up and running complaints procedures (National Consumer Council and National Institute for Social Work, 1988). The Patients' Association also published guidance for patients on the use of NHS complaints procedures (Patients' Association, undated). Many local authorities published their own guidance for people, including clients of the social services, wanting to make a complaint. Despite all this, Norman Warner's research for the Carers National Association showed that 44 per cent of carers did not know how to complain about services (Warner, 1994, p. 40), a discouraging finding in view of the fact that the sample was biased in any case towards better informed carers (Warner, 1994, p. 11).

The strength of complaints procedures is that they provide a support for the complainant. At their best, they are transparent and accessible, empowering complainants and not reinforcing professional defences against external critical scrutiny of services. But the practitioner has to be prepared for the fact that some complaints procedures are very formal, lengthy and therefore intimidating to the person not used to negotiating with organisations.

Inquiries and investigations
We have all witnessed media coverage of many investigations into shortcomings in health and social services. A great range of situations occurs in practice creating the necessity for an official inquiry or investigation. Sometimes, departmental officials carry out the investigation internally. A higher profile investigation on a more significant issue may lead to officially appointed investigators, as happened in Clwyd. Eventually, after more than a dozen investigations, the Clwyd situation attracted the

status of a judicial inquiry, where witnesses can be made subject to sub-poena to give evidence. Further along the line of independence, although not political power, there are reports by researchers or reporters from the mass media themselves.

Protests by people

There is little space in public services for discussion of the difficult, challenging client who resists. That is because, fundamentally, the system of client involvement, like the alleged commitment to empowering clients, is grudging and not embraced enthusiastically. Such a person is more likely than the conforming or apathetic person to be perceived as difficult or deviant and receive less of a quality service as a consequence. One reason for this is the lack of appropriate attention paid to resistance and protest of people receiving services, a fact which corresponds with the dominant political, policy and social culture in the UK, which rewards compliance or conformity more readily than questioning or rejection of dominant realities.

The SSI is driven not by clients' perceptions but by policy statements and ministers and relates primarily to professional and associated interests such as those based in education, training and research. The SSI bases its work on standards developed in-house as statements of expected quality of service. Local authorities are encouraged to use them for their own reviews and evaluations of services. These standards derive primarily from professional and political concerns and are not generated in the first place by clients, services users and carers.

Repeated evidence shows clients' perceptions and views are not attended to sufficiently, or taken sufficient account of. These need to be taken seriously and not ignored or responded to punitively. The key criterion which enables a judgement to be made about the effectiveness or otherwise of measures to empower citizens is whether their wishes and preferences are incorporated throughout the entirety of the way services are developed, organised, managed and delivered, and the context in which their wishes and preferences are reflected in decisions made by managers and practitioners about the services they receive.

Implications for social workers

The above discussion implies that as practitioners we should be

- more demanding of our employers
- unwilling to accept second best services

- unwilling to act as guardians of the status quo
- more assertive in our attempts to empower clients
- more supportive of people receiving services who wish to complain
- willing to accept the legitimacy of people's attempts to protest collectively.

Chapter summary

This chapter has considered the problems associated with implementing the ideal of citizen involvement in social services. Ultimately, efforts by governments to develop empowering policies, like empowering practice by the social worker, encounter the paradox that it is equally contradictory for politicians or professionals to facilitate people's empowerment. Experience of groups, such as protesters for example – whether about disability or environmental issues – suggests that their experience of self-empowerment needs to be taken on board and worked with.

Further reading

Beresford, P. and Croft, S. (1993) *Citizen Involvement: A Practice Guide for Change*, Macmillan, London – now Palgrave

King, D. and Stoker, G. (eds) (1996) *Rethinking Local Democracy*, ESRC and Macmillan, Basingstoke – now Palgrave

Rees, S. (1991) *Achieving power: Practice and Policy in Social Welfare*, London, Allen & Unwin

12

Future Trends

The political centre of gravity of social policy has shifted to the Right since 1979 when the Conservative government came into office. Assumptions about how much welfare the state should provide were modified during the New Right Conservative government and not restored when New Labour came to power in 1997. There is a question about how much further these assumptions will move, now that Labour has achieved a second landslide victory in June 2001, as it begins its second term in office, with a stated commitment to invest in the public services of education and health and work towards the abolition of child poverty.

One way to provide a benchmark against which to measure the 'social health' of the nation is with reference to an indicative incident which brings together most or all of the aspects of policy covered in this book. A convenient focus is provided by the urban riots of 1981 and 2001.

How have social conditions changed since 1981?

As this book was being being prepared for publication in the summer of 2001, riots erupted in Oldham, Rochdale and Bradford, as they had in Brixton, Toxteth and other urban areas in 1981.

Brixton in 1981

In 1981, Lord Scarman reported on the poverty, urban deprivation and racial discrimination, particularly by the police, which were accompaniments to those riots (Scarman, 1981). From contemporary inquiry reports, we can gather evidence to ascertain how far social policies have improved social conditions in the 20 years between these waves of rioting.

In Brixton in 1981, 'the general picture of housing provision both in the borough as a whole and in Brixton in particular is one of considerable stress' (Scarman, 1981, p. 5), the main problems being a shortage of houses and a waiting list of 18,000 households of which 37 per cent were black. An NDH survey confirmed that 10 per cent of households, or 12,000 households, were overcrowded and there was significant squatting in the large number of empty dwellings. Over 20,000 dwellings were regarded by the local authority as unfit or lacking at least one basic amenity. Nearly 80 per cent of the population lived in rented accommodation (Scarman, 1981, p. 5).

There was a lack of leisure and recreation facilities, especially for young people. Younger people and those in the professional and skilled working groups were moving out of Brixton, the population of which, Scarman notes, 'like many other inner city areas' had declined by 20 per cent between 1971 and 1981 (Scarman, 1981, p. 7).

There was

> a strikingly high figure of children in local authority care (2.3 per cent of the population aged 18 or less) and an incidence of single-parent families which, at one in six, is twice the national average. (Scarman, 1981, p. 7)

There was a high proportion of black people in the population and a disproportionate number of low-income households, young children and older people. Black children were underachieving, relative to white children, in schools (Scarman, 1981, p. 9). Young people from ethnic groups faced disproportionately high unemployment when they left school, the unemployment rate of young black men under 19 being 55 per cent (Scarman, 1981, p. 10). Mental illness rates and the incidence of physical and learning disability in the borough were higher than the national average. Social services spending in 1979/80, at £117.39, was the highest in England and twice the average for other London boroughs. Spending per head by the local area health authority in the same period, at £243, was also the highest in England, £230 being the average for other inner London health authorities (Scarman, 1981, p. 7).

There was evidence that discrimination in employment was 'a factor of considerable importance' (Scarman, 1981, p. 10). But

> discriminatory and hostile behaviour on racial grounds is not confined to the area of employment. There is evidence that it occurs not only among school children and in the street but, unintentionally no doubt, in the provision of some local authority services, principally housing. (Scarman, 1981, p. 11)

Scarman observed that:

> Many of the young people of Brixton are therefore born and raised in insecure
> social and economic conditions and in an impoverished physical environment.
> They share the desires and expectations which our materialist society encourages.
> At the same time, many of them fail to achieve educational success and on leaving
> school face the stark prospect of unemployment. (Scarman, 1981, p. 11)

Scarman commented that many of the other disturbances occurring in
other parts of England in the summer of 1981 – notably those in Southall,
Toxteth (Liverpool), Moss Side (Manchester) and the West Midlands –
shared similar features to Brixton:

> a high ethnic minority population, high unemployment, a declining economic
> base, a decaying physical environment, bad housing, lack of amenities, social
> problems including family breakdown, a high rate of crime and heavy policing.
> (Scarman, 1981, p. 12)

Bradford in 2001

After inter-communal riots in Bradford during July 2001, it emerged that
a report by Lord Herman Ouseley had been produced some two months
previously. This report raised a series of questions in a prophetic way,
notably: how can divisions in the community be improved and citizens
guaranteed a reasonable quality of life? The analysis by the report was
not as informed by external empirical evidence as the Scarman inquiry,
but it drew on the experiences of local people and presented a challenge
to policymakers, politicians and practitioners, including social workers.
Rhetoric about developing anti-discriminatory, anti-poverty, full employment, improved health, better housing, effective criminal and youth
justice and exemplary children and families policies appeared irrelevant
in the face of stark evidence of fragmented communities and deteriorating
relations between different cultural and ethnic communities.

The Bradford District Race Review was set up by Bradford Vision –
an umbrella group comprising key local organisations including
Bradford council, the police, health authority, local businesses, voluntary
groups and faith communities – to ensure local agencies and services met
their obligations under the Race Relations (Amendment) Act 2000 and
responded to the question: 'why is community fragmentation along
social, cultural, ethnic and religious lines occurring in the Bradford district?' (foreword to Ouseley, 2001). The aim of the review was – without

duplicating existing reports and outstanding recommendations – to advise on how to end racial discrimination, improve race and community relations and promote equality of opportunity. The 12 members of the review team included a majority of black members, seven being women and young people, two being pupils at Bradford schools.

The report identified strengths and positive features of the district, including the diversity represented in the cultures of people, local businesses, leisure, sports, community organisations and partnerships (Ouseley, 2001, p. 9). However, many common shortcomings were identified:

- the *negative image* of the district leading to 'white flight' of middle classes and more affluent Sikhs and Hindus moving out to preferred neighbourhoods 'leaving behind an underclass of relatively poor white people and visible minority ethnic communities' (Ouseley, 2001, p. 9)
- *inadequate leadership*, with self-styled community leaders 'in league with the establishment key people ... [to] maintain the status quo of control and segregation through fear, ignorance and threats' (Ouseley, 2001, p. 10)
- *divisions* (Ouseley, 2001, p. 10) and *conflicts* (Ouseley, 2001, p. 13) as different communities sought to protect their identities and culture by avoiding contact with others
- conflicting styles of *policing* which cause resentment and perpetuate stereotypes, by management promoting anti-racist policies, 'top down', 'while rank and file officers remain fearful of being called "racist" and damaging their career prospects if they tackle black and Asian offenders' (Ouseley, 2001, p. 11)
- *racial discrimination* in the labour market and workplace restricting equal opportunities for ethnic minorities (Ouseley, 2001, p. 12)
- *polarisation* of communities on racial, ethnic and religious lines, adversely affecting the education of young people (Ouseley, 2001, p. 13)
- *discrimination* and *self-segregation* through fear of harassment and violent crime
- *lack of facilities* to relieve boredom of young people and bring them together in multicultural activities
- *lack of consultation and participation* with minority ethnic communities over education
- *exclusion* of people – especially young people, women and Asian women in particular – from decision-making about policies and programmes to meet their needs (Ouseley, 2001, p. 11).

After the publication of the report and in the wake of the Bradford riots of July 2001, the chief executive of Bradford Vision, Martin Garratt, announced the setting up of a Bradford People Programme to respond to the main recommendations of the report to promote social and cultural mixing and good race relations, through: citizenship education in primary and secondary schools – to ensure all pupils learn about diversity and respect for others; creating a Centre for Diversity, Learning and Living to share resources and encourage development; a behavioural competency framework for the workplace, thereby ensuring organisations are aware of the diversity of social, cultural and religious communities; and adding equality and diversity conditions to all contracts for grant aid and public finance investments (Garratt, 2001, p. 4).

The Scarman and Ouseley reports illustrate significant changes occurring since the 1980s. Social problems of division and inter-communal conflict beset the inner cities as much now as 20 years ago. While concerns about racism and discrimination still endure, the debates about how to reduce them have shifted from global and general exhortations to specific initiatives aimed at promoting equality and celebrating diversity.

Two questions remain to be dealt with here: whether government policies can deliver significant improvements to people and what the implications of this are for social work.

Can government policies deliver improvements to the people?

Whether the Labour government can transform areas such as Brixton and Bradford described above is a difficult question to answer. The fact is that 20 years after the urban riots of 1981, such events are recurring, albeit in different towns, but where many of the social conditions of ethnic diversity and urban underachievement are similar. On one hand, the optimistic view holds out a radical prospect of empowered citizens meeting more of their potential because their needs are more adequately met. On the other hand, the pessimistic view is that existing policies risk continuing to exclude and stigmatise people.

There is no doubt that since 1998 the Labour government has focused social policy on strategic questions of how to regenerate deprived neighbourhoods. The SEU framework for consultation, published in 2000 (Social Exclusion Unit, 2000b, pp. 94–100), reiterates the intention to establish 'what works' and arrive at 'best value' strategies in neighbourhood renewal. It bases the proposed strategy on the main recommendations of the 18 PAT reports, summarised in Table 12.1.

Table 12.1 Summary of proposals in PAT reports

1.	Jobs	The disadvantages faced by unemployed people, especially those from ethnic minorities, in deprived areas need tackling by better engagement with and support for long-term unemployed people; anti-racist strategies in the labour market; more participation by employers in designing local employment schemes; removing disincentives to work; involving local bodies in services to unemployed people. (Policy Action Team 1, DfEE, 1999a)
2.	Skills	The disproportionate problems experienced by people in deprived areas in acquiring skills for the modern labour market can be tackled through more 'first-rung' provision to get people back into learning; locally run 'neighbourhood learning centres'; prioritising by the new Learning and Skills Council of skills needed in deprived areas. (Policy Action Team 2, DfEE, 1999b)
3.	Business	The revitalisation of deprived areas depends on the promotion of enterprise, through the leadership and support of the Small Business Service and finance for enterprise and self-employment from the government. (Policy Action Team 3, HM Treasury, 2000)
4.	Neighbourhood Management	Neighbourhood management should be developed on the basis of core principles; linking up local services to meet local needs; development through a pathfinder programme to test different models of implementation. (Policy Action Team 4, 2000)
5.	Housing Management	Deprivation can be tackled through high-quality, on-the-spot housing management: greater tenant involvement in self-managing their housing; more sensitive lettings policies; more use of caretakers; anti-discriminatory services. (Policy Action Team 5, DETR, 1999a)
6.	Neighbourhood Wardens	A dedicated team of neighbourhood wardens would help to reduce crime, disorder and the fear of crime; working closely with the police and promoting high standards agreed with the police. (Policy Action Team 6, Home Office, 2000)

Table 12.1 Continued

7. Unpopular Housing	Improved regional and local housing planning would result from comprehensive housing strategies covering home owners and tenants, linked with other services and with the involvement of ethnic minority communities; proactive housing management; increased flexibility in renting policies to encourage a social mix in social housing; selective demolition. (Policy Action Team 7, DETR, 1999b)
8. Antisocial Behaviour	Home Office and Crime and Disorder Partnerships would be responsible for addressing antisocial behaviour nationally and locally; Neighbourhood Agreements would set standards of behaviour; racist crime and harassment would be given priority attention. (Policy Action Team 8, SEU, 2000e)
9. Community Self-help	Grants for new and small community groups would be made from a new Community Resource Fund; the benefits system would be changed to encourage volunteering; the expertise of agencies working with local communities would be raised through a Community Charter Mark/Investors in Communities award; Neighbourhood Endowment Funds would be introduced; particular attention would be paid to ethnic minority groups in improving funding for capacity-building in local communities. (Policy Action Team 9, Home Office, 1999)
10. Arts and Sport	The contribution of arts and sport to regeneration would be enhanced; particular attention would be paid to activities promoting social inclusion. (Policy Action Team 10, DCMS, 1999)
11. Schools Plus	Reducing pupil underachievement in disadvantaged schools would involve a minimum of three hours a week study support for pupils; improving access to study support by extending school opening hours; creating Schools Plus Teams and activities; providing a range of support services through a network of school on-site Family Support Centres; improving teacher training in the area of Schools Plus; focusing Ofsted school and LEA inspections on community

Table 12.1   Continued

	activity; providing disadvantaged schools with adequate funds. (Policy Action Team 11, DfEE, 2000)
12. Young People	A shift from crisis intervention to prevention; improving existing services and creating new ones; involving young people in designing and delivering services. (Policy Action Team 12, DfEE, 2000a)
13. Shops	Efforts to halt the decline of shops in deprived areas would include more proactive community planning for local community needs; developing strategies for local retail; improving business and financial support; reducing tax and and other disincentives; prioritising measures to protect retailers against crime, including racist crime. (Policy Action Team 13, DH, 1999g)
14. Financial Services	The PAT report argued that access to financial services would make people's lives easier and save them money. Access to such services for the one and a half million low-income households who use no financial services would be improved by developing Post Offices, credit unions, Insurance with Rent schemes, reforming the Social Fund and widening access to financial advice and information. (Policy Action Team 14, HM Treasury, 1999)
15. Information Technology	Information and communication technologies (ICT) would be made available publicly in each neighbourhood; 'local champions' would encourage access to ICT; access to funding would be rationalised. (Policy Action Team 15, 2000)
16. Learning Lessons	Funding and peer training would be improved so that more local residents would be encouraged into becoming local community leaders and social entrepreneurs; national training would be overviewed to ensure that practitioners and professionals improved their working practices with each other and with local communities. (Policy Action Team 16, SEU, 2000g)
17. Joining it up Locally	Local strategic partnerships would be created within the new community planning

Table 12.1 Continued

	framework; neighbourhood renewal would be put onto the agenda of local government reform. (Policy Action Team 17, DETR, 2000a)
18. Better Information	Locally gathered neighbourhood statistics would be gathered by the Office for National Statistics (ONS), integrated into a coherent cross-government policy on relevant data and overseen by a ministerial group which would inform the development of the National Strategy for neighbourhood renewal. (Policy Action Team 18, SEU, 2000f)

Ethnic minorities

The Social Exclusion Unit has put forward proposals to address the deprivation of ethnic minorities:

> tackling racial discrimination in the labour market; involving people from ethnic minority communities more in the design and delivery of policies and services; implementing targeted programmes; tackling racist crime; and improving information about ethnic minority people. (Social Exclusion Unit, 2000b, p. 102)

Whether the Labour government adopts these, it still remains a matter for speculation whether they prove adequate to tackle the existing widespread racial discrimination which persists, in addition to problems of disproportionate deprivation affecting ethnic minorities. One problem is that the full extent of this discrimination and deprivation is not known. The SEU comments:

> There is a significant lack of data about ethnic minority groups. But it appears that people from ethnic minority backgrounds are disproportionately deprived. They are more likely than the rest of the population to live in poor areas, be unemployed, have low incomes, live in poor housing, have poor health and be victims of crime. (Social Exclusion Unit, 2000b, p. 101)

Social security: will poverty and gross inequalities be reduced significantly?

The categories of want have not changed significantly since Rowntree carried out the first survey of poverty (1901) and the first national insurance and pensions measures were legislated. They include: adults who become long-term unemployed and/or sick; disabled people; older people; families in poverty (family support); and children in poverty.

What can be learned from the problems of social security systems to date? Future social security policies need to address the issue of poverty and be less snarled up in complexities associated with the wish to prevent too many people benefiting when they are not in sufficient need. On the whole, the difficulties of social security systems are more associated with needy people not claiming benefits to which they *are* entitled.

We can use the six useful principles set out by John Ditch (1998, p. 276) as the basis for general statements about desirable social security provision:

- provision should be adequate to meet the needs of the individual, the household and the family
- benefits should be more comprehensive, on the grounds that reducing comprehensive benefits and relying more on safety net provision increases the possibility of people feeling stigmatised and not taking up benefits to which they are entitled
- benefits should be consistent across different areas such as criminal justice, employment, health and housing; people in similar circumstances should be dealt with in similar ways
- social security systems should respond flexibly to the circumstances of individuals rather than individuals having to meet the inflexible demands of the system
- benefits should be easy to understand, claim, apply and administer; benefits should be flexible and responsive at short notice to the changing circumstances, and sometimes crises, of individuals
- benefits should not be discriminatory between people, in terms of such aspects as gender, age, race, religion, where they are living, disability or sexual orientation.

Employment: will full employment be restored?

The SEU is putting faith in the goal of 'promoting enterprise in deprived areas' as a key to revitalising them. PAT 3 recommends that

> the Small Business Service should have a clear remit to promote enterprise and business growth in such areas by harnessing all available support and providing a clear lead; and the Government should encourage new initiatives to provide

finance for enterprise activity and promote self-employment. (Social Exclusion Unit, 2000b, p. 94)

However, the question as to how to attain full employment (see Chapter 3) remains wide open.

Healthcare: will the health of the nation be improved?

The failures of the health service to meet performance targets are well documented. The emphasis of Labour government policy is on increasing investment in privately funded healthcare (through PFI and PPPs) and encouraging private health insurance. But the rates of disease and death remain far higher in poorer households. Even if the government gave free school dinners to families receiving working families tax credit, which it has not, it is difficult to envisage this, or other modest benefit increases or health education measures significantly reducing the growing health and healthcare inequalities among children and young people, which impact on their learning and their future quality of life.

The major question, therefore, is whether the government can rely on partnerships between public and private funding to rectify the manifest shortcomings in the NHS and healthcare.

Social services for children and families and community care

The performance targets being demanded of the personal social services are being raised, yet the necessary resources to meet the identified levels of need are not being provided. If the personal social services, and social work, are to meet their targets, they should be adequately resourced and universalistic, throughout the life course, services for all (as they were more than half a century earlier), rather than a 'fire brigade' providing stigmatising services for a few so-called 'sad, mad, bad, needy or inadequate' people.

Youth justice

How far will youth justice policies go towards curbing youth crime? The central policies of Labour are a mixture of punitive custodial and community-based sentences plus individually focused programmes aimed at correcting cognitive deficits and modifying offending behaviour (see Chapter 7). The key question is whether these responses to crime will connect with the factors contributing to youth crime, especially those lying in the social environment of offenders.

What are the implications for social workers?

Finally, we consider the key questions arising from social policy changes which in future are likely to affect social workers. The general question is, what kind of social work will there be in the future? This raises further questions: How far will it be permeated by pan-European or global visions of social work? Will there be a social work profession or will social work be one of a number of adjuncts to other larger professional clusters, such as healthcare. Will social workers engage in significantly different activities in the future to tasks they carry out now?

What future for social services and social work?

The organisations called social services departments are undergoing radical metamorphoses. In England, some are combining with other departments such as housing, or are labelled with new titles such as environmental and public protection, remote from social care and social work. In some areas of practice such as community care, social services has become the collaborating partner with health services. By April 2002, aspects of education and social services will have merged into new integrated children's departments. In family work, youth justice and mental health work, it is often the role and responsibilities of the practitioner which is visible in job descriptions and advertisements for people to fill posts.

The Health Act 1999 encourages social care and health bodies to experiment with joint provision and pooled budgets. In localities with services judged as weak, the minister can intervene to direct health authorities and social services departments to form new care Trusts, accountable to the NHS. In theory, this would have the advantage of improving the coordination of health and social care in community care and work with older people requiring medical as well as social support. In practice, though, it might lead to geriatric services and community care moving lower down the list of priorities in the competition with high-profile medicine and surgery for scarce resources. Another possibility is that the unity in generic services achieved by Seebohm will be lost, as the diversity of services for families, children, people with mental health problems and disabilities are fragmented and distributed to newly created independent service-providing Trusts.

Some key social work services are prioritised on the basis of assessment of the degree of risk, to the individual or to relatives, friends or others, if no intervention takes place. Terms such as therapy and casework have been replaced by the culture of risk management, resource management, rationing, gatekeeping, person protection and social control.

Whatever legislative, organisational and professional context is provided, social work probably will continue to provide a service to clients which is distinct from other branches of the health and social services, including social care. Social workers are likely to continue to carry statutory responsibilities, unlike those of social care workers and agencies, when exercising powers and duties under legislation in childcare, mental health and criminal justice. These are practical reasons why, if social work was abolished today, it probably would be reinvented tomorrow. Specifically, social work duties and powers, particularly in childcare, criminal justice and mental health, are likely to continue to form the basis for the uniqueness of social work as a profession. Social work is likely to expand into new areas such as employment, guidance and counselling work. Proposed arrangements for the registration of social workers by the General Social Care Council (GSCC) which replaced CCETSW in October 2001 and the introduction of three-year qualifying courses for social workers reflects the likelihood that social work with particular client groups – in childcare and mental health, for example – will be a specialist activity in the wider continuum of social care functions at present carried out by local authority social services departments. Social work as a profession, therefore, will be subject to continuing change.

In some areas of work, such as community care and youth justice, the trend may be towards the creation of new meta-professionals – 'community care practitioner' and 'youth justice worker'. Collaboration and teamwork will become more extensive, where joint responsibilities make joint working appropriate.

There is a risk that the contract culture will lead to the cheapest service being developed rather than the best value service, as the report of the King's Fund inquiry chaired by Julia Unwin concludes that urgent action is needed to improve the status, image, training threshold and financial rewards to care staff, including social services spending at least an additional £700 m per year (Unwin, 2001).

Chapter summary

This chapter has considered the major factors affecting the future of social policy and social work. It has reviewed the current government goals of different policy areas examined in this book and the likelihood of services fulfilling the needs of clients. It has examined some of the main implications for the future of social work, of working in the context of the persistent problems of poverty, urban decay, inequality, divisions and racism which permeate society.

Further reading

Giddens, A. (1998) *The Third Way: The Renewal of Social Democracy*, Polity Press, Cambridge

Lewis, G., Gewirtz, S. and Clarke, J. (eds) (2000) *Rethinking Social Policy*, Open University, Buckingham with Sage, London.

Appendices

Appendix 1

Abbreviations

ACPO	Association of Chief Police Officers
ACU	Active Community Unit
ADHD	attention deficit hyperactivity disorder
AHA	Area Health Authority
AIDS	acquired immune deficiency syndrome
ASW	Approved Social Worker (England)
Bid	Bail for Immigration Detainees
BLs	Business Links
CBI	Confederation of British Industry
CC	County Council
CCT	compulsory competitive tendering
CDP	community development project
CEPR	Centre for Economic Policy Research
CFI	Community Finance Initiative
CHE	community home with education (on the premises)
CHI	Commission for Health Improvement
CND	Campaign for Nuclear Disarmament
COS	Charity Organisation Society
CPA	Care Programme Approach
CPS	Centre for Policy Studies
CRE	Commission for Racial Equality
C(RS)A	Carers (Recognition and Services) Act 1995
CSA	Child Support Agency
CSDPA	Chronically Sick and Disabled Persons Act 1970
CSJ	Commission on Social Justice (led to Borrie Report 1994)
DCMS	Department for Culture, Media and Sport
DES	Department of Education and Science
DETR	Department of the Environment, Transport and the Regions

DfEE	Department for Education and Employment
DH	Department of Health
DHA	District Health Authority
DHSS	Department of Health and Social Security
DMT	District Management Team
DPEA	Disabled Persons (Employment) Act 1958
DP(SCR)A	Disabled Persons (Services, Consultation and Representation) Act 1986
DRC	Disability Rights Commissioner
DSO	Direct Service Organisation
DSS	Department of Social Security
DTI	Department of Trade and Industry
DTTO	drug treatment and testing order
EC	European Community
EEC	European Economic Community
eLSC	Electronic Library for Social Care
EMU	European Monetary Union
EOC	Equal Opportunities Commission
EPA	educational priority area
ESRC	Economic and Social Research Council
EU	European Union
FHSA	Family Health Service Authority
FIS	Family Income Supplement
FLA	Family Law Act 1996
FMI	Financial Management Initiative
FPC	Family Practitioner Committee
FSA	Financial Services Authority
GDP	gross domestic product
GGE	general government expenditure
GLC	Greater London Council
GMC	General Medical Council
GNP	gross national product
GP	general practitioner
GSCC	General Social Care Council
HEA	Health Education Authority
HIV	human immuno-deficiency virus
HMT	HM Treasury
HSPHA	Health Services and Public Health Act 1968
ICT	information and communication technology
IdeA	Improvement and Development Agency
IEA	Institute for Economic Affairs

IFS	Institute for Fiscal Studies
IGO	intergovernmental organisation
IISS	International Institute for Strategic Studies
ILO	International Labour Organisation
IPPR	Institute for Public Policy Research
IRS	Industrial Relations Service
IS	Income Support
JSA	Jobseeker's Allowance
LASSA	Local Authority Social Services Act 1970
LEA	Local Education Authority
LETs	Local Exchange Trading Schemes
LGA	Local Government Association
LGIU	Local Government Information Unit
LPC	Low Pay Commission
LPU	Low Pay Unit
MAP	Management Action Plan (under Quality Protects)
MBC	Metropolitan Borough Council
MHA	Mental Health Act 1959 or 1983
MHO	Mental Health Officer (Scotland)
MoH	Ministry of Health
MP	Member of Parliament
MPH	methylphenidate (ritalin)
NAA	National Assistance Act 1948
NAYJ	National Association for Youth Justice
NAPO	National Association of Probation Officers
NCH	National Children's Homes
NCQA	National Commission for Quality Assurance
NCR	New Commitment to Regeneration
NCSC	National Care Standards Commission
NDC	New Deal for Communities
NDDP	New Deal for Disabled People
NEDC	National Economic Development Council
NEDO	National Economic Development Office
New TSN	New Targeting Social Need (Initiative) (Northern Ireland)
NGO	nongovernmental organisation
NHS	National Health Service
NHSA	National Health Services Act 1977
NHSCCA	National Health Service and Community Care Act 1990
NHSME	National Health Service Management Executive

NSPCC	National Society for the Prevention of Cruelty to Children
OECD	Organisation for Economic Co-operation and Development
Ofsted	Office for Standards in Education
ONS	Office for National Statistics
PACE	Police and Criminal Evidence Act 1984
PAF	Performance Assessment Framework
PAT	Policy Action Team (of SEU)
PEP	Priority Estates Project
PFI	private finance initiative
PI	performance indicator
PIU	Performance and Innovation Unit
PHC	Primary Health Care
PO	Probation Officer
PPP	public private partnership
PRP	Performance Related Pay
PSBR	Public Sector Borrowing Requirement
PSI	Promoting Social Inclusion (Northern Ireland)
PSO	Probation Service Officer
QP	Quality Protects (programme)
RDA	Regional Development Agency
RHA	Regional Health Authority
RHA	Registered Homes Act 1984
RLC	Refugee Legal Centre
RSL	registered social landlord
SB	Supplementary Benefit
SBA	Supplementary Benefits Act 1976
SBS	Small Business Service
SCG	Social Care Group
SCR	Social Care Region/s
SEU	Social Exclusion Unit
SRB	Single Regeneration Budget
SSI	Social Services Inspectorate
SSIN	Scottish Social Inclusion Network
TEC	Training and Enterprise Council
TQM	Total Quality Management
UA	Urban Alliance
UK	United Kingdom
UN	United Nations
UNHCR	United Nations High Commissioner for Refugees

USSR	Union of Soviet Socialist Republics
VAT	value added tax
WFTC	Working Families Tax Credit
WHO	World Health Organization
YJB	Youth Justice Board
YOI	young offender institution
YOT	youth offending team

Appendix 2

Key Dates: Legislation

1834   Poor Law Amendment Act
1882   Married Women's Property Act
1908   Children Act
1911   National Insurance Act
1920   Dangerous Drugs Act
1926   Adoption of Children Act
1933   Children and Young Persons Act
1934   Unemployment Act
1944   Disabled Persons (Employment) Act
1946   National Insurance Act
1948   National Assistance Act
1948   Children Act
1948   The United Nations Universal Declaration of Human Rights
1958   Disabled Persons (Employment) Act
1959   Mental Health Act
1963   Children and Young Persons Act
1968   Health Services and Public Health Act
1968   Social Work (Scotland) Act
1969   Children and Young Persons Act
1970   Chronically Sick and Disabled Persons Act
1970   Law Reform Miscellaneous Provisions Act
1970   Local Authority Social Services Act
1971   Immigration Act
1971   Misuse of Drugs Act
1972   Local Government Act
1973   Matrimonial Causes Act
1973   Powers of Criminal Courts Act
1975   Child Benefit Act
1975   Social Security Benefit Act
1975   Sex Discrimination Act

1976	Adoption Act
1976	Race Relations Act
1976	Supplementary Benefits Act
1977	National Health Services Act
1977	Rent Act
1977	Protection from Eviction Act
1978	Domestic Proceedings and Magistrates' Courts Act
1980	Children Act
1980	Registered Homes Act
1982	Criminal Justice Act
1983	Health and Social Services and Social Security Adjudications Act
1983	Mental Health Act
1984	Police and Criminal Evidence Act
1984	Health and Social Security Act
1984	Public Health (Control of Disease) Act
1984	Registered Homes Act
1985	Landlord and Tenant Act
1985	Housing Act
1985	Public Order Act
1985	Prosecution of Offences Act
1986	Social Security Act
1986	Disabled Persons (Service, Consultation and Representation) Act
1988	Criminal Justice Act
1988	Housing Act
1988	Local Government Finance Act
1988	Social Security Act
1989	Children Act
1990	National Health Service and Community Care Act
1991	Child Support Act
1991	Criminal Justice Act
1991	Criminal Procedure (Insanity and Unfitness to Plead) Act
1992	Education (Schools) Act
1992	Local Government Finance Act
1993	Probation Services Act
1993	Asylum and Immigration Appeals Act
1994	Criminal Justice and Public Order Act
1995	Carers (Recognition and Services) Act
1995	Children (Scotland) Act
1995	Child Support Act

1995   Criminal Injuries Compensation Act
1995   Disability Discrimination Act
1995   Mental Health (Patients in the Community) Act
1996   School Inspections Act
1996   Asylum and Immigration Act
1996   Community Care (Direct Payments) Act
1996   Direct Payments Act
1996   Education Act
1996   Family Law Act
1996   Housing Act
1996   Sex Offenders' Act
1997   The Housing (Homeless Persons) Act
1997   Protection from Harassment Act
1997   Crime (Sentences) Act
1997   Police Act
1998   Crime and Disorder Act
1998   Human Rights Act
1998   National Minimum Wage Act
1998   School Standards and Framework Act
1998   Social Security Act
1999   Health Act
1999   Access to Justice Act
1999   Local Government Act
1999   Protection of Children Act
1999   Welfare Reform and Pensions Act
2000   Child Support, Pensions and Social Security Act
2000   Local Government Act
2000   Youth Justice and Criminal Evidence Act
2000   Care Standards Act
2001   Criminal Justice and Police Act

Appendix 3

Internet Addresses of Main Sources of Information on Policy and Research

Barnardo's	www.barnardos.org.uk
Children's Society	www.the-childrens-society.org.uk
Commission for Racial Equality	http://www.cre.gov.uk/
Daycare Trust	http://www.daycaretrust.org.uk
Department of the Environment, Transport and the Regions	http://www.detr.gov.uk
Department of Health	http://www.doh.gov.uk
EOC (Scotland)	http://www.scotland.gov.uk/inclusion/ssin09.htm
Electronic Library for Social Care	info@elsc.org.uk
Employment Service	http://www.employmentservice.gov.uk
Government Information and Departments	http://www.open.gov.uk
Government (London) Treasury	http://www/hm-treasury.gov.uk
Joseph Rowntree Foundation	http://www.jrf.org.uk/bookshop/
King's Fund, The	www.kingsfund.org.uk
Legislation in process	http://www.parliament.the-stationery-office.co.uk
Low Pay Commission	http://www.lowpay.gov.uk
Mental Health Foundation	www.mentalhealth.org.uk
NACRO Youth Crime Section	info@nacroycs.demon.co.uk
National Association for Youth Justice	www.nayj.org.uk
New Deal	http://www.newdeal.gov.uk
Northern Ireland Information Service	http://www.nio.gov.uk
New TSN and PSI (N. Ireland)	www.dfpni.gov.uk
NSPCC	http://www.nspcc.org.uk

OECD   www.oecd.org/publications
Policy Press   tpp@bristol.ac.uk
Scottish Office/Scottish Executive   http://www.scotland.gov.uk
Social Exclusion Unit (London)
                                    www.cabinet_office.gov.uk/seu/index.htm
Visible Women Campaign   www.open.gov.uk/cre/crehome
Web Journal of Current Legal
    Issues No. 1   http://webjcli.ncl.ac.uk
Who Cares Trust   http://www.thewhocarestrust.org.uk

Bibliography

Abel-Smith, B. and Townsend, P. (1965) *The Poor and the Poorest*, Bell & Son, London

Adams, R. (1991) *Protests by Pupils: Empowerment, Schooling and the State*, Falmer, Brighton

Adams, R. (1994) *Prison Riots in Britain and the USA*, Macmillan, Basingstoke – now Palgrave

Adams, R. (1996a) *The Personal Social Services: Clients, Consumers or Citizens?* Addison Wesley Longman, Harlow

Adams, R. (1996b) *Social Work and Empowerment*, BASW/Macmillan, Basingstoke – now Palgrave

Adams, R. (1997) 'Empowerment, Marketisation and Social Work', in L. Bogdan (ed.) *Change in Social Work*, Arena, Aldershot, pp. 69–87

Adams, R. (1998a) *Quality Social Work*, Macmillan, Basingstoke – now Palgrave

Adams, R. (1998b) 'Empowerment and Protest', in L. Bogdan (ed.) *Challenging Discrimination in Social Work*, Ashgate, Aldershot

Adams, R. (1998c) *The Abuses of Punishment*, Macmillan, Basingstoke – now Palgrave

Adams, R., Dominelli, L. and Payne, M. (1998) 'Introduction', in R. Adams, L. Dominelli and M. Payne (eds) *Social Work: Themes, Issue and Critical Debates*, Macmillan, Basingstoke – now Palgrave, pp. xv–xviii

Adams, A., Erath, P. and Shardlow, S. (eds) (2000) *Fundamentals of Social Work in Selected European Countries*, Russell House, Lyme Regis

Alcock, P. (1996) *Social Policy in Britain: Themes and Issues*, Basingstoke, Macmillan – now Palgrave

Alcock, P. (1997) *Understanding Poverty*, 2nd edn, Basingstoke, Macmillan – now Palgrave

Alcock, P., Erskine, A. and May, M. (eds) (1998) *The Student's Companion to Social Policy*, Blackwell, Oxford

Allen, I. (2001) *Stress Among Ward Sisters and Charge Nurses*, Policy Studies Institute, London

Allsop, J. (1995) *Health Policy and the NHS: Towards 2000*, 2nd edn, Pearson, Harlow

Altenstetter, C. and Björkman, J.W. (eds) (1997) *Health Policy Reform, National Variations and Globalization*, Macmillan, with International Political Science Association, London

Amnesty (1994) *Prisoners without a Voice: Asylum-seekers Detained in the United Kingdom*, Amnesty International, London

Anderson, E. (1990) *The Three Worlds of Welfare Capitalism*, Princeton University Press, Princeton

Arnold, M. and Laskey, H. (1985) *Children of the Poor Clares: The Story of an Irish Orphanage*, Appletree Press, Belfast

Ascher, K. (1987) *The Politics of Privatisation: Contracting Out in Public Services*, Macmillan, Basingstoke – now Palgrave

Atkinson, M. and Elliott, L. (2000) 'UK Fails to Provide Path from School to Work', *The Guardian*, 11 February, p. 6

Atkinson, R. and Durden, P. (1994) 'Housing Policy Since 1979: Developments and Prospects' in S. Savage, R. Atkinson and L. Robins (eds) *Public Policy in Britain*, Macmillan, Basingstoke – now Palgrave, pp. 182–202

Auckland, R. (1997) 'Women and Protest', in C. Barker and M. Tyldesley (eds) *Third International Conference on Alternative Futures and Popular Protest*, Vol. 1, Manchester Metropolitan University, Manchester, pp. 1–12

Audit Commission (1986) *Making a Reality of Community Care*, HMSO, London

Audit Commission (1992) *The Community Revolution: Personal Social Services and Community Care*, HMSO, London

Audit Commission (1996) *Misspent Youth. Young People and Crime*, Audit Commission, London

Audit Commission (2000) *Another Country*, Audit Commission, London

Awaih, J., Butt, S. and Dorn, H. (1990) 'The Last Place I Would Go: Black People and Drug Services in Britain', *Druglink*, Sept/Oct

Awaih, J., Butt, S. and Dorn, H. (1992) *Race, Gender and Drug Services*, Research Monograph No. 6, Institute for the Study of Drug Dependence, London

Bailey, R. and Williams, B. (2000) *Inter-agency Partnerships in Youth Justice: Implementing the Crime and Disorder Act 1998*, Social Service Monograph, Department of Sociological Studies, Sheffield University, Sheffield

Bains Report (1972) *The New Local Authorities: Management and Structure*, HMSO, London

Balding, J. (1998) *Young People and Illegal Drugs in 1998*, Schools Health Education Unit, London

Baldock, J. and Ungerson, C. (1994) *Becoming Consumers of Community Care*, Joseph Rowntree Foundation, York

Ball, C., Harris, R., Roberts, G. and Vernon, S. (1988) *The Law Report: Teaching and Assessment of Law in Social Work Education*, CCETSW, London

Balogh, T. (1941) 'Work For All', *Picture Post*, 4 January, pp. 10–12

Barker, K., Chalkley, M., Malcomson, J.M. and Montgomery, J. (1997) 'Contracting in the National Health Service: Legal and Economic Issues', in R. Flynn and G. Williams (eds) *Contracting For Health: Quasi-Markets and the National Health Service*, Oxford University Press, Oxford, pp. 82–97

Barker, R., Jones, J., Saradjian, J. and Wardell, R. (1998) *Abuse in Early Years: Report of the Independent Inquiry into Shieldfield Nursery and Related Events*, Newcastle upon Tyne City Council, Newcastle upon Tyne

Bateman, N. (2000) 'Making a Hard Life Harder', *Community Care*, 20–26 April, (1318):29

Becker, S. (ed.) (1995) *Young Carers in Europe: An Exploratory Cross-national Study in Britain, France, Sweden and Germany*, Loughborough University, Loughborough

Becker, S. and Aldridge, J. (1995) 'Young Carers in Britain', in S. Becker (1995), pp. 1–25

Bereseford, P. and Croft, S. (1993) *Citizen Involvement: A Practical Guide for Change*, BASW/Macmillan, Basingstoke – now Palgrave

Berridge, D. (1997) *Foster Care: A Research Review*, Stationery Office, London

Berridge, D. and Broide, I. (1998) *Children's Homes Revisited*, Jessica Kingsley, London

Bertoud, R., Brown, J.C. and Cooper, S. (1981) *Poverty and the Development of Anti-Poverty Policy in the UK*, Policy Studies Institute, London

Beveridge, W. (1942) *Social Insurance and Allied Services*, Cmnd 6404, HMSO, London

Beveridge, W. (1944) *Full Employment in a Free Society*, Allen & Unwin, London

Bilton, K. (2000) 'Making Choices on Our Children's Future', *Professional Social Work*, October, p. 2

Bird, L. (1999) *The Fundamental Facts*, Mental Health Foundation, London

Björkman, J.W. and Altenstetter, C. (1997) 'Globalized Concepts and Localized Practice: Convergence in National Health Policy Reforms', in C. Altenstetter and J.W. Björkman (eds) *Health Policy Reform, National Variations and Globalization*, Macmillan, with International Political Science Association, London, pp. 1–16

Blom-Cooper, L. (1985) *A Child in Trust: the Report of the Panel of Inquiry into the Circumstances Surrounding the Death of Jasmine Beckford*, London Borough of Brent, London

Blom-Cooper, L., Murphy, E. and Hally, H. (1995) *The Falling Shadow*, South Devon Health-Care Trust, Torquay

Bluglass, R. and Bowden, P. (1990) *Principles and Practice of Forensic Psychiatry,* Churchill Livingstone, Edinburgh

Booth, C. (1889) *Life and Labour of the People in London* (17 volumes) Macmillan, Basingstoke – now Palgrave

Bowlby, J. (1951) *Maternal Care and Mental Health*, World Health Organization, Geneva

Bowlby, J. (1965) *Child Care and the Growth of Love*, Penguin, Harmondsworth

Boyd, W.D. (1994) *A Preliminary Report on Homicide*, Steering Committee of the Confidential Inquiry into Homicides and Suicides by Mentally Ill People, London

Boynton, Sir J. (1980) *Report of the Review of Rampton Hospital* (Chairman Sir John Boynton) Cmnd 8073, HMSO, London

Bradley, G. and Manthorpe, J. (1997) *Dilemmas of Financial Assessment*, Venture Press, Birmingham

Bradshaw, J. (1998) 'Lone Parents', in P. Alcock, A. Erskine and M. May (eds) pp. 263–9

Brandon, D. (1993) *Advocacy: Power to People with Disabilities*, Venture Press, Birmingham

Braye, S. and Preston-Shoot, M. (1990) 'On Teaching and Applying the Law in Social Work: It is not that simple', *British Journal of Social Work*, **20**(4):333–53.

Brayne, H. and Martin, G. (1999) *Law for Social Workers*, Blackstone Press, London

Brechin, A. (2000) 'Introducing Critical Practice', in A. Brechin, H. Brown and M.A. Eby (eds) *Critical Practice in Health and Social Care*, Sage, London, pp. 25–47

Brindle, D. (1999) 'Despite the Red Nose Jollity', *The Guardian*, 13 March, p. 4

British Association of Social Workers (BASW) (1995) *Statement: Mental Health (Patients in the Community) Act 1995*, BASW, Birmingham

British Association of Social Workers (BASW) (1997) *Whistleblowers: Guidance for Social Services on Free Expressions of Staff Concerns*, BASW, Birmingham

British Association of Social Workers Scotland (2000) *Response to the Consultation Paper on Modernising Social Work Services: Workforce Regulation and Education*, BASW Scotland, Edinburgh

Brown, D. (1990) *Black People, Mental Health and the Courts*, NACRO, London

Brown, E., Bullock, R., Hudson, C. and Little, M. (1998) *Making Residential Care Work: Structure and Culture in Children's Homes*, Ashgate, Aldershot

Browne, K. (1995) 'Child Abuse: Defining, Understanding and Intervening', in K. Wilson and A. James (eds) *The Child Protection Handbook*, Baillière Tindall, London pp. 43–65

Bullock, R., Little, M. and Millham, S. (1998) *Secure Treatment Outcomes*, Ashgate, Aldershot

Burchardt, T., Hills, J. and Propper, C. (1999) *Private Policy and Public Welfare*, Joseph Rowntree Foundation, York

Burden, T., Cooper, C. and Petrie, S. (2000) *Modernising Social Policy: Unravelling New Labour's Welfare Reforms*, Ashgate, Aldershot

Burnett, R. (1996) *Fitting Supervision to Offenders: Assessment and Allocation Decisions in the Probation Service: Home Office Research Study 153*, Home Office, London

Butler-Sloss, E., Right Honourable Lord Justice, DBE (1987) *Report of the Inquiry into Child Abuse in Cleveland*, Cm 412, HMSO, London

Campbell, B. (1984) *Wigan Pier Revisited: Poverty and Politics in the 80s*, Virago, London

Campbell, B. (1999) 'Second-class Citizens', *Community Care*, 7–13 October, (1293):14

Cannan, C. and Warren, C. (eds) (1997) *Social Action with Children and Families: A Community Development Approach to Child and Family Welfare*, Routledge, London

Cannan, C., Berry, L. and Lyons, K. (1992) *Social Work and Europe*, BASW/Macmillan, Basingstoke – now Palgrave

Carlen, P. (1994) 'The Governance of Homelessness', *Critical Social Policy*, **14**:18–33

Carlen, P. and Tchaikovsky, C. (1996) 'Women's Imprisonment in England at the End of the Twentieth Century: Legitimacy, Realities and Utopias', in R. Matthews and P. Francis (eds) *Prisons 2000: An International Perspective on the Current State and Future of Imprisonment*, Macmillan, Basingstoke – now Palgrave, pp. 201–18

Carling, A. (1991) *Social Division*, Verso, London

Cavadino, P. and Bell, T. (1999) *Going Straight Home*, NACRO, London

Cavadino, M. and Dignan, J. (1997) *The Penal System: An Introduction*, 2nd edn, Sage, London

Central Advisory Council for Education (1967) *Children and Their Primary Schools: A Report of the Central Advisory Council for England* (Plowden Committee) HMSO, London

Chadda, D. (2000) 'A Long Overdue Review', *Community Care*, 2–8 November, (1346):12

Chapman, T. and Hough, M. (1998) *Evidence Based Practice: A Guide to Effective Practice*, Home Office, London

Chetwynd, M. and Ritchie, J. (1996) *The Cost of Care: The Impact of Charging Policy on the Lives of Disabled People*, Joseph Rowntree Foundation, York

Church Hill House Hospital Inquiry (1979) *Inquiry into Allegations Made in Respect of Church Hill House Hospital, Bracknell*, Berkshire Area Health Authority, Reading

Church, J. and Summerfield, C. (1996) *Social Focus on Ethnic Minorities*, HMSO, London

Clarke, M. and Stewart, J.D. (1992) 'Empowerment: A Theme for the 1990s', *Local Government Studies*, **18**(2):18–26

Clements, L. (1999) 'Screening Service Users', *Community Care*, 21–27 October, (1295):28

Clothier, C., MacDonald, C.A. and Shaw, D.A. (1994) *The Allitt Inquiry, Independent Inquiry Relating to Deaths and Injuries on the Children's Ward at Grantham and Kesteven General Hospital During the Period February to April 1991*, HMSO, London

Cochrane, A. (1996) 'From Theories to Practices: Looking for Local Democracy in Britain', in D. King and G. Stoker (eds) *Rethinking Local Democracy*, Macmillan, Basingstoke – now Palgrave, pp. 193–213

Cohen, S. (2001) *Immigration Controls, the Family and the Welfare State*, Jessica Kingsley, London

Commission for Racial Equality (1992) *Cautions v. Prosecutions'*, Commission for Racial Equality, London

Commission of the European Communities (1993) *Employment in Europe*, Commission of the European Communities, Brussels

Commission on Social Justice (1994) *Social Justice: Strategies for National Renewal: The Report of the Commission on Social Justice* (The Borrie Report), Vintage, Random House, London

Committee of Inquiry (1992) *Report of the Committee of Inquiry into Complaints About Ashworth Hospital*, HMSO, London

Community Care (2000) Editorial Comment, (1310):15

Confidential Inquiry (1996) *Report of the Confidential Inquiry into Homicides and Suicides by Mentally Ill People*, Royal College of Psychiatrists, London

Cooke, J. and Marshall, J. (1996) 'Homeless Women', in K. Abel, S. Buszewicz, S. Davison, S. Johnson and E. Staples (eds) *Planning Community Mental Health Services for Women*, Routledge, London

Cookson, H. (1992) 'Alcohol Use and Offence Type in Young Offenders', *British Journal of Criminology*, **32**(3):352–60

Corner, L. (1997) Women's Participation in Decision-making and Leadership: A Global Perspective. Paper given at Conference on Women in Decisionmaking in Cooperatives held by Asian Women in Cooperative Development Forum (ACWF) and the International Co-operative Alliance Regional Office for Asia and the Pacific (ICAROAP) on 7–9 May at Tagatay City, Phillippines. Published as *Women in Decision-Making in Co-operatives: Report of a Regional Conference* by ACWF and ICAROAP.

Cosis Brown, H. (1998) *Social Work with Lesbian Women and Gay Men*, Macmillan, Basingstoke – now Palgrave

Costhill Hospital Inquiry (1980) *Report of the Committee of Inquiry into Mental Handicap Services*, Oxfordshire Area Health Authority, Oxford

Cox, L. (1997) 'Reflexivity, Social Transformation and Counter Culture', in C. Barker and M. Tyldesley (eds) *Third International Conference on Alternative Futures and Popular Protest*, Vol. 1, Manchester Metropolitan University, Manchester pp. 1–15

Craig, G. (1998) 'The Privatization of Human Misery', *Critical Social Policy*, **18**(1):51–76

Craig, G. and Manthorpe, J. (1999a) 'Small but Imperfectly Formed', *Community Care*, 14–20 October, (1294):25

Craig, G. and Manthorpe, J. (1999b) *Unfinished Business: Local Government Reorganisation and Social Services*, Policy Press, Bristol

Creighton, S.J. (1995) 'Patterns and Outcomes', in K. Wilson and A. James (eds) *The Child Protection Handbook*, Baillière Tindall, London, pp. 5–26

Crichton, J. (ed.) (1995) *Psychiatric Patient Violence: Risk and Response*, Duckworth, London

Croft, S. and Beresford, P. (1995) 'Whose Empowerment? Equalising the Competing Discourses in Community Care', in R. Jacks (ed.) *Empowerment in Community Care*, Chapman Hall, London, pp. 59–73

Crowley, A. (1998) *A Criminal Waste: A Study of Child Offenders Eligible for Secure Training Centres*, Children's Society, London

Curtis, M., CBE (1946) *Report of the Care of Children Committee*, Cmnd 6922, HMSO, London

Darlington Memorial Hospital Inquiry (1976) *Report of the Committee of Inquiry*, Northern Regional Health Authority, Newcastle upon Tyne

Darvill, G. and Smale, G. (eds) (1990) *Partners in Empowerment: Networks of Innovation in Social Work*, NISW, London

Davies, N., Lingham, R., Prior, C. and Sims, A. (1995) *Report of the Inquiry into the Circumstance Leading to the Death of Jonathan Newby (a volunteer worker) on 9 October 1993 in Oxford*, Oxfordshire Health Authority, Oxford

Dean, H. (ed) (1999) *Begging Questions*, Policy Press, Bristol

Dearden, C. and Becker, S. (2000) *Growing Up Caring: Vulnerability and Transition to Adulthood – Young Carer's Experiences*, National Youth Agency, Leicester

Department for Culture, Media and Sport (DCMS) (1999) *Report of Policy Action Team 10: Arts and Sport*, DCMS London

Department for Education and Employment (DfEE) (1988) *Learning to Succeed*, White Paper, Stationery Office, London

Department for Education and Employment (DfEE) (1999a) *Report of Policy Action Team 1: Jobs for All*, TSO, London

Department for Education and Employment (DfEE) (1999b) *Report of Policy Action Team 2: Skills for Neighbourhood Renewal – Local Solutions*, TSO, London

Department for Education and Employment (2000) *Report of Policy Action Team 11: School Plus: Building Learning Communities: Improving the Educational Chances of Children and Young People from Disadvantaged Areas*, Department for Education and Employment, London

Department for Education and Employment (DfEE) (2000a) *Report of Policy Action Team 12: Young People*, TSO, London

Department of the Environment, Transport and the Regions (1998) *Modern Local Government: In Touch with the People*, White Paper, Cm 4014, Stationery Office, London

Department of the Environment, Transport and the Regions (DETR) (1999a) *Report of Policy Action Team 5: Housing Management*, DETR, London

Department of the Environment, Transport and the Regions (1999b) *Report of Policy Action Team 7: Unpopular Housing*, DETR, London

Department of the Environment, Transport and the Regions (2000) *Quality and Choice: A Decent Home for All*, The Housing Green Paper, Summary, DETR, London

Department of the Environment, Transport and the Regions (2000a) *Report of Policy Action Team 17: Joining It Up Locally*, DETR, London

Department of Health (1989) *Caring for People: Community Care in the Next Decade and Beyond*, White Paper, Cmnd 849, HMSO, London

Department of Health (1990) *Care in the Community, Making it Happen*, HMSO, London

Department of Health (1992a) *The Health of the Nation – A Strategy for Health in England*, White Paper, Cmnd 1986, HMSO, London

Department of Health (1992b) *Choosing with Care: The Report of the Committee of Inquiry into the Selection, Development and Management of Staff in Children's Homes*, HMSO, London

Department of Health (1992c) *The Patient's Charter*, Department of Health, London

Department of Health (1998) *New Ambitions for our Country: A New Contract for Welfare*, Green Paper, Cm 3805, Stationery Office, London

Department of Health (1998a) *Modernising Social Services*, White Paper, Cm 4169, Stationery Office, London

Department of Health (1998b) *The Government's Response to the Children's Safeguards Review*, Cm 4105, HMSO, London

Department of Health (1998c) *Partnership for Equality*, HMSO, London

Department of Health (1999) *A New Contract for Welfare: Children's Rights and Parents' Responsibilities*, White Paper, Cm 4349, Stationery Office, London

Department of Health (1999) *A New Contract for Welfare: Partnership in Pensions*, Green Paper, Cm 4179, Stationery Office, London

Department of Health (1999a) *Regulating Private and Voluntary Healthcare: The Way Forward*, Department of Health, London

Department of Health (1999b) *Children Looked After in England, 1998/99* Bulletin 1999/26 update 17 March 2000, Department of Health, London

Department of Health (1999c) *Modern Social Services – A Commitment to Improve*, The 8th Annual Report of the Chief Inspector of Social Services 1998/1999, Department of Health, London

Department of Health (1999d) *Caring About Carers: A National Strategy for Carers*, Stationery Office, London

Department of Health (1999e) *A New Approach to Social Services Performance*, Consultation Document, Department of Health, London

Department of Health (1999f) *Still Building Bridges*, Department of Health, London

Department of Health (1999g) *Report of Policy Action Team 13: Improving Shopping Access for People living in Deprived Neighbourhoods*, Department of Health, London

Department of Health, (2000a) *Protecting Children, Supporting Parents*, Green Paper, Department of Health, London

Department of Health (2000b) *The Children Act Report 1995–1999*, Cm 4579, Stationery Office, London

Department of Health (2000c) *Learning the Lessons – The Government's Response to Lost in Care: Report of the Tribunal of Inquiry into the Abuse of Children in Care in the Former County Council Areas of Gwynedd and Clwyd since 1974*, Stationery Office, London

Department of Health (2000d) *The NHS Plan – A Plan for Investment. A Plan for Reform*. Cm 4818, Department of Health, London

Department of Health (2001) *Better Care, Higher Standards – Guidance for 2001/02*, Department of Health, London

Department of Health/Department of Education and Employment and Home Office (2000) *Framework for the Assessment of Children in Need and Their Families*, Stationery Office, London

Department of Health, Home Office, Department for Education and Employment (1999) *Working Together to Safeguard Children: A Guide to Inter-Agency Working to Safeguard and Promote the Welfare of Children*, Stationery Office, London

Department of Health and Social Security (1971) *Better Services for the Mentally Handicapped*, White Paper, HMSO, London

Department of Health and Social Security (1980a) *Inequalities in Health: A Report of a Research Working Group*, (Chaired by Sir Douglas Black, known as the Black Report), DHSS, London

Department of Health and Social Security (1980b) *Report of the Review of Rampton Hospital*, (Chairman Sir John Boynton), Cmnd 8073, HMSO, London

Department of Health and Social Security (1981) *Care in Action* HMSO, London

Department of Health and Social Security (1988) *Community Care: Agenda for Action*, (Griffiths Report), HMSO, London

Department of Health/Social Services Inspectorate (1991a) *Care Management and Assessment: Practitioners' Guide*, HMSO, London

Department of Health/Social Services Inspectorate (1991b) *The Right to Complain: Practice Guidance on Complaints Procedures in Social Services Departments*, HMSO, London

Department of Health/Social Services Inspectorate (1991c) *Complaints About the Social Services Department: Ideas for Practice Booklet for Clerks, Receptionists and Telephonists*, HMSO, London

Department of Health/Social Services Inspectorate (1999) *The Work of the Social Care group*

Dews, V. and Watts, J. (1995) *Review of Probation Officer Recruitment and Qualifying Training* (Dews Report), HMSO, London

Dickens, Charles (1946) *Bleak House*, Thomas Nelson, London

Dickinson, D. (1994) *Crime and Unemployment*, Department of Applied Economics, University of Cambridge, Cambridge

Ditch, J. (1998) 'Income Protection and Social Security', in P. Alcock, A. Erskine and M. May (eds) *The Student's Companion to Social Policy*, Blackwell, Oxford, pp. 273–9

Dodd, V. (2000) 'Malicious Racism in Youth Prison', *The Guardian*, 22 January, pp. 1–2

Dominelli, L. (1990) *Women and Community Action*, Venture Press, Birmingham

Dominelli, L. (1997) *Sociology for Social Work*, Macmillan, Basingstoke – now Palgrave

Dominelli, L. and McLeod, M. (1989) *Feminist Social Work*, Macmillan, Basingstoke – now Palgrave

Donahue, J.D. (1989) *The Privatization Decision: Public Ends, Private Means*, Basic Books, New York

Doré, G. and Jerrold, B. (1872) *London: A Pilgrimage*, Grant & Co., London

Douglas, A. (1997) 'No Speech Therapy', Inside Community Care, *Community Care*, 22–28 May, (1173):11

Doyal, L. (ed.) (1998) *Women and Health Services: An Agenda for Change*, Buckingham, Open University Press

Drake, R.F. (1999) *Understanding Disability Policies*, Macmillan, Basingstoke – now Palgrave

Drakeford, M. and Sachdev, D. (2001) 'Financial Exclusion and Debt Redemption', *Critical Social Policy*, **21**(2): 209–30

Durand, V. (1960) *Disturbances at the Carlton Approved School on 29th and 30th August 1959, Report of an Inquiry*, Cmnd, 937, HMSO, London

Dutt, R. (1999) 'Placing Refugee Children', *Community Care*, 29 April–5 May, (1270):30

Eaton, M. (1993) *Women After Prison*, Open University Press, Buckingham

Elcock, H. (1993) 'Local Government', in D. Farnham and S. Horton (eds) *Managing the New Public Services*', Macmillan, Basingstoke – now Palgrave, pp. 150–71

Ensor, R.C.K. (1936) *England 1870–1914*, Clarendon Press, Oxford

Equal Opportunities Commission (1990) *Women and Men in Britain*, Equal Opportunities Commission, London

Equal Opportunities Commission (1993) *Women and Men in Society*, Equal Opportunities Commission, Manchester

Fallon, P., Bluglass, R., Edwards, B. and Daniels, G. (1999) *Report of the Committee of Inquiry into the Personality Disorder Unit, Ashworth Special Hospital*, Cm 4194, Stationery Office, London

Farmer, E. and Pollock, S. (1998) *Sexually Abused and Abusing Children in Substitute Care*, John Wiley & Sons/Department of Health, Chichester

Farnham, D. (1993) 'Human Resources Management and Employee Relations', in D. Farnham and S. Horton (eds) *Managing the New Public Services*, Macmillan, Basingstoke – now Palgrave, pp. 99–124

Farnham, D. and Horton, S. (1993a) 'The Political Economy of Public Sector Change', in D. Farnham and S. Horton (eds) *Managing the New Public Services*', Macmillan, Basingstoke – now Palgrave, pp. 3–26

Farnham, D. and Horton, S. (1993b) 'The New Public Service Managerialism: an Assessment', in D. Farnham and S. Horton (eds) *Managing the New Public Services*', Macmillan, Basingstoke – now Palgrave, pp. 237–54

Farrington, D.P., Gallagher, B., Morley, L., St Ledger, R.J. and West, D.J. (1986) 'Unemployment, School Leaving and Crime', *British Journal of Criminology*, **26**: 335–56

Fernando, S. (1991) *Mental Health, Race and Culture*, Macmillan, in association with MIND, London

Ferri, E. and Smith, K. (1998) *Step-Parenting in the 1990s*, Family Policy Studies Centre and Joseph Rowntree Foundation, London

Fetterman, D.M., Kaftarian, S.J. and Wandersman, A. (eds) (1996) *Empowerment Evaluation: Knowledge and Tools for Self-assessment and Accountability*, Sage, London

Fleischmann, P. and Wigmore, J. (2000) *Nowhere Else to Go*, Mental Health Foundation, London

Fletcher, H. (1999) 'Call for Resources for the Service', *NAPO News*, November, (114):1

Flynn, R. and Williams, G. (eds) (1997) *Contracting for Health: Quasi-markets and the National Health Service*, Oxford University Press, Oxford

Ford, J., Burrows, R., Wilcox, S., Cole, I. and Beatty, C. (1998) *Social Housing Rent Differentials and Processes of Social Exclusion*, Centre for Housing Policy, University of York, York

Fox Harding, L. (1996) *Family, State and Social Policy*, Macmillan, Basingstoke – now Palgrave

Fox Harding, L. (1997) *Perspectives in Child Care Policy*, Longman, Harlow

Franklin, B. (ed.) (1995) *The Handbook of Children's Rights – Comparative Policy and Practice*, Routledge, London

Franklin, B. (1999) *Hard Pressed, National Newspaper Reporting of Social Work and Social Services*, Community Care, London

Franklin, B. (ed.) (2000) *Social Policy, The Media and Misrepresentation*, Routledge, London

Fraser, D. (1984) *The Evolution of the British Welfare State*, 2nd edn, Macmillan, Basingstoke – now Palgrave

Fratter, J. (1991) 'Parties in the Triangle', *Adoption and Fostering*, **15** (4):91–8

Fryer, D. (1992) *The Psychological Effects of Unemployment*, British Psychological Society, Leicester

Gaskell, E. (1970) *North and South*, Harmondsworth, Penguin

George, M. (2000) 'Act of Cruelty', *The Guardian, Guardian Society*, 8 November, pp. 5–6

George, V. (1968) *Social Security: Beveridge and After*, Routledge & Kegan Paul, London

George, V. and Taylor-Gooby, P. (eds) (1996) *European Welfare Policy: Squaring the Welfare Circle*, Macmillan, Basingstoke – now Palgrave

George, V. and Wilding, P. (1976) *Ideology and Social Welfare*, Routledge & Kegan Paul, London

George, V. and Wilding, P. (1999) *British Society and Social Welfare: Towards a Sustainable Society*, Macmillan, Basingstoke – now Palgrave

Giddens, A. (1998) *The Third Way: The Renewal of Social Democracy*, Polity Press, Cambridge

Ginsburg, N. (1999) 'Housing', in R. M. Page and R. Silburn (eds) *British Social Welfare in the Twentieth Century*, Macmillan, Basingstoke – now Palgrave, pp. 223–46

Glendinning, C. and Millar, J. (1992) *Women and Poverty in Britain in the 1990s*, Harvester Wheatsheaf, Hemel Hempstead

Glennerster, H. and Hills, J. (1998a) 'Lifting the Lid on Pot Luck', *The Guardian, Guardian Society*, 22 April, pp. 2–3

Glennerster, H. and Hills, J. (eds) (1998b) *The State of Welfare: The Economics of Social Spending*, 2nd edn, Oxford University Press, Oxford

Goffman, E. (1961) *Asylums: Essays on the Social Situations of Mental Patients and Other Inmates*, Penguin, Harmondsworth

Golding, P. and Middleton, S. (1982) *Images of Welfare: Press and Public Attitudes to Poverty*, Martin Robertson, Oxford

Goldson, B. (ed.) (2000) *The New Youth Justice*, Russell House, Lyme Regis

Goldson, B. and Peters, E. (2000) *Tough Justice*, Children's Society, London

Gooding, C. (2000) 'Disability Discrimination Act: From Statute to Practice', *Critical Social Policy*, **20** (4): 533–49

Gordon, D., Adelman, L., Ashworth, C. et al. (2000) *Poverty and Social Exclusion in Britain*, Joseph Rowntree Foundation, York

Gould, M. (2001) 'Lives Trapped in Limbo', *The Guardian, Guardian Society*, 24 Jan, p. 7

Graham, J. and Bowling, B. (1995) *Young People and Crime*, Home Office Research Study No. 145, Stationery Office, London

Green, D. (2000) *An End to Welfare Rights*, Institute of Economic Affairs, London

Green, H., Deacon, K., Iles, N. and Down, D. (1997) *Housing in England 1995/96*, Stationery Office, London

Green, L. (2000) 'Anti-poverty Plans Lack Workers' Input', *Community Care*, 22–28 June, (1327): 10–11

Green, L. (2000) 'Anti-Smacking Campaigners Vow to Continue Their Fight', *Community Care*, 27 April–3 May, (1319): 9

Greenhalgh, C. and Gregory, H. (1997) 'Why Manufacturing Still Matters: Working with Structural Change', in J. Philpott (ed) *Working for Full Employment*, Routledge, London, pp. 96–108

Griggs, A., Hogg, D. and Hunt, S. (2000) 'Our Friends in the North', *Community Care*, 4–10 May, (1320): 23

Hadley, R. and Hatch, S. (1981) *Social Welfare and the Failure of the State*, Allen & Unwin, London

Hall, S. (2001) 'Charge for Nursery Place Rises to £6000 a year', *The Guardian*, 5 Feb., p. 9

Halmos, P. (1978) *The Personal and the Political: Social Work and Political Action*, Hutchinson, London

Ham, C. (1985) *Health Policy in Britain*, Macmillan, Basingstoke – now Palgrave

Hanmer, J. and Statham, D. (1999) *Women and Social Work: Towards Woman-centred Practice*, Macmillan, Basingstoke – now Palgrave

Harris, R. (1995) 'Child Protection, Care and Welfare', in K. Wilson and A. James (eds) *The Child Protection Handbook*, Baillière Tindall, London, pp. 27–42

Hasler, F. (1999) 'Excercising the Right to Freedom of Choice', *Professional Social Work*, June, pp. 6–7

Hattenstone, S. (2001) 'Frankly, I'm Appalled', *The Guardian*, Friday Supplement, 2 Feb., pp. 8–9

Head, A. (1995) 'The Work of the Guardian *Ad Litem*', in K. Wilson and A. James (eds) *The Child Protection Handbook*, Baillière Tindall, London, pp. 281–94

Hewitt, P. (1993) *About Time: The Revolution in Work and Family Life*, IPPR/Rivers Oram, London

Hewitt, P. (1997) Full Employment for Men and Women', in J. Philpott (ed) *Working for Full Employment*, Routledge, London, pp. 81–95

Hill, M. (1993) *The Welfare State in Britain: A Political History Since 1945*, Edward Elgar, Aldershot

Hills, D. and Child, C. (2000) *Leadership in Residential Child Care: Evaluating Qualification Training*, John Wiley & Sons, Chichester

Hills, J. (1995) *Income and Wealth – The Latest Evidence*, Joseph Rowntree Foundation, York

Hirst, P. (1994) *Associative Democracy: New Forms of Economic and Social Governance*, Polity Press, Oxford

HM Government (1944) *Employment Policy*, White Paper, Cmnd 6527, HMSO, London

HM Inspectorate of Probation (1995a) *Probation Orders with Additional Requirements. Report of a Thematic Inspection*, Home Office, London

HM Inspectorate of Probation (1995b) *Dealing with Dangerous People: The Probation Service and Public Protection*, Home Office, London

HM Inspectorate of Probation (1996) *Probation Services Working in Partnership: Increasing Impact and Value for Money. Report of a Thematic Inspection*, Home Office, London

HM Inspectorate of Probation (1998) *Strategies for Effective Offender Supervision. Report of the "What Works" Project*, Home Office, London

HM Prison Service (1999) *Annual Report and Accounts 1998 to March 1999*, Stationery Office, London

HM Treasury (1999) *Report of Policy Action Team 14: Access to Financial Services*

HM Treasury (2000) *Report of Policy Action Team 3: Enterprise and Social Exclusion*, Her Majesty's Treasury, London

Holihead, M. (2000) 'Whistling the Same Tune', *Community Care*, 20–26 Jan., (1305): 20–1

Holman, B. (2000) 'Think Local, Gordon', *Community Care*, 22–8 June, (1327): 22

Home Office (1946) *Report of the Committee on the Care of Children* (Curtis Report) Cmnd 6922, HMSO, London

Home Office (1965) *The Child, the Family and the Young Offender* (White Paper) Cmnd 2742, HMSO, London

Home Office (1968) *Children in Trouble* (White Paper) Cmnd 3601, London, HMSO

Home Office (1988) *Punishment, Custody and the Community*, Green Paper, Cm 424, HMSO, London

Home Office (1990) *Provisions for the Mentally Disordered Offender*, Circular 66/90, HMSO, London

Home Office (1990a) *Crime, Justice and Protecting the Public: The Government's Proposals for Legislation*, Cm 965, HMSO, London

Home Office (1999) *Report of Policy Action Team 9: Community Self-Help*, Home Office, London

Home Office (1999a) *Living Without Fear – An Integrated Approach to Tackling Violence Against Women*, Home Office and Women's Unit, London

Home Office (2000) *Report of Policy Action Team 6: Neighbourhood Wardens*

Home Office (2000a) *Policing and Reducing Crime Briefing Note 1/00*, Home Office, PRC Unit Publications, London

Home Office (2001) *New Strategies to Address Youth Offending: The National Evaluation of the Pilot Youth Offending Teams*, RDS Occasional Paper No. 69, Home Office, London

Homer, A. and Gilleard, C. (1975) 'Abuse of Elder People by their Carers', *British Medical Journal*, 301: 1359–62

Hood, R. and Shute, S. (2000) *The Parole System at Work: A Study of Risk Based Decision Making*, Home Office Research Study 202, Home Office, London

Hope, M. and Chapman, T. (1998) *Evidence Based Practice: A Guide to Effective Practice*, London, Home Office

House of Commons, (1992) *Report of the Inquiry into the Removal of Children from Orkney in February 1991*, House of Commons ([HC]; 195, 1992–93)

Howarth, C., Kenway, P., Palmer, G. and Miorelli, R. (1998) *Monitoring Poverty and Social Exclusion: Labour's Inheritance*, New Policy Institute/Joseph Rowntree Foundation, York

Huber, N. (2000) 'Made to Measure', *Community Care*, 18–24 May, (1322): 20

Hughes, B. (1995) *Older People and Community Care: Critical Theory and Practice*, Open University Press, Buckingham

Hugman, R. (1991) *Power in Caring Professions*, Macmillan, Basingstoke – now Palgrave

Hunt, R. (2000) *Quality Protects Research Briefing 1: The Educational Performance of Children in Need and Children Looked After*, Department of Health, London

Husbands, C. (1983) *Racial Exclusionism and the City*, Allen & Unwin, London

International Labour Organisation (1995) *World Employment Report*, ILO, Geneva

Jackson, S. and Thomas, N. (1999) *On the Move Again? What Works in Creating Stability for Looked After Children*, Barnardo's, Barkingside, Ilford

Jacobs, B.D. (1992) *Fractured Cities Capitalism, Community and Empowerment in Britain and America*, Routledge London

Jacobs, J. (1992) *Beveridge 1942–1992: Papers to Mark the 50th Anniversary of the Beveridge Report*, Whiting & Birch, London

Jenkins, S. and Hill, M. (2000) *Poverty Among British Children: Chronic or Transitory*, Institute for Social and Economic Research, University of Essex, Colchester

Joseph Rowntree Foundation (1995) *Inquiry into Income and Wealth*, Vol. 1, Joseph Rowntree Foundation, York

Jupp, B. (1999) *Living Together: Community Life on Mixed Tenure Housing Estates*, Demos, London

Kegley, C.W. Jr and Wittkopf, E.R. (1997) *World Politics: Trend and Transformation*, 6th edn, St Martin's Press, New York

Kennedy, H. (1995) *Banged up, Beaten up, Cutting up: Report of the Howard League Commission of Inquiry into Violence in Penal Institutions for Teenagers under 18*, Howard League, London

Kennett, P. and Marsh, A. (eds) (1999) *Homeless: Exploring the New Terrain*, Policy Press, Bristol

Kent Area Health Authority (1977) *St Augustine's Hospital Committee of Inquiry: Report of Emergency Panel*, Kent Area Health Authority, Maidstone

Kershaw, C. and Renshaw, G. (1997) *Reconviction Rates of Prisoners Discharged from Prison in 1993*, HMSO, London

Keynes, J.M. (1961, first published 1935) *The General Theory of Employment Interest and Money*, Macmillan, Basingstoke – now Palgrave

Kincaid, J.C. (1975) *Poverty and Equality in Britain: A Study of Social Security and Taxation*, Penguin, Harmondsworth

Kincaid, S. (1973) *A New Approach to Homelessness and Allocations*, Shelter London

King, D. and Stoker, G. (eds) (1996) *Rethinking Local Democracy*, Macmillan, Basingstoke – now Palgrave

Kirkwood, A., QC. (1992) *The Leicestershire Inquiry. The Report of an Inquiry into Aspects of the Management of Children's Homes in Leicestershire between 1973 and 1986*, Leicestershire County Council, Leicester

La Fontaine, J. (1994) *The Extent and Nature of Organised Ritual Abuse*, HMSO, London

Lampard, R. (1994) 'An Examination of the Relationship Between Marital Dissolution and Unemployment', in D. Gallie, C. Marsh and C. Vogler (eds) *Social Change and the Experience of Unemployment*, Oxford University Press, Oxford

Lane, M. and Walsh, T. (1995) 'Court Proceedings' in K. Wilson and A. James (eds) *The Child Protection Handbook*, Baillière Tindall, London, pp. 226–80

Langan, J. and Means, R. (1996) 'Financial Management and Elderly People with Dementia in the UK: As Much a Question of Confusion as Abuse?' *Ageing and Society*, (16): 287–314

Le Grand, J. (1982) *The Strategy of Equality*, Allen & Unwin London

Leicester County Council (1985) *Report of an Independent Inquiry into the Provision and Co-ordination of Services to the Family of Carly Taylor by the Relevant Local Authorities and Health Services and by the Persons or Agencies to Leicestershire County Council and Leicester Area Health Authority Teaching*, Leicester County Council, Leicester

Levin, E. and Webb, S. (1997) *Social Work and Community Care: Changing Roles and Tasks*, NISW, London

Levitas, R. (1998) *The Inclusive Society? Social Exclusion and New Labour* Macmillan, Basingstoke – now Palgrave

Levy, A. and Kahan, B. (1991) *The Pindown Experience and the Protection of Children: the Report of the Staffordshire Child Care Inquiry 1990*, Staffordshire County Council, Stafford

Lewis, J. (1997) 'The Paradigm Shift in the Delivery of Public Services and the Crisis of Professionalism', in R. Adams (ed.) *Crisis in the Human Services, National and International Issues*, Policy Studies Research Centre, Lincoln pp. 67–74

Lewis, J. (1999) 'Voluntary and Informal Welfare' in R.M. Page and R. Silburn (eds) *British Social Welfare in the Twentieth Century*, Macmillan, Basingstoke – now Palgrave, pp. 249–70

Lewis, O. (1965) *The Children of Sánchez*, Penguin, Harmondsworth

Lindblom, C.E. (1977) *Politics and Markets: The World's Political Economic Systems*, Basic Books, New York

Lindsey, E. (2001) 'Willing and Able', *The Guardian*, 10 Jan., pp. 2–3

Lister, R. (1997) *Citizenship: Feminist Perspectives*, Macmillan, Basingstoke – now Palgrave

Lister, R. (2000) 'Strategies for Social Inclusion: Promoting Social Cohesion or Social Justice?', in P. Askonas and A. Stewart (eds) *Social Inclusion: Possibilities and Tensions*, Macmillan, Basingstoke – now Palgrave, pp. 37–54

Local Government Association (2000) *The New Commitment to Regeneration*, LGA, London

Local Government Information Unit (LGIU) (1997a) *Citizens' Panels: A New Approach to Citizen Consultation*, LGIU, London

Local Government Information Unit (LGIU) (1997b) *Community Involvement: Neighbourhood Groups, Redditch Case Study*, LGIU, London

Local Government Information Unit (LGIU) (1997c) *Capacity Building Programme for Urban Regeneration: Sandwell Case Study*, LGIU, London

Local Government Information Unit (LGIU) (1998) *Use of Focus Groups in Local Government: Newham Case Study*, London, LGIU

Local Government Information Unit (1999a) *The New Regional Development Agencies* LGIU/SEEDS, London

Local Government Information Unit (1999b) *Social Services and the New Public Services Agenda*, LGIU, London

London Borough of Greenwich (1987) *A Child in Mind: Protection of Children in a Responsible Society. The Report of the Commission of Inquiry into the*

Circumstances Surrounding the Death of Kimberley Carlile, London Borough of Greenwich and Greenwich Health Authority

London Borough of Lambeth (1987) *Whose Child? The Report of the Panel Appointed to Inquiry into the Death of Tyra Henry*, London Borough of Lambeth

Low Pay Commission (1998) *The National Minimum Wage: First Report of the Low Pay Commission*, Stationery Office, London

Low Pay Commission (2000) *The National Minimum Wage: The Story so Far: Second Report of the Low Pay Commission*, Stationery Office, London

Lowe, R. (1993) *The Welfare State in Britain Since 1945*, Macmillan, Basingstoke – now Palgrave

Lyon, C.M. (1995) 'Child Protection and the Civil Law', in K. Wilson and A. James (eds) *The Child Protection Handbook*, Baillière Tindall, London, pp. 153–69

Mack, J. and Lansley, S. (1985) *Poor Britain*, George Allen & Unwin, London

McCarthy, M. (ed.) (1989) *The New Politics of Welfare: An Agenda for the 1990s?*, Macmillan, Basingstoke – now Palgrave

McCreadie, C. (1991) *Elder Abuse: An Exploratory Study*, Age Concern, London

McCurry, P. (1999) 'Courting New Roles', *Community Care*, 2–8 Sept., (1288): 22–3

McGregor, C. (1999) 'Care and Control in Mental Health Social Work', *Professional Social Work*, May, pp. 4–5

McGuire, J. (ed.) (1995) *What Works: Reducing Reoffending: Guidelines from Research and Practice*, John Wiley, Chichester

McIvor, G. (ed.) (1996) *Working with Offenders*, Jessica Kingsley, London

McKay, R. (2000a) 'Does Devolution Deliver?', *Community Care*, 10–16 February, (1308): 24–5

McKay, R. (2000b) 'Are These Dangerous Liaisons?', *Community Care*, 11–17 May, (1321): 12

McLean, S., Balloch, S. and Fisher, M. (1999) *Social Services Working Under Pressure*, National Institute for Social Work/Policy Press, London

Macpherson, Sir William (1999) *The Stephen Lawrence Enquiry*, Stationery Office, London

McVeigh, T. (2001) 'Soaring Cost of Childcare Hits Families', *The Guardian*, 4 Feb., p. 12

Malin, N. (1994) *Implementing Community Care*, Open University Press, Buckingham

Mares, P. (1996) *Business Skills for Care Management: A Guide to Costing, Contracting and Negotiating*, Age Concern, London

Marlow, A. and Pearson, G. (1999) *Young People, Drugs and Community Safety*, Russell House, Lyme Regis

Marshall, T.H. (1970) *Social Policy*, 3rd edn, Hutchinson, London

Martell, R. (2000) 'No Champion for English Children', *Community Care*, 6–12 July, (1329): 10–11

Mary Dendy Hospital Inquiry (1977) *Report of a Committee of Inquiry*, Mersey Regional Health Authority, Liverpool

Mathiesen, T. (1974) *The Politics of Abolition*, Martin Robertson, Oxford

Matthews, R. and Francis, P. (eds) (1996) *Prisons 2000: An International Perspective on the Current State and Future of Imprisonment*, Macmillan, Basingstoke – now Palgrave

Maud Report (1967) *Report of Committee: The Management of Local Government*, HMSO, London

Mayhew, H. and Binney, J. (1862) *The Criminal Prisons of London and Scenes of Prison Life*, Griffin, Bohn, London

Means, R. and Smith, R.(1994) *Community Care: Policy and Practice* Macmillan, Basingstoke – now Palgrave

Merton, Sutton and Wandsworth Area Health Authority (1975) *St Ebba's Hospital Inquiry Report*, Merton, Sutton and Wandsworth Area Health Authority

Millham, S., Bullock, R. and Cherrett, P. (1975) *After Grace – Teeth! A Comparative Study of the Residential Experience of Boys in Approved Schools*, Human Context Books, London

Millham, S., Bullock, R. and Hosie, K. (1978) *Locking Up Children: Secure Provision within the Child Care System*, Saxon House, Farnborough

MIND (1999) *Creating Accepting Communities: Report of the Mind Inquiry into Social Exclusion and Mental Health Problems*, MIND, London

Ministerial Group on the Family (1998) *Supporting Families: A Consultation Document*, Stationery Office, London

Ministerial Group on the Family (1999) *Supporting Families: A Consultation Document*, Stationery Office, London

Mishra, R. (1981) *Society and Social Policy: Theories and Practice of Welfare*, 2nd edn, Macmillan, Basingstoke – now Palgrave

Mishra, R. (1984) *The Welfare State in Crisis: Social Thought and Social Change*, Harvester Wheatsheaf, Brighton

Mishra, R. (1999) *Globalisation and the Welfare State*, Edward Elgar, Cheltenham

Mjijen, M. (1996) 'Scare in the Community: Britain in Moral Panic', in T. Heller, J. Reynolds, R. Gomm. R. Muston and S. Pattison (eds) *Mental Health Matters: A Reader*, Macmillan with Open University, Basingstoke, pp. 143–56

Morris, J. (1993) *Independent Lives? Community Care and Disabled People*, Macmillan, Basingstoke – now Palgrave

Murie, A. (1998) 'Housing', in P. Alcock, A. Erskine and M. May (eds) *The Student's Companion to Social Policy*, Blackwell/Social Policy Association, Oxford, pp. 299–305

Murray, C. (1994) *Underclass: The Crisis Deepens*, IEA Health Unit, West Sussex

Myers, F. (1999) *Social Workers as Mental Health Officers*, Research Highlights 28, Jessica Kingsley, London

National Association for the Care and Resettlement of Offenders (2000) *Some Facts About Young Offenders*, NACRO Youth Crime Section Factsheet, NACRO, London

National Association for the Care and Resettlement of Offenders (2001) *Some Facts About Young People Who Offend*, Youth Crime Factsheet, NACRO, London

National Association for Youth Justice (NAYJ) (2000) *Manifesto for Youth Justice*, Hampshire County Council, Winchester

National Audit Office (1994) *Looking After the Financial Affairs of People with Mental Incapacity*, National Audit Office, London

National Consumer Council and National Institute for Social Work (1988) *Open to Complaints: Guidelines for Social Services Complaints Procedures*, National Consumer Council, London

National Health Service (1969) *Report of the Committee of Inquiry into Allegations of Ill-treatment of Patients and other Irregularities at the Ely Hospital, Cardiff*, Cmnd 3975, HMSO, London

Newman, P. and Smith, A. (1997) *Social Focus on Families*, Stationery Office, London

Nolan, Lord (1995) *First Report of the Committee on Standards in Public Life*, HMSO, London

Oakley, A. (1999) People's Ways of Knowing: Gender and Methodology, in B. Mayal and S. Oliver (eds) *Critical Issues in Social Research*, Oxford University Press, Oxford

O'Connor, D., Pollitt, P., Brook, C., Reiss, B. and Roth, M. (1991) 'Does Early Intervention Reduce the Number of Elderly People with Dementia Admitted to Institutions for Long Term Care?', *British Medical Journal*, 13 April, **302**: 871–4

Office for National Statistics (1998) *Social Trends 28*, Stationery Office, London

Office for National Statistics (1999) *Social Trends 29*, Stationery Office, London

Oldfield, M. (1993) 'Assessing the Impact of Community Service: lost opportunities and the politics of punishment', in D. Whitfield and D. Scott (eds) *Paying Back Twenty Years of Community Service*, Waterside Press, Winchester

Oliver, M. (1990) *The Politics of Disablement: Critical Texts in Social Work and the Welfare State*, Macmillan, Basingstoke – now Palgrave

Oliver, M. (1998) 'Disabled People', in P. Alcock, A. Erskine and M. May (eds) *The Student's Companion to Social Policy*, Blackwell, Oxford, pp. 257–62

Oppenheim, C. and Harker, L. (1996) *Poverty: The Facts*, CPAG, London

Orwell, G. (1940) *Down and Out in Paris and London*, Penguin, Harmondsworth

Orwell, G. (1967) *The Road to Wigan Pier*, Penguin, Harmondsworth

Ouseley, Sir H. (2001) *Community Pride Not Prejudice – Making Diversity Work in Bradford*, Bradford Vision, Bradford

Owens, P., Carrier, J. and Horder, J. (eds) (1995) *Interprofessional Issues in Community and Primary Health Care*, Macmillan, Basingstoke – now Palgrave

Page, R.M. and Silburn, R. (1999) *British Social Welfare in the Twentieth Century*, Macmillan, Basingstoke – now Palgrave

Palmer, S. (2000) 'Rights the UK Won't Give', *The Guardian*, 22 Nov., p. 21

Parker, H., Bakx, K. and Newcombe, R. (1988) *Living with Heroin*. Open University Press, Milton Keynes

Parker, J. (1975) *Social Policy and Citizenship*, Macmillan, Basingstoke – now Palgrave

Parsloe, P. (ed.) (1996) *Pathways to Empowerment*, Venture Press, Birmingham

Parton, N. (1991) *Governing the Family: Child Care, Child Protection and the State*, Macmillan, Basingstoke – now Palgrave

Parton, N. (ed.) (1997) *Child Protection and Family Support: Tensions, Contradictions and Possibilities*, Routledge, London

Patients' Association (undated) *NHS Complaints Procedures: A Guide for Patients*, Patients' Association, London

Payne, M. (2000a) *Anti-bureaucratic Social Work*, Venture, Birmingham

Payne, M. (2000b) *Teamwork in Multiprofessional Care*, Macmillan, Basingstoke – now Palgrave

Peay, J. (1995) 'Mental Disorders and Violence: the Lessons of the Inquiries', *Criminal Justice Matters*, Autumn, (21): 21–2

Peay, J. (1997) 'Mentally Disordered Offenders' in M. Maguire, R. Morgan, and R. Reiner (eds) *Oxford Handbook of Criminology*, Clarendon Press, Oxford

Pearson, G. (1975) *The Deviant Imagination: Psychiatry, Social Work and Social Change*, Macmillan, Basingstoke – now Palgrave

Pearson, G. and Patel, K. (1998) 'Drugs, Deprivation and Ethnicity: Outreach Among Asian Drug Users in a Northern English City', *Journal of Drug Issues*, **28** (1): 199–224

Petrie, S. and James, A. L. (1995) 'Partnership with Parents', in K. Wilson and A. James (eds) *The Child Protection Handbook*, Baillière Tindall, London, pp. 313–33

Phillipson, C., Biggs, S. and Kingston, P. (1995) *Elder Abuse in Perspective*, Open University Press, Buckingham

Philo, G., Henderson, L. and McLaughlin, G. (1993) *Mass Media Representation of Mental Health/Illness; Report for Health Education Board for Scotland*, Glasgow University Media Group, Glasgow

Philpott, J. (1997) 'Looking Forward to Full Employment', in J. Philpott (ed.) *Working for Full Employment*, Routledge, London, pp. 1–29

Piachaud, D. (1997) 'A Price Worth Paying? The Costs of Unemployment', in J. Philpott (ed.) *Working for Full Employment*, Routledge, London, pp. 49–62

Piachaud, D. (2000) 'Sickly Youth' article based on address to UK Public Health Association Annual Forum in Harrogate, on Partnership, Participation and Power, *The Guardian*, 29 March, p. 7

Pierson, C. (1992) *Beyond the Welfare State*, Polity Press, Cambridge

Pleace, N., Jones, A. and England, J. (2000) *Access to General Practice for People Sleeping Rough*, Centre for Housing Policy, University of York, York

Porporino, F.J. (1995) 'Intervention in Corrections: Is "Cognitive" Programming an Answer or Just a Passing Fashion?', State of Corrections Proceedings of the 125th ACA Congress of Corrections, Cincinnati, 1995, Cincinnati, USA

Powell, M. (2000) 'New Labour and the Third Way in the British Welfare State: A New and Distinctive Approach', *Critical Social Policy*, **20**(1): 39–60

Power, A. (1999) *Estates on the Edge: The Social Construction of Mass Housing in Northern Europe*, Macmillan, Basingstoke – now Palgrave

Power, M. (1997) *The Audit Society: Rituals of Verification*, Oxford University Press, Oxford

Priestly, M. (1999) *Disability Politics and Community Care*, Jessica Kingsley, London

Prison Reform Trust (1999) *A Fiscal and Economic Analysis of the Crime (Sentences) Act*, Prison Reform Trust, London

Ramon, S. (ed.) (1991) *Beyond Community Care: Normalisation and Integration Work*, Macmillan/MIND, London

Ratcliffe, P. (2000) 'Is the Assertion of Minority Identity Compatible with the Idea of a Socially Inclusive Society?', in P. Askonas and A. Stewart (eds) *Social Inclusion: Possibilities and Tensions*, Macmillan, Basingstoke – now Palgrave, pp. 169–85

Raynsford, N. (1989) 'Housing', in M. McCarthy (ed.) *The New Politics of Welfare: An Agenda for the 1990s*, Macmillan, Basingstoke – now Palgrave, pp. 82–103

Read, J. and Reynolds, J. (eds) (1996) *Speaking Our Minds: An Anthology*, Macmillan, Basingstoke – now Palgrave

Redcliffe-Maud, Lord (1969) (chairman) *Royal Commission on Local Government in England 1966–69*, Vol. 1 (Report), Cmnd 4040, HMSO, London

Rees, S. (1991) *Achieving Power: Practice and Policy in Social Welfare*, Allen & Unwin, Sydney

Regional Trends 33 (1998) Stationery Office, London

Report of the Committee on Children and Young Persons (1960) (Ingleby Report) Cmnd 1191 London, HMSO

Revans, L. (2000) 'Commission Seeks to Add to its Remit', *Community Care*, 14–20 September, (1340): 12

Rickford, F. (1999) 'Stressed Out', *Community Care*, 26 Aug–1 Sept., (1287): 22–3

Rickford, F. (2000) 'The Best Way of Driving Quality?', *Community Care*, 7–13 Dec., (1351): 20–1

Ritchie, J. (1990) *Thirty Families: Their Living Standards in Unemployment*, Department of Social Security Research Report No. 1, HMSO, London

Ritchie, J.H., Dick, D. and Lingham, R. (1994) *The Report of the Inquiry into the Care and Treatment of Christopher Clunis*, (The Ritchie Report) HMSO, London

Robbins, D. (ed.) (1993) *Community Care: Findings from Department of Health Funded Research 1988–1992*, HMSO, London

Roberts, K. (1995) *Youth and Employment in Modern Britain*, Oxford University Press, Oxford

Robinson, D. (1995) *The Impact of Cognitive Skills Training on Post-Release Recidivism Among Canadian Federal Offenders*, Correctional Service of Canada, Ottawa

Ross, R.R. and Fabiano, E. (1985) *Time to Think: A Cognitive Model of Delinquency Prevention and Offender Rehabilitation*, Institute of Social Sciences and Arts Inc., Johnson City, Tennessee

Rowe, J., Davies, K., Baburaj, V. and Sinha, R. (1993) 'F.A.D.E. The Financial Affairs of Dementing Elders and Who is the Attorney?', *Journal of Elder Abuse and Neglect*, **5**(2): 73–9

Rowntree, B.S. (1901) *Poverty: A Study of Town Life*, Macmillan, Basingstoke – now Palgrave

Rowntree, B.S. (1941) *Poverty and Progress*, Longmans, Green, London

Rowntree, B.S. and Lavers, G.R. (1951) *Poverty and the Welfare State: A Third Social Survey of York dealing only with Economic Questions*, Longmans, Green, London

Rubery, J. (1997) 'What do Women Want from Full Employment?' in J. Philpott (ed.) *Working for Full Employment*, Routledge, London, pp. 63–80

Rugg, J. (1996) *Opening Doors: Helping People on Low Income Secure Private Rented Accommodation*, Centre for Housing Policy, University of York, York

Rugg, J. (1997) *Closing Doors? Access Schemes and the Recent Housing Changes*, Centre for Housing Policy, University of York, York

Sandhill Park Hospital Inquiry (1981) *Member Enquiry into Sandhill Park Hospital, Interim and Final Reports*, Somerset Area Health Authority, Taunton

Savage, S., Atkinson, R. and Robins, L. (eds) (1994) *Public Policy in Britain*, Macmillan, Basingstoke – now Palgrave

Sayce, L. (1995) 'Response to Violence: A Framework for Fair Treatment', in J. Crichton (ed.) *Psychiatric Patient Violence: Risk and Response*, Duckworth, London, pp. 127–50

Scarman, The Rt Hon. Lord (1981) *The Brixton Disorders 10–12 April 1981*, Cmnd 8427, HMSO, London

Schaffer, H. (1990) *Making Decisions About Children*, Blackwell, Oxford

Scottish Executive (2000) *The Same as You? Review of Services for People with Learning Difficulties*, Scottish Executive, Edinburgh

Scottish Home and Health Department/Scottish Education Department (1964) *Children and Young Persons: Scotland* (Kilbrandon Report), Cmnd 2306, HMSO, Edinburgh

Scottish Office (1998) *Social Exclusion in Scotland*, Consultation Paper, Scottish Office, Edinburgh

Scottish Office (2000) *Social Inclusion: Opening the Door to a Better Scotland*, Scottish Office, Edinburgh

Secretary of State for Health (1998) *Modernising Social Services: Promoting Independence, Improving Protection, Raising Standards*, Cm 4169, Stationery Office, London

Secretary of State for Social Security and Minister for Welfare Reform (1998) *New Ambitions for Our Country: A New Contract for Welfare*, Green Paper, Cm 3805, Stationery Office, London

Secretary of State for Social Services (1974) *Report of the Committee of Inquiry into the Care and Supervision Provided in Relation to Maria Colwell*, HMSO, London

Seebohm, F. (1968) *Report of the Committee on Local Authority and Allied Personal Social Services* (Seebohm Report), Cmnd 3703, HMSO, London

Seldon, A. (1960) *Pensions for Prosperity*, Institute of Economic Affairs, London

SeQueria, R. (1997) 'Size Does Matter', Inside Community Care, *Community Care*, 24–30 April: 8

Servian, R. (1996) *Theorising Empowerment: Individual Power and Community Care*, Policy Press, Bristol

Shelter (1999) *From Pillar to Post: Failing to Meeting the Support and Housing Needs of Vulnerable People*, Shelter, London

Shelter (2000a) *Shelterline: One Year On*, Shelter, London

Shelter (2000b) *Latest News*, Shelter, London

Sheppard, M. (1995) *Care Management and the New Social Work: A Critical Analysis*, Whiting & Birch, London

Sherrard, M. (1978) *Report of the Committee of Inquiry into Normansfield Hospital*, Cmnd 7357, HMSO, London

Sinclair, I. and Gibbs, I. (1998) *Children's Homes: A Study in Diversity*, John Wiley & Sons, Chichester

Sinclair, I., Parker, R., Leat, D. and Williams, J. (1990) *The Kaleidoscope of Care: A Review of Research on Welfare Provision for Elderly People*, NISW HMSO, London

Slack, K.M. (1966) *Social Administration and the Citizen*, Michael Joseph, London

Smith, A., Griffin, R., Hill, C. and Symmonds, T. (1998) *Social Focus on the Unemployed*, Stationery Office, London

Smith, C. (2001) 'Trust and Confidence: Possibilities for Social Work in "High Modernity"', *British Journal of Social Work*, **31** (2): 287–305

Smith, J., Gilford, S. and O'Sullivan, A. (1998) *The Family Background of Homeless Young People*, Family Policy Studies Centre/Joseph Rowntree Foundation, London

Smith, K. (1995) 'Social Work and Resettlement, *Journal of Social Work Practice*, **9** (1): 53–62

Social Care News (2000) 'The NHS Plan and You', Aug., pp. 3–4

Social Exclusion Unit (1998a) *Bringing Britain Together: A National Strategy for Neighbourhood Renewal*, Cm 4045, The Stationery Office, London

Social Exclusion Unit (1998b) *Rough Sleeping*, TSO, London

Social Exclusion Unit (1998c) *Truancy and School Exclusion*, TSO, London

Social Exclusion Unit (1999a) *Teenage Pregnancy*, TSO, London

Social Exclusion Unit (1999b) *Bridging the Gap: New Opportunitites for 16–18-year-olds not in Education, Employment or Training*, TSO, London

Social Exclusion Unit (2000a) *Minority Ethnic Issues in Social Exclusion and Neighbourhood Renewal: A Guide to the Work of the Social Exclusion Unit and the Policy Action Teams so far*, The Cabinet Office, London

Social Exclusion Unit (2000b) *National Strategy for Neighborhood Renewal: A Framework for Consultation*, The Cabinet Office, London

Social Exclusion Unit (2000c) *National Strategy for Neighborhood Renewal: A Framework for Consultation: Executive Summary*, The Cabinet Office, London

Social Exclusion Unit (2000d) *National Strategy for Neighborhood Renewal. Policy Action Team Report Summaries: A Compendium*, The Cabinet Office, London

Social Exclusion Unit (2000e) *Report of Policy Action Team 8: Anti-Social Behaviour*, TSO, London

Social Exclusion Unit (2000f) *Report of Policy Action Team 18: Better Information*, TSO, London

Social Exclusion Unit (2000g) *Report of Policy Action Team 16: Learning Lessons*, TSO, London

Social Services Inspectorate (1992) *Confronting Elder Abuse* London, HMSO

Social Services Inspectorate (1993) *No Longer Afraid: The Safeguard of Older People in Domestic Settings* London, HMSO

Social Services Inspectorate (1998) *Social Services Facing the Future: The Seventh Annual Report of the Chief Inspector, Social Services Inspectorate*, Department of Health, London

Social Services Inspectorate (2000a) *Social Services in Wales 1998–1999*, The Report of the Chief Inspector of the SSI for Wales, Stationery Office, Cardiff

Sontag, S. (1991) *AIDS and its Metaphors*, Penguin, Harmondsworth

South Ockendon Hospital Inquiry (1974) *Report of the Committee of Inquiry into South Ockendon Hospital*, H.C.124, HMSO, London

Spurgeon, P. (2000) 'Implications of Policy Development for the Nursing Profession', in D. Hennessy and P. Spurgeon (eds) *Health Policy and Nursing: Influence, Development and Impact*, Macmillan, Basingstoke – now Palgrave, pp. 190–200

St Augustine's Hospital Enquiry (1976) *Report of a Committee of Enquiry St Augustine's Hospital, Chatham, Canterbury*, South East Thames Regional Health Authority, Croydon

St Mary's Hospital (1979) *Report of the Inquiry Relating to St Mary's Hospital* (Stannington Inquiry), Gateshead Area Health Authority, Gateshead

Standing Inquiry Panel (1985) *Report of the Standing Inquiry Panel into the Case of Reuben Carthy*, Nottinghamshire County Council, Nottingham

Stedman Jones, G. (1976) *Outcast London: A Study in the Relationship Between Classes in Victorian Society*, Penguin, Harmondsworth

Stein, M. and Carey, K. (1986) *Leaving Care*, Blackwell, Oxford

Stevenson, O. (1998) 'Law and Social Work Education: A Commentary on the Law Report', *Issues in Social Work Education*, **8**(1): 37–45

Stone, E. (1997) *Women and Housing*, Shelter, London

Surrey Area Health Authority (1980) *Report of the Committee of Inquiry into Standards of Care at Brookwood Hospital*, (Chairman C. Beaumont), West Surrey/North East Hampshire Health District, Woking

Sutherland, D. (2001) 'Abolishing Care Charges', *Professional Social Work*, January, p. 5

Sutherland, Professor, Sir S. (1999) *With Respect to Old Age: Long Term Care – Rights and Responsibilities, Report of the Royal Commission on Long Term Care for the Elderly*, Stationery Office, London

Tarling, R. (1993) *Analysing Offending: Data, Models and Interpretation*, HMSO, London

Taylor, D. (1996) *Critical Social Policy*, Sage, London

Taylor, M. (2000) 'The Devolution Blues', *Community Care*, 6–12 April, (1316): 14

Taylor, M. and Vigars, C. (1993) *Management and Delivery of Social Care*, Longman, Harlow

Taylor-Gooby, P. (1981) 'The New Right and Social Policy', *Critical Social Policy* **1**(1): 18–31

Taylor-Gooby, P. (1996) 'The United Kingdom: Radical Departures and Political Consensus', in V. George and P. Taylor-Gooby (eds) *European Welfare Policy: Squaring the Welfare Circle*, Macmillan, Basingstoke – now Palgrave, pp. 95–116

Taylor-Gooby, P. and Dale, J. (1981) *Social Theory and Social Welfare*, Edward Arnold, London

Thomas, M., Walker, A., Wilmot, A. and Bennett, N. (1998) *Living in Britain: Results from the 1996 General Household Survey*, Stationery Office, London

Thompson, A. (1999) 'Cinderella Service', *Community Care*, 9–15 December, (1302): 20–1

Thompson, A. and Hirst, J. (1999) 'We've Seen the Future', *Community Care*, 28 October–3 November, (1296): 22–3

Thompson, N. (1998) *Promoting Equality: Challenging Discrimination and Oppression in the Human Services*, Macmillan, London – now Palgrave

Titmuss, R.M. (1976a) *Essays on 'The Welfare State'*, 3rd edn, George Allen & Unwin, London

Titmuss, R.M. (1976b) *Commitment to Welfare*, 2nd edn, Allen & Unwin, London

Townsend, P. (1979) *Poverty in the United Kingdom: A Survey of Household Resources and Standards of Living*, Penguin, Harmondsworth

Travis, A. (2000) 'Racist Probation Service Shocks Inspectors', *The Guardian*, 23 June, p. 9

Travis, A. (2001a) 'Jails Chief Threatens to Resign', *The Guardian*, 6 Feb., p. 1

Travis, A. (2001b) 'Technical Rebuffs for 30% of Asylum Seekers', *The Guardian*, 26 Jan., p. 9

Triseliotis, J. and Russell, J. (1984) *Hard to Place: The Outcome of Adoption and Residential Care*, Heinemann, London

Triseliotis, J., Shireman, J. and Hundleby, M. (1997) *Adoption: Theory, Policy and Practice*, Cassell, London

Troke, A. (1994) 'Financial Abuse', *Action on Elder Abuse Bulletin*, 8 Nov/Dec London, Action on Elder Abuse, p. 3

TUC (1994) *Black Workers in the Labour Market*, Trades Union Congress, London

TUC (1995a) *The TUC Charter on Race and Social Security*, Trades Union Congress, London

TUC (1995b) *Black and Betrayed*, Trades Union Congress, London

Tyler, A. (1995) (rev. edn) *Street Drugs*, Coronet Books, Hodder & Stoughton, London

Ungerson, C. (1987) *Policy is Personal: Sex, Gender and Informal Care*, Tavistock, London

Unwin, J. (2001) *Future Imperfect?*, The King's Fund, London

Utting, Sir W. (1991) *Children in the Public Care: A Review of Residential Child Care*, HMSO, London

Utting, Sir W. (1997) *People Like Us: The Report of the Review of the Safeguards for Children Living Away from Home* (The Utting Report) Stationery Office, London

Vaughn, P.J. and Badger, D. (1995) *Working with the Mentally Disordered Offender in the Community*, Chapman & Hall, London

Vertovec, S. (ed.) (1999) *Migration and Social Cohesion*, Edward Elgar, Cheltenham

Vidal, J. (1999) 'The Endless Diaspora', *The Guardian*, 2 April, p. 19

von Hayek, F. (1944) *The Road to Serfdom*, Routledge & Kegan Paul, London

von Hayek, F. (1960) *The Constitution of Liberty*, Routledge & Kegan Paul, London

Wade, J., Biehal, N. with Clayden, J. and Stein, M. (1998) *Going Missing: Young People Absent from Care*, John Wiley & Sons, Chichester

Walker, A. and Walker, C. (1997) *Britain Divided*, CPAG, London

Wallcraft, J. (1996) 'Becoming Fully Ourselves', in Jim Read and Jill Reynolds (eds) *Speaking Our Minds: An Anthology*, Macmillan, Basingstoke – now Palgrave, pp. 191–6

Ward, L. (2001) 'MPs Attack Emergency Loans to Poor', *The Guardian*, 4 April, p. 10

Warlingham Park Hospital Inquiry (1976) *Report of the Committee of Inquiry*, Croydon Area Health Authority, Croydon

Warner, N. (1994) *Community Care: Just a Fairy Tale?*, Carers National Association, London

Waterhouse, Sir R. (2000) *Lost in Care: Report of the Tribunal of Inquiry into the Abuse of Children in Care in the former County Council Areas of Gwynedd and Clwyd since 1974*, HC 201, Stationery Office, London

Watson, S. and Doyal, L. (eds) (1998) *Engendering Social Policy*, Buckingham, Open University Press

Webb, S. (2001) 'Some Considerations on the Validity of Evidence-based Practice in Social Work', *British Journal of Social Work*, **31** (1): 57–79

Wellard, S. (2000) 'Leeds Delivers Services to Refugees', *Community Care*, 13–19 May, (1272): 8–9

Wertheimer, A. (ed.) (1991) *A Chance to Speak Out: Consulting Service Users and Carers about Community Care*, London, King's Fund Centre

West, D.J. and Farrington, D.P. (1977) *The Delinquent Way of Life*, Heinemann, London

Whitaker, D., Archer, L. and Hicks, L. (1998) *Working in Children's Homes: Challenges and Complexities*, John Wiley & Sons, Chichester

Who Cares Trust (1999) *Right to Read Project*, General Information Leaflet, Who Cares Trust, London

Williams, J. (1995) 'Child Protection and the Criminal Justice System', in K. Wilson and A. James (eds) *The Child Protection Handbook*, Baillière Tindall, London, pp. 295–308

Williams, V. and Robinson, C. (2000) *In Their Own Right: The Carers Act and Carers of People with Learning Disabilities*, Policy Press, Bristol

Willmott, P. and Young, M. (1960) *Family and Class in a London Suburb*, Routledge & Kegan Paul, London

Willow, C. (1997) *Hear! Hear!* Local Government Information Unit (LGIU), London

Wilson, G. (1994) 'Abuse of Elderly Men and Women Among Clients of a Community Psychogeriatric Service', *British Journal of Social Work*, (24): 681–700

Winchester, R. (2000) 'Government Meets Adoption Wish-List', *Community Care*, 13–19 July, (1330): 8–9

Winn, L. (ed.) (1992) *Power to the People: The Key to Responsive Services in Health and Social Care*, King's Fund, London

Winterton Hospital Inquiry (1979) *Report to Durham Area Health Authority*, Durham Area Health Authority, Durham

Wolfensberger, W. (1972) *The Principle of Normalisation in Human Services*, National Institute of Mental Retardation, Toronto

Wolfensberger, W. (1982) 'Social Role Valorisation: A proposed new term for the principle of normalisation', *Mental Retardation*, **21** (6): 234–9

World Health Organization (1946) *Constitution: Basic Documents*, World Health Organization, Geneva

Worrall, A. (1997) *Punishment in the Community: the Future of Criminal Justice*, Longman, Harlow

Young, J. (1999) *The Exclusive Society*, Sage, London

Zamble, E. and Porporino, F.J. (1988) *Coping, Behaviour and Adaptation in Prison Inmates*. Springer-Verlag, Secaucus, NJ

Index

A

absolute poverty 43
Adam Smith Institute 30
adopted 10
adoption 112, 120, 123
Adoption of Children Act 1926 116
Adult Training Centres (ATCs) 103
Afro-Caribbean 167
age, crime and substance abuse 143
age-discrimination 160
alcohol use 142–3
anti-discrimination 169–70
anti-psychiatry 19
antisocial behaviour orders 88
Arkansas 10
Ashworth special hospital inquiry (1992) 100
Asian 5, 9, 10
Association of Chief Officers of Police (ACOP) 137
Asylum and Immigration Act 1996 164
Asylum and Immigration Appeals Act 1993 164
asylum seeker/s 88, 163–4
Audit Commission 22, 95, 105, 183, 191

B

bailiffs 90
Bains Report (1972) 177
Bangladeshi 57, 81, 158
Barnardo's 29, 115
Beckford, Jasmine 4
Benefits Agency 197
Berlin Wall 30
Beveridge Report (1942) 17, 20, 46, 189
Beveridge, Sir William 17, 62, 66, 173
Black Report (1980) 94, 153
Blair government 20, 52, 136
Blair, Tony 19, 21, 25, 68, 201
Boer War 93
Booth, Charles 41
Borrie Report (1994) 20–1
    see also Commission on Social Justice
Bourneville 75
Bowlby, John 122
Bradford riots 215–17
British Nationality Act 1981 165
Brixton riots 213–15
Broadwater Farm Estate 66
Bulger, Jamie 138

C

Campaign for Nuclear Disarmament (CND) 168
Campaign for Racial Equality (CRE) 170
Campbell, Beatrix 49
Canada 135–6
Care Commissioners 7
Care Programme Approach (CPA) 101, 145
carers 107
Carers (Recognition and Services) Act 1995 93, 201
carers, young 107
Care Standards Act 2000 104, 105, 182–3
Caribbean 9
caring 9
Carlton Approved School 116
case reviews 7
Cathy Come Home 79
central government 15, 21
Chadwick, Edwin 74
charging for services 194–7
Charity Organisation Society (COS) 50
Child Abduction Acts 1984 and 1985 116
child abuse 23, 104, 116–17
    see also nonaccidental injury
child benefit 47–8
Child Benefit Act 1975 47
childcare 67, 110–26
Childcare Commission 114
childminding 24, 180
Child Protection Register 120
children 7, 15, 37, 51, 223
Children Act 1908 116
Children Act 1948 8, 18, 116
Children Act 1980 116
Children Act 1989 14, 31, 110, 113, 114, 115, 116, 118, 120, 124, 129, 137
Children and Young Persons Act 1933 110, 116, 137
Children and Young Persons Act 1963 110, 116, 137
Children and Young Persons Act 1969 110, 116, 121, 132, 137, 140, 190
Children First 119
children's rights 116
Children's Rights Commissioner 122
Children's Complaints Officer 122
children's services 22, 23, 32
Children's Society 115
Child Support Act 1991 53, 110, 116

Child Support Act 1995 52, 53, 110
Child Support Agency (CSA) 52–3
Child Support, Pensions and Social Security Act 2000 52
Chronically Sick and Disabled Persons Act 1970 92, 102
citizenship 206
citizen's rights *see* rights
civil rights 102
civil service 19
class, social 153–4
Cleveland 117
Clunis, Christopher 101, 144
cognitive-behavioural work 135–6
collective pay bargaining 66
collectivism 187–8
Colwell, Maria 24
Commission on Social Justice 20, 44, 61
     see also Borrie Report
commissioning 97, 98
communities 72
community care 15, 20, 92–109, 188, 191
Community Care (Direct Payments) Act 1996 38, 93, 103
community development 65
community development projects 42, 45, 65
community work 65
complaints 209–10
compulsory competitive tendering (CCT) 114
conservatism 20
Conservative government 30, 52, 62, 66, 68, 77, 80, 84, 132, 133, 139, 140, 165, 175, 178, 179, 182, 193, 201, 213
Conservative Party 138
Conservative/s 19, 30, 112
contract culture 96–8
council houses/ing 45, 74, 78, 85
Council of Europe 151
Crime and Disorder Act 1998 31, 137, 140
criminal activity 60
criminal justice 127–48
Criminal Justice Act 1948 18, 132
Criminal Justice Act 1972 133
Criminal Justice Act 1991 138
Criminal Justice and Court Services Act 2000 133
Criminal Justice and Public Order Act 1994 31, 129, 139
criminal justice system/s 3
Criminal Procedure (Insanity and Unfitness to Plead) Act 1991 145

criminal violence in the home 88
Crisis (voluntary organisation) 86
critical practice 33

D
Darwin, Charles 49
Darwinist 15, 74
daycare 120
Daycare Trust 114
debt management 196
Debt Redemption Initiative 196
dementia 105–6
demographic trends 9–10
denationalisation 65
Denmark 181–2
Department for Education and Employment 47
Department of Economic Affairs 65
Department of Health 15, 22, 104, 119, 122, 182, 205
Department of Health and Social Security 22, 94, 95, 104, 178
Department of Social Security 47
Department of the Environment, Transport and the Regions 82
Department of Work and Pensions 47
Dews Report 133
Direct Service Organisation/s (DSO) 180
disabilities, people with 102–4
disability 162–3, 222
Disability Discrimination Act 1995 93, 102, 161
disability movement 201
disabled people 15
Disabled Persons (Employment) Act 1944 102
Disabled Persons (Employment) Act 1958 92
Disabled Persons (Service, Consultation and Representation) Act 1986 102
disadvantage 42
discrimination 6, 158–65
Disraeli, Benjamen 48
diversity 69
divisions 151–60
divorce 51
doctor/s 24
Domestic Proceedings and Magistrates' Courts Act 1978 110
domiciliary care 99
Doré, Gustave 73
drug treatment and testing orders 143
drug use 129, 142–3

E

East, the 10
Economic and Social Research Council
  (ESRC) 97
education 24, 67–9, 167
Education Act 1870 62
Education Act 1944 18, 116
educational priority area (EPA) 42, 45, 65
Education Reform Act 1988 174
Ely Hospital 103
emancipation 159
employment 17, 24, 55–71, 157
Employment Action Plan 68
empowerment 202–7
Equal Opportunities Commission (EOC)
  156, 161, 167, 170
Equal Pay Act 1970 162
ethical duty and social work 33
ethnic minorities 83, 167
Europe 10, 14
  unemployment in 57
European Atomic Energy Community 11
European Coal and Steel Community
  (ECSC) 11
European Community (EC) 11
European Convention on Human Rights
  151, 170
European Court of Human Rights
  14, 170
European Economic and Monetary Union
  64
European Parliament 11
European Union 10, 11–12, 68, 158, 190
European Working Time Directive 12, 63
exclusion, racial 60
  see also social exclusion

F

Fabianism 29
Factory Act 1819 62
families 8, 9, 42, 51, 72, 80, 223
  single parent 52
  work with 110–26
  see also lone parent
family
  break up 89
  care 15
  changing 110–12
  Income Supplement (FIS) 60
  policy 21
  poverty 44
  social security 38
  support 6, 67
Federation of British Industry (FBI) 65

feminist 19, 29
financing services 186–99
First World War 8, 13, 17, 78
fiscal measures 65
foster care 120
foster homes 123
France 83
Friedman, Milton 12, 62

G

garden cities 75
Gaskell, Elizabeth 48
gay 112, 156–7
gender 154–6
General Strike 66
George, David Lloyd 76
General Social Care Council (GSCC)
  225
Germany 83
globalisation 10, 12–13
Great Depression 39, 48, 57, 64
Griffiths Report (1988) 95–6
Griffiths, Sir Roy 95

H

Hayek, F. von 62
health 92–109, 223
Health Act 1999 224
Health Action Zones 78, 168
Health and Community Care Committee
  (Scotland) 106
health and social services 7, 12, 20, 98
health authorities 182
healthcare 13, 23
Health Services and Public Health Act
  1968 38
Her Majesty's Inspectors of Probation
  (HMIP) 137
Her Majesty's Inspectors of Schools 23,
  183
higher education 70
HIV/AIDS 157–8
homelessness 85–8
Home Office 135, 145
Home Office Probation Unit 137
homophobic attitudes 157
household/s 73–4, 81, 89
House of Commons Public Accounts
  Committee 84–5
housing 49, 72–91
  associations 45, 80–2
  benefit 70, 84, 90
  department 6
  officer 90

Housing Act 1924 76
Housing Act 1957 80
Housing Act 1974 80
Housing Act 1980 80
Housing Act 1985 86
Housing Act 1986 72
Housing Act 1996 81, 84, 88
Housing and Town Planning Act 1909 76
Housing and Town Planning Act 1919 76
Housing Benefit (General) Regulations 1987 38
Housing Finances Act 1972 80
Housing (Homeless Persons) Act 1977 86, 88
human rights, *see* rights
Human Rights Act 1998 102, 151, 170–1
Hungary 61

I
immigrants 163–4
Immigration Act 1971 164
Immigration and Asylum Act 1999 164
income 43–4, 49, 54
Income Support 47, 51, 60, 70
Independent Living Scheme 103
Industrial Training Act 1964 68
informal care 106–7
Institute of Economic Affairs (IEA) 19
intergovernmental organisation (IGO) 13
intermediate treatment 130
International Institute for Strategic Studies 163
International Labour Organisation (ILO) 55, 64
Invalidity Benefit 63
investigations 210–11
Iraq 88
Irish 9
Isle of Man 174

J
jeopardy, double and triple 145, 155–6
Jewish people 10
Jobseeker's Allowance 70
justice 137–8

K
Keynes, J M 62, 64
Keynsian 65
key performance indicators (KPIs) 137
Kilshaw, Alan and Judith 10, 117
Kurdish family example 171–2

L
Labour government 19, 47, 48, 50, 61, 62, 65, 66, 69, 77, 78, 81, 84, 88, 93, 99, 113, 114, 132, 133, 139, 140, 166, 172, 189, 200, 201, 207, 217, 221
Labour Party 20, 30, 61
laissez-faire 187
Lawrence, Stephen 138
learning disability *see* disability
legalism and social work 32
lesbian 112, 157
less eligibility 195
Lewis, Oscar 42
liberal 17, 30
Liberal Democrats 20, 21
liberalism 29
local authority/ies 8, 15, 23–6, 77, 80, 86, 187
Local Authority Social Services Act 1970 3, 28, 178
local government 177–82
reorganisation 15, 181
Local Government Act 1888 174
Local Government Act 1899 174
Local Government Act 1929 45
Local Government Act 1963 174
Local Government Act 1972 174, 178
Local Government Act 1985 174
Local Government Act 1988 129
Local Government Act 1992 174
Local Government Act 1999 23, 204
Local Government Finance Act 1992 194
Local Government Planning and Land Act 1980 179
local housing companies 84–5
lone parent/s 50, 51, 81, 113
see also families, single parent
long-term care 105
looked after children 120–3

M
Maastricht Treaty 12, 63
Macmillan, Harold 65
Macpherson Report (1999) 139, 159–60
macroeconomic policy 64
maintenance 51
managerialism 176
Marxist/s 17, 19, 29, 30, 187–8, 207
Matrimonial Causes Act 1973 72
Maud Report (1967) 177
means test 195

mental health 71, 100–1, 162
  legislation 92
Mental Health Act 1959 92, 100, 144, 191
Mental Health Act 1983 31, 92, 100, 101,
  145, 191
Mental Health (Patients in the Community)
  Act 1995 100
mentally disordered offenders 143–6
mentoring 146
Mexico 61
Middle East 10, 62, 188
mid-Victorians 19, 50, 75
  see also Victorian/s
Milton Keynes 75
MIND 205
miners' strike (1984–5) 66
minimum wage 24, 63, 64
minimum wage councils 66
Ministerial Group on the Family 21,
  113–14
Ministry of Health 94
Ministry of Labour 46
Ministry of Social Security 94
Ministry of Technology 65
Modernisation Agency 99
modernisation programme 200
Modernising Government initiative 106
monetarist 19
Monopolies Commission 66
Municipal Corporations Act 1835 173
Murray, Charles 154

N
National Assistance Act 1948 8, 18, 38, 51,
  62, 72, 92
National Association for Youth Justice
  (NAYJ) 138, 141, 147
National Association of Probation Officers
  134
National Audit Office 85
National Care Standards Commission
  24, 183
National Children's Homes (NCH) 29
National Economic Development Council
  (NEDC) 65
National Family and Parenting Institute 124
National Front 60
National Health Service (NHS) 94, 194,
  224
National Health Service Act 1946 18
National Health Service and Community
  Care Act 1990 23, 31, 92–3, 96–7,
  104, 105, 180, 186, 192, 210
National Insurance 47

National Insurance Act 1911 62
National Insurance Act 1946 62
nationalism 65–6
National Literacy Association 122
National Minimum Wage Act 1998 162
National Probation Service 128
  see also probation service
National Society for the Prevention of
  Cruelty to Children (NSPCC) 29
Netherlands 130
New Deal 24, 68
New Labour 16, 20–2, 168, 188
New Lanark 75
New Left 19
New Right 7, 19, 30, 50, 111, 112, 187, 213
nonaccidental injury 117
  see also child abuse
nongovernmental organisations (NGOs) 13
normalisation 103
Northern Ireland 9, 10, 11, 22, 28, 76, 151,
  166, 167, 174, 177, 181, 183
north-south divide 48–9
nurseries 114

O
Office of Fair Trading 66
older people 104–6
Old Labour 21
Ombudsman *see under* Parliamentary
  Commissioner for Administration
Organisation for Economic Cooperation and
  Development (OECD) 61
organising services 173–85
Orkney 117
Orwell, George 48, 49
Ouseley, Lord Herman 215
Owen, Robert 75, 204
owner occupation 78–9

P
Pakistani 57, 81, 158
Parliamentary Commissioner for
  Administration (Ombudsman) 84
participation 200–12
patients 24
Patients' Association 94
pauperism 40, 45, 50
pensions 47–8, 222
Performance Assessment Framework 119,
  183
performance indicators 23–4
persistent young offenders 142
Policy Action Team/s (PAT) of the Social
  Exclusion Unit 25, 83, 217–21

Poor Law/s 8, 39, 51, 173
Elizabethan 86
Poor Law Amendment Act 1834 45, 60, 62, 195
poor people 8–9
population 9–10
Port Sunlight 75
Portugal 61
poverty 6, 19, 25, 37, 39–40, 41–2, 54, 61, 71, 128
Powers of Criminal Courts (Sentencing) Act 2000 141
Priority Estates Project 66
prison 130–1
private finance initiative (PFI) 84, 99
private providers 12, 180
private sector 8, 15
privatisation 19, 193–4
probation service 176
see also National Probation Service
Probation Services Act 1993 3
providers 15
Public Assistance Board 51
public expenditure 19
Public Health Act 1848 75
public sector 8, 15
purchaser 15

Q

quality assurance 22–4, 84, 182–4, 209–11
Quality Protects 22–3, 119, 141–2

R

Race Relations Act 1965 160
Race Relations Act 1976 159, 160, 169, 129, 161
racism 60, 132, 158–60
see also exclusion and social exclusion
Reagan government 187
Reagan, Ronald 12, 62
reasoning and rehabilitation programmes 135–6
reflexivity 206–7
Refugee Convention 163
refugees 10, 163–4
Regional Development Agencies 77
Registered Homes Act 1980 92
Registered Homes Act 1984 24, 92
rehousing 146
relative poverty 43
religious discrimination 163
Rent Act 1915 76
repossessions 79–80
research 7–8

respite care 105
Restrictive Trade Practices Court 66
rights, children's 14, 16
rights, human 13
riots 213–17
risk management 101
Romania 10
Rome 151
Rowntree, Seebohm 41, 221

S

Saltaire 75
Scandinavia 130
Scarman, Lord 213
Scarman Report (1981) 213–15, 217
school 146
Scilly Isles 174
Scotland 9, 10, 11, 22, 28, 49, 76, 106, 130, 151, 161, 166, 167–74, 177, 181–2, 183
Scottish Executive 49
Scottish Social Exclusion Network 166
scroungers 40–1, 54, 61
Second World War 8, 17, 47, 76, 78, 175
Seebohm Report (1968) 28, 94, 178, 179
selective benefits 19
self-help 19, 50, 67, 159
service users 24
severe personality disorders, people with 100
Sex Discrimination Act 1975 129, 161, 162
sexism 132
among working-class men 49
sexuality 156–8
Sexual Offences Act 1967 129
single parent *see under* lone parent
Single Regeneration Budget 78
social administration 26–7, 28
social care 28
Social Care Group 182
Social Chapter of the European Union 63
social democratic 31
social divisions 51
see also divisions
social exclusion 25, 45, 201
definition of 166
policies in Scotland and Northern Ireland 166
see also exclusion
Social Exclusion Unit 25, 50, 69, 83, 124, 166–8, 221–3
social housing 80–2
see also council houses/ing

socialism 20
socialist 29, 31, 187
socially excluded people 85
social policy 26
social role valorisation 103
social security 6, 17, 27, 37–54, 221
Social Security Act 1975 48
Social Security Act 1986 38, 47
Social Security Contributions and Benefits
    Act 1992 38
social services 8, 19, 27–8, 180
social services department/s 3, 23, 192
Social Services Inspectorate (SSI) 15, 22,
    104, 205, 211
social work and the law 32–3
Social Work Service 22
Spain 61
Supplementary Benefits Act 1976 72
Supplementary Benefits Commission 48
Sure Start 124
Survivors Speak Out 205
Sutherland Report (1999) 106

T
taxation 45, 194–5
taxes 67
tax subsidies 74
Thatcher government 18, 19, 21, 65, 81,
    112, 168, 187
Thatcherism 16
Thatcher, Margaret 12, 62
Townsend, Peter 41–2
Transport and General Workers Union
    (TGWU) 63
travellers 167

U
Uganda 165
Ugandan Asian people 10
underclass 49–50, 154
unemployment 44, 55–72, 222
unemployment trap 60
Union of Soviet Socialist Republics
    (USSR) 11, 30
unitary authority/ies 8, 15
United Nations (UN) 13–14
    Convention on the Rights of the Child
        115
    enactments (on many aspects) 13–14
    High Commissioner for Refugees 163
    Universal Declaration of Human Rights
        (1948) 13
universalistic benefits 19

urban aid 42, 45
Urban Alliance 168
urban degeneration, theory of 49
USA 11–12, 14, 68, 117, 187, 190
utopian communities 75

V
Victorian/s 39, 40, 49, 73, 75
    see also mid-Victorians
Vietnam 10
violence against women 155
Visible Women Campaign 161
voluntary providers 12, 180
voluntary sector 8, 15

W
Wages Act 1986 68
Wales 9, 10, 11, 22, 28, 29, 49, 76, 115,
    116, 119, 151, 174, 181–2, 183
Waterhouse Report (2000) 118, 121
wealth 19, 43, 54, 94
welfare benefits 67
welfare pluralism 19
Welfare Services Act 1947 18
welfare state 6, 16–18, 19, 27, 51
    critical history of 173, 175
Welfare to Work 67, 68, 168
West Indies 165
whistleblowing 209
women carers 106–7
Woodward, Louise 117
workfare 68
workhouse 50
    test 195
Working Families Tax Credit 24, 67
World Health Organization (WHO) 93

Y
young offender institutions (YOIs) 131,
    140, 143
youth justice 6, 127–8, 223–4
    manifesto for 138, 147
    National Association for Youth Justice
        (NAYJ) 147
Youth Justice and Criminal Evidence Act
    1999 141
Youth Justice Board 141
youth offending team (YOT) 128, 140, 141,
    143, 147
Yugoslavia 10, 88

Z
Zito, Jonathan 101, 144